Ancient History

Forgotten Stories of Egypt, Greece, and Rome

Free Bonus from Captivating History
(Available for a Limited time)

Hi History Lovers!

Now you have a chance to join our exclusive history list so you can get your first history ebook for free as well as discounts and a potential to get more history books for free!

Simply visit the link below to join.

Or, Scan the QR code!

captivatinghistory.com/ebook

Also, make sure to follow us on Facebook, X, and YouTube by searching for Captivating History.

Table of Contents

Part 1: Ancient Egypt

Discovering Lost Stories from Egyptian History

Introduction

Without a doubt, Egypt is one of the most famous ancient civilizations in the world. Whenever we think of ancient history's greatest empires, many immediately think of Greece and Rome because of their great military campaigns, philosophers, and heroes, both historical and mythical. However, whenever Egypt is mentioned, one cannot help but immediately picture an image of Cleopatra or the Pyramid of Giza. While they are both iconic symbols of ancient Egypt, they barely scratch the surface of what Egypt truly was.

This kingdom along the Nile existed for over five thousand years. Egypt's story is more or less like a marathon rather than a sprint. Unlike Greece and Rome, which had clear beginnings, golden ages, and eventual declines, Egyptian history is far more complex. Throughout the years, there were many episodes where dynasties rose and fell, foreign rulers took the throne, resulting in the kingdom either falling into chaos or flourishing, and traditions that continued to evolve but never disappeared. Suffice it to say, but the length of the Egyptian story is astonishingly long—perhaps never-ending. Even when Cleopatra reigned, she lived closer to our present day than to the time when the first foundations of the Great Pyramid of Giza were being laid.

Of course, at the heart of the kingdom was the pharaoh. These rulers were viewed by the Egyptians as divine and the earthly embodiment of the sacred gods. These pharaohs commanded armies, commissioned grand temples, and made every decision that shaped the course of Egyptian history. Some, like Ramesses II and Hatshepsut, are still celebrated today. However, there are still many others who remain obscure or overshadowed by famous pharaohs despite their astonishing achievements or, in some cases, their bizarre reigns.

For instance, the Old Kingdom ruler, Pepi II, is known for his reign, which defied all expectations. Unlike other kings of his time, like Djoser or Khufu, who left their legacies through the construction of the Step Pyramid and the Great Pyramid of Giza, Pepi II is best known for his long reign. Typically, most Egyptian rulers sat on the throne for a few decades at most. Their lives were often cut short either by war, political intrigue, or, for those lucky enough, natural causes. However, according to ancient records, Pepi II ruled for over ninety years—some suggest sixty—earning him a place on the list of the longest monarchs in history. He wore the crown when he was only a child. While Pepi inherited a kingdom that was already flourishing, his long life also forced him to witness Egypt's power and stability gradually weakening. His later years saw the creeping decline of central authority, the rise of ambitious local governors, and the eventual fragmentation of the kingdom.

Although the names of the pharaohs are highlighted in the many books about ancient Egypt, it is impossible to dismiss that the kingdom's story is far greater than the rulers who sat on its throne. Yes, they were viewed as the earthly embodiment of the gods, but in reality, their rule depended on their thousands of subjects, from the artisans who carved and painted the walls of their tombs to the priests who maintained the grand temples and from the scribes who recorded protective hymns to the soldiers who defended Egypt's borders.

Egypt was considered a mighty empire known for its engineering and architectural wonder, wealth, trade, and successful war campaigns and invasions. However, the kingdom was not always blessed. There were times when chaos constantly loomed on the horizon. Cities were sacked, monuments were defaced, armies disappeared, and even those who built Egypt's royal tombs once laid down their tools in defiance.

Beyond the well-known tales of pharaohs and pyramids lie stories of lost structures, forgotten battles, and moments of rebellion that shook the kingdom from within. Some mysteries have lingered for millennia, while others were deliberately erased from history. This book seeks to uncover these hidden episodes and offer a clearer glimpse into a side of Egypt rarely told.

Chapter 1 – Imhotep: God or Man?

Some may have heard of the name Imhotep, perhaps through films or books that talk about the pyramids and ancient Egypt in general. Pharaohs are often remembered since their names were etched in history unless a ruler decided a past ruler should be forgotten, but there were also figures like Imhotep who contributed greatly to the ancient civilization. However, his name was seldom mentioned or even remembered by those outside the realm of Egyptology. Unlike the kings and pharaohs of Egypt, whose power was typically inherited, Imhotep was a man who earned his status through his intellect and skills.

Imhotep was not born with a silver spoon in his mouth. In fact, he lived in a rather humble village along the fertile banks of the Nile. Being born into a family of modest means, Imhotep was well aware that his path to success was not easy. He had neither connections nor privileges that could boost him up the ranks. It is well known that Egyptian society, much like every other ancient civilization in the world, had a rigid hierarchy. More often than not, birthright determined one's opportunities and fate in life.

However, there were also times when one's origin and background were put second. The ancient Egyptians also valued merit, especially in important roles tied to the kingdom and religion. Individuals with exceptional talents and skills could also have a chance to ascend the social ladder, though their path was not as straightforward compared to those with a better birthright. These people had to earn the trust of royals and court officials through their service, skill, and loyalty. Craftsmen could carve a better life if their creations and innovations were exceptional enough that they attracted the attention of the nobles, while priests could build a name for themselves if they could navigate and solve a crisis involving a god's wrath. Scribes could rise in status as well via their mastery of writing and record-keeping. Horemheb, for instance, was a royal scribe before becoming a pharaoh in the New Kingdom. As for Imhotep, he charted his course by doing nearly everything. He ventured into the worlds of architecture, religion, and administration.

Imhotep had an uncanny ability to observe the world around him. He was fascinated by the magnificent temples that dotted the kingdom. However, in his eyes, these temples were not merely places of worship. They were masterpieces that blended the sacred and the practical. Imhotep also spent his early years observing the intricate rituals performed by priests. He understood not only their symbolic meaning but also realized the ultimate precision and discipline needed to execute them.

Imhotep's first known role was that of priest of Ptah. As the creator god and patron deity of both craftsmen and architects, Ptah was highly revered in Memphis, which was also Egypt's administrative and spiritual heart at the time. Of course, in a kingdom that prioritized religion above all else, the role of a priest was a position of immense respect and authority. The responsibilities and tasks, though, were far from easy. As a priest of Ptah, Imhotep was tasked with typical religious duties, but he was also expected to preserve the sacred knowledge of architecture, medicine, and art. So, he often spent most of his time studying sacred texts in order to hone his understanding of the physical and metaphysical worlds.

His talent and devotion never went unnoticed. Imhotep was soon promoted to the position of high priest of Ptah, where he became the spiritual and intellectual leader of Memphis. With a higher position came greater responsibilities, and his role demanded rigorous devotion. He was expected to possess deep knowledge of rituals and theology, as well as the ability to manage complex temple affairs. He needed to fulfill these responsibilities, all while maintaining the favor of both the gods and the people. He was the head of elaborate religious ceremonies, but Imhotep was also the one responsible for managing the temple's extensive resources and workforce.

A depiction of Imhotep dressed in a leopard-skin robe, a ritual garment typically worn by priests.[1]

Imhotep's influence began to grow, eventually catching the attention of the reigning king, Djoser. As one of the most influential rulers of the Third Dynasty, Djoser often had his name listed as a visionary king. He sought to elevate Egypt's architectural and cultural achievements. After recognizing Imhotep's unique combination of skills, Djoser made the decision to appoint him to oversee the construction of his eternal home.

Unlike many other cultures around the globe, ancient Egyptians saw tombs as far more than just resting places for the dead. To them, tombs and burial chambers were the portals to the afterlife, a realm that was full of challenges. It was a must for these Egyptian tombs to be meticulously designed so that the deceased would be left with a safe passage for them to continue their existence in the next world.

It was clear to the ancient Egyptians that death was not the end but rather a transition to another plane of existence. However, one could only enjoy eternal life if they were given the proper rituals. For their kings especially, rituals and ceremonies were more pronounced. After all, these rulers were considered divine intermediaries, so their well-being in the afterlife was very important to maintain cosmic order. Tombs of Egyptian kings were typically constructed in the grandest way possible. Their chambers were filled with treasures and provisions, which the spirits of these kings would use during their journey through the underworld. These tombs had to be perfect to ensure the safety of the deceased kings, so the construction typically began years, if not decades, before the king's death. Djoser's decision to entrust Imhotep with this task showed the trust and respect he held for the high priest.

Long before Imhotep's innovations—or even his birth—the standard design for royal tombs was called the mastaba. Built using mudbricks, the mastaba was rectangular in shape and had flat roofs and sloping sides. This form of eternal resting place was reserved for kings and nobles. Of course, despite its simple exterior, the mastaba also featured inscriptions and carvings that typically detailed the life and achievements of the deceased.

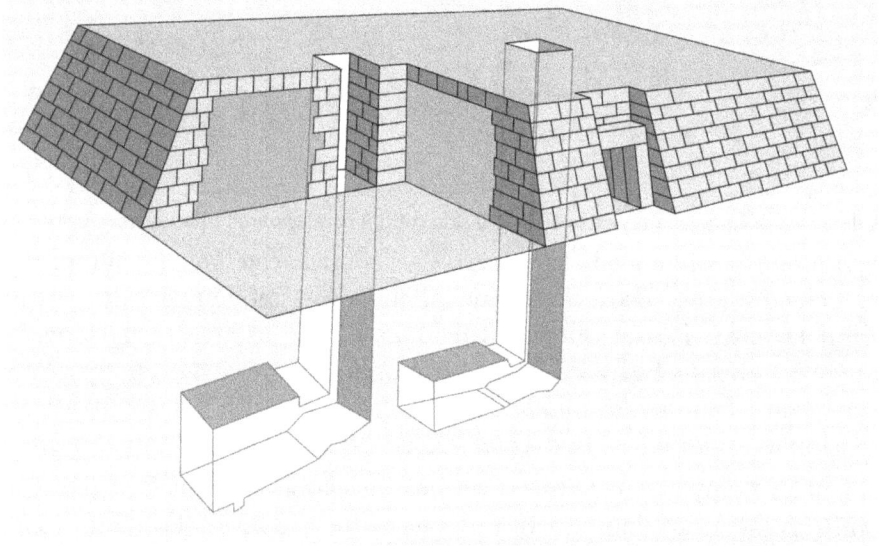

Structure of a mastaba.'

Interestingly, Imhotep decided to deviate from this traditional design. The reasons behind this remain a mystery, yet many agree its implications were revolutionary. Now known as the Step Pyramid, Imhotep designed Djoser's tomb with a square foundation, which was a striking difference from the mastabas, which had rectangular bases. He then stacked six mastaba-like layers on top of one another, each smaller than the one below. This allowed Imhotep to create a tower-like monument that appeared as if it was reaching for the heavens. This design presumably symbolized a divine ascent, which further reinforced the Egyptian belief that their king was connected to the gods.

Imhotep also came up with the idea of using stones to build Djoser's Step Pyramid; in the past, the Egyptians constructed tombs using mudbricks. However, despite his decision to come up with a different design, the priest and architect did not completely stray away from the traditional mastabas. Instead, he retained the old ideas but turned them into a better structure. For instance, similar to the mastabas, the pyramid complex featured walls that had patterns and little indents as decorations. He also proposed the idea of stone columns, which were carved to resemble bundles of reed and papyrus. Since the Step Pyramid was taller than its predecessors, it was crucial for Imhotep to innovate a way to ensure the pyramid never collapsed. He placed the stones at a slight inward angle, making the entire structure more stable and able to hold its own weight.

The Step Pyramid of Djoser.[3]

It took two decades for the builders to finally hang their tools. Upon completion, the Step Pyramid—the first Egyptian pyramid—stood proudly on the Saqqara necropolis at an astonishing height of over two hundred feet. It was the tallest structure to have ever been built at the time. The pyramid was surrounded by an impressive complex that spanned at least forty acres. Temples, courtyards, shrines, and living quarters for the priests dotted the complex, and the entire site was surrounded by a thirty-foot-high wall. A total of thirteen false doors were also installed to confuse tomb robbers. The only real entrance was built in the southeastern corner. The complex was further protected by a trench beyond the wall, which measured around 2,460 feet long and 131 feet wide.

Apart from serving as the eternal resting place for the Egyptian king (Djoser died sometime in 2649 BCE or 2611 BCE, depending on the chronology used), the Step Pyramid also became a template for future pyramids. It is safe to say that Imhotep's achievements were not just a tribute to his king but also a legacy that transformed the landscape and architecture of Egypt.

Imhotep was made Djoser's most trusted advisor. He was expected to be by the king's side during important decisions to assist him in navigating through various periods of crisis. Perhaps one of the most well-known crises during Djoser's reign was the seven-year famine that plagued the land. It all began when the Nile refused to inundate. This plunged the kingdom into complete chaos. Crops withered and refused to grow. As a kingdom that relied heavily on agriculture, it was a difficult time. Hunger spread, and many of the Egyptians resorted to robbing each other in the name of survival. Temples were closed, and shrines were no longer used.

The Famine Stela.'

According to their ancient beliefs, the annual inundation was a gift from Hapi, the god of the Nile (some scholars suggest Hapi was not a god but rather a personification of the flood itself). So, when the land failed to receive the flood for seven years straight, the Egyptians deduced that the god was somehow enraged by them. According to the Famine Stela (an ancient inscription carved centuries following the disaster), Djoser turned to Imhotep to solve the problem. He asked his advisor to search for the birthplace of Hapi himself, believing that by learning of the god's origins, he could also learn the ways to appease the god. Imhotep set out on a journey to find the answer. His first stop was the Temple of Thoth (also known as the House of the Net), where he spent hours reading through sacred texts.

His effort soon paid off. His investigation revealed that the flooding of the Nile was under the dominion of Khnum, the ram-headed god who was also believed to have created humankind on his potter's wheel. Khnum was said to have been the one who guarded the sacred spring that fed the Nile's waters. Imhotep's next step to save his people was now clear: he must journey to Elephantine, the home of the deity. Upon his arrival, Imhotep wasted no time in purifying himself before praying to Khnum. He also made offerings, hoping for the god to restore the Nile's flow and end his people's sufferings.

Perhaps exhausted from his long journey and continuous praying and rituals, Imhotep fell into a deep sleep within the sacred temple. He then dreamed of the god himself. In this dream, the mighty and kind Khnum appeared before him and spoke of his power over the Nile and the creation of life. The god promised to end the suffering of Egypt and its people by letting the waters flow once again. However, there was one condition: the Egyptians must increase their effort in worshiping the god.

When Imhotep finally awoke, he immediately recorded the details of his dream and made haste to King Djoser. The king was relieved and grateful to hear of this. Aiming to fulfill the god's demand, Djoser issued a decree to restore and enrich the Temple of Khnum. He even went to the extent of granting the temple the lands between Aswan and Tachompso. A share of imports from Nubia was also given to the temple. This way, the god would be pleased, and Egypt would be forever showered with prosperity and wealth. As if the god was pleased with the king's actions, Egypt was rewarded with the annual inundation, bringing life and abundance back to the land.

Following this episode, Imhotep's reputation continued to grow. Over time, legends and myths painted him as a figure of unparalleled wisdom who also possessed extraordinary supernatural prowess. One such record from the Tebtunis Temple Library, which dates back to the Roman period, described Imhotep as a court magician. Although heavily exaggerated and fictionalized to suit Egyptian and Roman cultural ideas, this type of narrative showed that Imhotep was regarded for a very long time, even centuries after his passing.

A seated figurine of Imhotep, possibly created during the Ptolemaic period.[5]

According to this legend, Imhotep actually had a divine lineage. His father was none other than Ptah. As a talented court magician, Imhotep was believed to have played a role in the myth of the god Osiris.

Known as the god of the afterlife, fertility, and resurrection, Osiris's most famous story begins with the betrayal of his brother, Set. Based on the myth, Osiris was a compassionate king who earned the love of his subjects. This sparked jealousy and rage within Set. So, planning to usurp the throne, Set murdered Osiris. He then dismembered his brother's body and scattered the pieces across the world.

The first rule of resurrecting a god was to ensure that he was in one piece. The myth goes on to tell how Osiris's sister-wife, Isis, retrieved Osiris's lost body parts. The records from the Tebtunis Temple Library detailed Imhotep's role in addressing this catastrophe. He was tasked with retrieving Osiris's scattered pieces. His challenging quest eventually brought him to Assyria. Here, he encountered a certain Assyrian sorceress who planned to thwart his mission. Ancient writings narrate the two confronting each other, with them using their wit and supernatural power to gain the upper hand. Imhotep ultimately emerged victorious.

The myth also narrated how Imhotep, after securing Osiris's body parts, performed sacred rites to honor and bring the god back to life. It was believed that these rites symbolized the restoration of Maat, the cosmic balance, and reaffirmed the divine authority of Osiris. With his task accomplished, Imhotep returned to Egypt, where he was celebrated as a restorer of divine harmony.

Other than the realms of myth and architecture, Imhotep was also held in high regard in the world of medicine. To this day, some acknowledge him as the first physician of the ancient world. Imhotep had been writing on the subject of medicine for over two thousand years prior to the birth of the "Father of Medicine," Hippocrates. Before Imhotep's time, Egyptian healers typically relied heavily on magic and prayers to treat illnesses. They made use of spells, charms, and incantations to help their patients. In their eyes, most diseases were caused by supernatural forces or by the patient displeasing the divine.

Imhotep, despite his pious background, embraced a more empirical approach. Although he still acknowledged the divine's work in healing, he also knew it was not enough to rely strictly on a god's intervention. Instead of using only spells and charms, he emphasized diagnosis and treatment based on careful observation. Patients were typically questioned about their symptoms, injuries, and pain. Before giving remedies, physical examinations needed to be done, which included touching, prodding, and analyzing the affected areas. This practice is reminiscent of modern medical consultations.

Imhotep is credited with diagnosing and treating perhaps as many as two hundred diseases, from tuberculosis to appendicitis and from gout, gallstones, to even arthritis. Scholars suggested that he might have had experience in performing surgeries. His techniques would not be too out of place in contemporary medical practices. This claim was further cemented by the discovery of the Edwin Smith Papyrus. Believed to be authored by Imhotep himself, this ancient text included remarkable insights into his methods and techniques. Known to be the oldest written medical document, the papyrus provided instructions for forty-eight cases of wounds, fractures, dislocations, and tumors. It also contained detailed instructions for suturing wounds and managing infections using only honey and resins.

Imhotep never planned to keep his knowledge to himself. The physician later founded the first-ever school of medicine in Memphis, where aspiring physicians often flocked to, eager to study under his guidance. His teachings and techniques undoubtedly laid the foundation for Egyptian medicine and, by extension, ensured that his legacy endured for generations.

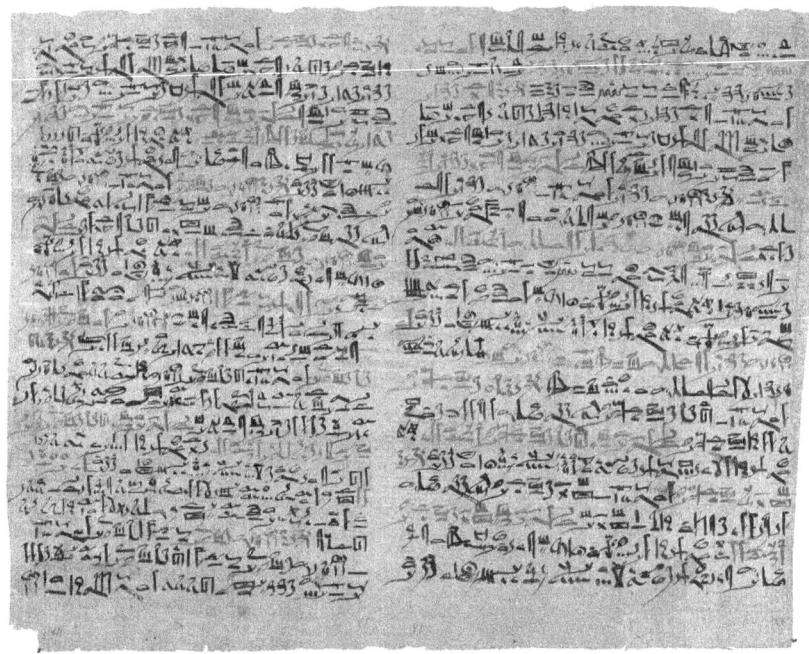

A page of the Edwin Smith Papyrus.[6]

Djoser was beyond impressed with Imhotep's contributions. His architectural accomplishments, in particular, were highly appreciated by the king to the point where Djoser allowed Imhotep's name to be carved alongside his own on different monuments. When the king eventually died, his remains were interred in the burial chamber right beneath the Step Pyramid, just as he had wished.

As for Imhotep, his career did not end with Djoser's departure. He was believed to have continued his service under a few more rulers of the Third Dynasty, including Sekhemkhet (c. 2650 BCE), Khaba (c. 2640 BCE), and Huni (c. 2630). However, this claim is debated by scholars. Nevertheless, Imhotep lived a remarkably long life. His talents were highly sought after for many years.

His exact year of death has yet to be confirmed. Historians and scholars believe that he lived for much of the 26th century BCE, but there are no definitive records that detail his final years.

His reputation and legacy grew stronger over time, though. When the Egyptians saw the start of the New Kingdom, Imhotep's name was still remembered. Since he was highly revered for his wisdom and mastery of written knowledge, he was eventually celebrated as a patron of scribes. So, not only did his image often appear on scribal palettes, but his name was also invoked in prayers, especially by those seeking inspiration and guidance in their works.

By the Late Period, Imhotep's legacy had been cemented. He was deified and worshiped as a god of medicine and healing. Temples dedicated to him were constructed, and there was a dedicated priesthood. His cult began on a local level in Saqqara, where he had made his greatest architectural contributions. As the years passed by, his cult expanded. His status grew beyond merely a healer to an intermediary between the divine and mortal realms. Even the Greeks, who held the Egyptian culture in high regard, acknowledged his deification. They identified Imhotep with their own god of medicine, Asclepius.

However, for someone who was once held in high esteem, it is surprising that the location of Imhotep's tomb remains one of Egypt's greatest unsolved mysteries. Just like the tombs of Alexander the Great and even Cleopatra and Mark Antony, archaeologists have never found the exact site of his tomb despite years of investigations. Only theories remain about the resting place of the man who elevated Egyptian architecture and medicine to new levels.

Theories suggest that Imhotep's tomb is located either within Djoser's burial complex or somewhere in North Saqqara, which was also the site where many significant tombs of the Third Dynasty were discovered. British archaeologist W. B. Emery, for one, conducted extensive excavations at North Saqqara. The tomb he labeled as S 3518 may be Imhotep's final resting place. This conclusion—or speculation—was based on Emery's hypothesis about the tomb's elaborate structure. Not only did the tomb contain various votive offerings, but it also had a system of cult rooms. The most convincing evidence of all was seal imprints bearing King Djoser's name.

This conclusion has never been officially confirmed. While some scholars are open to the suggestion, others argue that Imhotep's eternal home might have been destroyed long ago. There are also historians who suggest that the tomb may have been uncovered without anyone knowing. Nevertheless, even without the discovery of his lost tomb, Imhotep succeeded in immortalizing his name. To this day, he is considered a symbol of innovation, intellect, and devotion. Many agree that he was a man ahead of his time.

Chapter 2 – Unas: The Pharaoh Who Consumed Gods

The year was 1881. There had been a new discovery at Saqqara, the vast necropolis of Egypt. Buried deep beneath the sands was a pyramid. However, unlike the grand pyramids of Giza, this one seemed rather unremarkable at first glance. Its limestone casing had long eroded, leaving the pyramid to appear as if it was nothing more than just a huge mound in the middle of the desert. However, as the team ventured into the pyramid, they uncovered something far more extraordinary. The walls of the burial chamber were adorned with rows of hieroglyphs, all carved in meticulous detail. From these inscriptions, the archaeologists learned that the pyramid was the eternal resting place for Unas, a pharaoh whose name was unfamiliar to many.

The hieroglyphs not only told the archaeologists the name of the individual buried within the tomb but also narratives of the afterlife. Known as the Pyramid Texts, these rows of hieroglyphs are today considered one of the oldest known religious writings in the world. Instead of recounting battles or listing royal titles, these walls carry a series of magic spells, hymns, and prayers meant to guide the soul of the dead pharaoh through the daunting journey across the Duat (the Egyptian underworld). They spoke of encounters with gods, battles with chaotic forces, and the ultimate union with the divine.

Pyramid Texts carved onto the walls of Unas's pyramid.[7]

To put it simply, the Pyramid Texts were a map to immortality. It narrated the journey of how the soul of the pharaoh would ascend to the heavens, where he would later merge with the great god of the sun, Ra. Other than the narrative of the journey, the walls of the burial chamber were also full of spells. Historians suggest that these spells served as protection for the deceased pharaohs. They were thought to have the ability to ward off serpents, demons, and other dangers lurking in the afterlife.

The ancient Egyptians were strong believers in the afterlife; they believed that death was far from the conclusion of a person's life. The journey to enjoy the next life was filled with peril and potential, even for the greatest ruler of the kingdom. However, the Pyramid Texts explain that whatever danger awaited a person in the Duat—be it a massive serpent or other vicious creatures—they could all be vanquished. One's eternal union with the gods was confirmed, given that one's tomb was adorned with such texts.

Unas, the Last King of the Fifth Dynasty

The Old Kingdom is often referred to as the golden era of pyramid building. Just as this name suggests, the period witnessed the construction of some of the most impressive monuments in human history. For centuries, the mighty pharaohs were the central figure in Egyptian society. They were viewed as more than a king; they were seen as a living god who controlled the vast lands, economy, and military. The Old Kingdom, in particular, thrived on this model of centralized authority. Pharaohs were the ones who oversaw the construction projects and agricultural surpluses that supported the kingdom. So, whenever the construction project of a pyramid was launched, the Egyptians made sure to put a lot of effort into it. To them, the pyramids were more than just tombs for their leader; they were also grand statements of the pharaohs' divine authority.

What remains of the Pyramid of Unas.'

The Fourth Dynasty was the peak of pyramid building, with the pyramids of Giza being the most famous of all, even to this day. These tombs were so massive and built with the utmost precision that they eventually became symbols of ancient Egypt. Then, when the Egyptians saw the beginning of the Fifth Dynasty—to which Pharaoh Unas belonged—Egypt saw a slight change in the focus of its construction projects. This era was where religious innovations and the worship of Ra were more emphasized, which was why the kingdom saw more sun temples and grand complexes dedicated to the god being built.

However, these massive projects were expensive. Building such intricate structures needed a lot of workers, and the continuous demand for labor and resources eventually strained Egypt's economy. When Unas ascended the throne as the last pharaoh of the Fifth Dynasty, Egypt was still at the height of its cultural and architectural achievements. But at the same time, the kingdom was also on the brink of significant change. Egypt was facing a gradual decentralization of power.

During this time, Egypt's provinces, also referred to as nomes, were managed by nomarchs (similar to governors). Initially, these nomarchs acted as representatives of the pharaoh, but as time went by, things began to change. The nomarchs gradually accumulated wealth and authority over the years, and they began to stray away from the central government. By the time Unas wore the crown, the balance of power was already shifting away from the pharaoh. Combined with Egypt's economic challenges, the times when monumental pyramids dotted the land had ended. The Pyramid of Unas at Saqqara reflected this change; it was significantly smaller than those that housed his predecessors.

Nevertheless, Egypt under Unas remained a powerful kingdom. Despite its economy being strained, the kingdom was still supported by flourishing trade networks. The pharaoh's mortuary temple featured evidence of this; archaeologists have discovered reliefs that depict Unas launching trade missions to Punt, a mysterious land renowned for its precious and invaluable resources, such as incense, myrrh, ebony, gold, and an array of exotic animals. There were also inscriptions that talked about military campaigns into Canaan or Nubia during his reign. Scholars debate the details of these campaigns—some claim they were more symbolic than factual—but these inscriptions portrayed the traditional image of the pharaoh as both a powerful warrior and the protector of the realm.

Although his pyramid and mortuary temple were considered modest in scale, these structures appeared as if they were constructed by the most skilled craftsmen in the kingdom. It is safe to assume that Unas's administration, despite its challenges, was still capable of mobilizing talented artisans. Other reliefs from his temple featured scenes of daily life, agricultural abundance, and various religious rituals. These images offer us a glimpse into the society he once ruled.

Unas's reign also marked a turning point in the realm of religion. Although Ra remained the central figure of the Egyptian pantheon, Osiris, the god of the underworld and resurrection, rose in influence. Osiris represented a shift in focus from the solar deities to those associated with death, renewal, and the afterlife. Perhaps it was this change that drove Unas to introduce the first-ever Pyramid Texts.

Unas's Pyramid Complex

The pharaoh's pyramid was built sometime in 2375 BCE. During its golden age, the structure stood at a height of forty-three meters. However, when erosion struck the structure many centuries later, Unas's once-grand pyramid was reduced to only a weathered mound of rubble. However, this state was only on its exterior; the pyramid's interior and its surrounding complex still is mostly intact.

Believe it or not, Unas's pyramid was the first to feature inscriptions in its burial chamber, which set it apart from its predecessors. True, the ancient Egyptians were always known for their innovations and creativity, especially when it came to architecture. However, the decorations in this specific pyramid brought their skills to a whole new level, especially since it was constructed over four thousand years ago. The walls of the chamber were lined with polished white alabaster, invoking a sense of elegance, and the contrasting hieroglyphs painted with blue pigment further added to the chamber's intricacy. One can only imagine the ethereal look of the chamber when it was freshly constructed.

The main highlight of the chamber was the Pyramid Texts, which transformed the pyramid from a mere tomb into a spiritual sanctuary. The walls were not the only ones adorned with inscriptions and images. Above, the chamber's ceiling was painted with golden stars set against a dark background. Scholars suggested that the dark background symbolized the night sky, with the stars representing the gods as well as the pharaoh himself, who was thought to have earned a place among the celestial beings.

The restored causeway at Unas's pyramid complex.[9]

The pyramid complex also featured a causeway, which is easily comparable to the one at Khufu's Pyramid. Stretching almost 750 meters from the pyramid's eastern side to the valley temple, the causeway was initially roofed, and its walls were heavily decorated with reliefs depicting an array of scenes, from agricultural activities to trade expeditions to religious rituals. The most intriguing image along the causeway shows a rather dark scene. The humans appeared emaciated. Scholars interpreted this as evidence of a famine that struck the Egyptians during Unas's reign. This relief was unique, as it contrasted with the usual depictions of abundance and prosperity, providing us with a rare peek into the misfortune faced by the kingdom. Unfortunately, the majority of the causeway is now in ruins. However, archaeologists were able to save portions of its reliefs, such as the images of famine. These are now preserved in the Imhotep Museum, which is located nearby.

A relief recovered from the causeway, depicting starving Egyptians.[10]

Interestingly, to the south of the upper causeway, one can find two boat pits. Measuring about forty-five meters long each, these pits were designed to hold wooden ceremonial boats. Although these boats have long since disappeared, historians suggest that back then, these boats were probably viewed as a symbol of Ra's solar barque, which the sun god sailed in during his journey through the sky and the Duat.

The pyramid complex also boasted a bustling necropolis. To this day, over two hundred tombs have been excavated in the vicinity. The tombs of Unas's queens were also uncovered, along with other prominent officials of the Fifth and Sixth Dynasties. While two of Unas's queens, Nebet and Khenut, were buried in a double mastaba near the pyramid, his daughter Princess Idut's tomb was adorned with beautifully preserved carvings and paintings. Not far from Unas's eternal home were also the tombs of Mehu, the royal vizier from the Sixth Dynasty, and Nefer, whose titles included the supervisor of artisans and director of choir singers. Similarly, both of their tombs featured images of courtly life and religious practices during Unas's time.

The Cannibal Hymn, a Collection of Inscriptions That Sparked Controversies

Perhaps the most startling feature of the Pyramid Texts carved onto the walls of Unas's burial chamber is the Cannibal Hymn. This inscription was popular for its vivid yet unsettling imagery. The hymn describes a deceased king who had been deified engaging in an act of cannibalism. Instead of eating the flesh of mortals, though, the deified king is devouring the gods themselves to absorb their powers and assert his supremacy in the divine realm.

Historians agree that the Cannibal Hymn is unique; it is known for its obvious divergence from the more orderly and serene imagery typically associated with Egyptian funerary texts. While other spells included in the typical Pyramid Texts often focused on harmony, purification, and the journey to eternal peace, this specific hymn showed a far more aggressive vision of the pharaoh's afterlife. The hymn pictured the pharaoh as a conqueror not only on earth but also in the celestial realm, where he had to assert his place among the divine through acts of symbolic violence and assimilation.

However, the discovery of this dark inscription has sparked debates among the scholars and historians who have sought to interpret the meaning of the hymn. While many scholars agree that the hymn is symbolic, some have proposed controversial ideas about its origins and meaning. Ernest Alfred Wallis Budge, for instance, proposed one such theory. This early 20th-century Egyptologist earned his reputation through his work on various ancient Egyptian texts, including the famed Papyrus of Ani (also known as the Book of the Dead). In 1911, the Egyptologist authored his book called *Osiris and the Egyptian Resurrection*, in which he suggested that the Osiris myth—and, by extension, the Cannibal Hymn—was purposely created by the early Egyptians to discourage cannibalistic practices. Budge suggested that the image from the Cannibal Hymn, where the pharaoh consumed gods to gain their power, actually symbolized the practice of consuming human flesh. To eliminate this practice altogether, the state priests of the Old Kingdom invented the story of Osiris's death and resurrection to introduce the practice of mummification. This was thought to replace the practice of cannibalism, ensuring that bodies were preserved in the best condition possible rather than being consumed.

Although the theory initially gained some traction, it has been largely dismissed. Later scholars had trouble finding conclusive evidence that cannibalism was ever practiced by the ancient Egyptians, be it ritually or otherwise. The Cannibal Hymn is now believed to have been nothing more than a metaphor; it simply symbolized the pharaoh's ultimate dominance over his realm and his divine nature.

Another renowned Egyptologist, Miriam Lichtheim, also proposed a theory that focused more on the hymn's political and symbolic themes. According to Lichtheim, the phrases in the hymn that described Unas "eating the Red" and "swallowing the Green" are not references to flesh and blood like many others suggested. Instead, it was actually a metaphor symbolizing the unification of Upper and Lower Egypt. The word "Red" could refer to the Red Crown of Lower Egypt, while "Green" might have symbolized the Wadjet, the cobra goddess of Upper Egypt. Therefore, by depicting the pharaoh consuming these symbols, it meant that Unas was the ultimate ruler of the two lands.

Last but not least, the hymn can also be seen as part of the theological innovations of the Fifth Dynasty, a time when the pharaoh's connection to Ra was increasingly emphasized. Scholars have suggested that despite the Cannibal Hymn's aggressive imagery, the meaning behind it probably was far from how it looked. The inscriptions might have symbolized the king's triumph over chaos, with the imagery of the pharaoh consuming the gods simply meaning he had assimilated with the deities, becoming a unifying cosmic force. Instead of an act of destruction, the inscription might be talking about transformation and integration.

Ancient Egypt after Unas's Departure

After the death of Unas, the ancient Egyptians saw the end of the Fifth Dynasty. While his predecessors had their legacies tied to sun temples and pyramids the size of enormous mountains, Unas left behind a different kind of legacy—one that was rooted in innovation rather than scale. It is safe to say that his reign marked a period of transition, where the focus shifted from outward displays of power to the deeper spiritual needs of the afterlife.

The political landscape of the kingdom during the time of his reign was also growing more complex. As the years passed by, the pharaoh's authority was chipped away bit by bit by the nomarchs who controlled the nomes. This was not an immediate crisis, but the gradual decentralization of the government set in motion the eventual fragmentation of the Old Kingdom. Although the kingdom was still unified when Unas left the world, the balance of power was already tilting. The nomarchs, who continued to expand their wealth and influence, soon created a network of regional power centers that would challenge the authority of the pharaohs of the Sixth Dynasty.

Unas was succeeded by Teti, the first ruler of the Sixth Dynasty. Records are scarce, but historians are confident that his ascension to power went smoothly. Under Teti's watchful eyes, the Egyptians continued many of the traditions established during the Fifth Dynasty. Pyramids continued to be constructed, and the Egyptians also placed emphasis on religious practices involving Ra and Osiris. However, the pyramids constructed during this period became increasingly modest due to the kingdom's economic constraints.

Nevertheless, the practice of including Pyramid Texts in burial chambers continued to be adopted and expanded by later kings. Initially, the funerary texts were reserved only for the royals, but later on, these inscriptions also were etched on the walls of tombs belonging to non-royal elites. When Egypt entered the era of the Middle Kingdom, the Pyramid Texts went through an evolution. The Coffin Texts were also used by commoners. Instead of being inscribed on the walls of burial chambers, the Coffin Texts were typically painted on the inside of coffins—hence the name. This way, even the most ordinary citizens could gain the same protections and guidance in the afterlife. Although resurrection, purification, and cosmic unity remained the central theme of these texts, not every spell appeared the same. They were also adjusted and personalized to fit different individuals.

The Pyramid Texts were the foundation for the creation of the Book of the Dead, which first emerged during the New Kingdom. This funerary text was often written on papyrus scrolls and buried with the deceased. Similar to its precursor, the scrolls also featured spells, incantations, rituals, and prayers to overcome the hurdles thrown to the deceased in the Duat. The only difference was that it was in a more portable format. The most famous of this text is the Papyrus of Ani, which was discovered in 1888. This scroll, which is full of cursive hieroglyphs, is considered the finest, best-preserved, and most detailed Egyptian funerary text to ever exist.

Chapter 3 – The Mystery of the Sea Peoples

The Late Bronze Age (c. 1600–1200 BCE) was a period of prosperity and interconnectedness. Powerful kingdoms of the ancient Mediterranean, such as the Egyptians, the Hittites, and the Mycenaeans, grew tremendously. While these kingdoms clashed swords with each other from time to time, warfare was not constant. More often than not, diplomacy was practiced, useful innovations were shared, and precious goods were traded with each other. Cyprus, for instance, was known for its copper, while the Levant (the modern-day areas of Lebanon and Syria) had plenty of cedar trees. The Egyptians, on the other hand, were rich in gold. Much of this precious mineral, however, was extracted from Nubia, a region under Egyptian control during the New Kingdom. These goods moved across vast distances, allowing these kingdoms to achieve even greater heights as time passed by.

Of course, ancient Egypt, under the New Kingdom pharaohs, was the center of this interconnected world. The Egyptians peaked as early as the 13th century BCE, with their kingdom stretching from Nubia in the south to Canaan in the north. Egypt's influence grew even more following the reign of Ramesses II. The kingdom did not only see territorial expansion but also major growth in its economy and culture. It is safe to conclude that the pharaohs of the New Kingdom emphasized diplomatic efforts. The Amarna Letters are evidence of this; the preserved documents revealed a world of royal alliances and rivalries where gifts were often exchanged between rulers in order to ensure peace or leverage power.

Egyptian territories during the New Kingdom period.[11]

Meanwhile, the Hittite Empire based in Anatolia (modern-day Turkey) was also growing into a formidable empire. With control over vital trade routes that linked the eastern Mediterranean to the lands of the Near East, the Hittites were able to gain immense wealth and resources. But, of course, this dominance also caused problems. Conflicts were brewing on the horizon, and the Hittites eventually turned into one of Egypt's greatest rivals. These two powers vied for control over Canaan. Their rivalry reached a climax in the Battle of Kadesh, which erupted in 1274 BCE. This was the bloody episode where the Egyptian pharaoh, Ramesses II, faced the Hittite king, Muwatalli II. Despite being known as one of the most famous battles of the ancient world, the Battle of Kadesh ended in a stalemate.

However, wars and battles were not the only things that exposed the vulnerabilities of kingdoms. While trade routes brought wealth to these ancient civilizations, they could just as easily spread instability when they were disrupted. The Egyptians enjoyed an era of prosperity, but they were not free from obstacles. Maintaining such a massive empire required substantial effort. Immense resources and a well-trained military were needed to ensure its borders and secure trade routes from impending threats. Rebellions were still a common occurrence during this time, and there were also foreign threats spearheaded by those driven by the tantalizing wealth of the kingdom.

Egypt also had to deal with its own internal issues. Succession in Egypt was not always smooth, and there were multiple times when the kingdom struggled with the inconsistent inundation of the Nile. Mother Nature has never been known for her mercy. Ancient Egypt was not the only kingdom to have experienced her wrath; cities like Ugarit (an ancient port city in northern Syria), for example, were terrorized by earthquakes, leaving them vulnerable and an easy target for invaders. Back then, rulers relied on complex, centralized governments to keep order. However, as their territories grew, these kingdoms also saw the rise of local rulers who began acting on their own. This decentralized governing structure undoubtedly weakened the unity of great powers like Egypt and the Hittite Empire, thus leaving the door open for invaders to strike.

The first signs of trouble could be seen by the late 13th century BCE. Reports of raids constantly came in from coastal cities that had long thrived in the region. Interestingly, these cities were unfamiliar with the groups that launched these vicious raids. Following these attacks, trade networks began to falter, and many settlements that had once enjoyed prosperity were silenced. Later known as the Sea Peoples, these groups moved swiftly across the Mediterranean, their raids shaking the very foundations of the Late Bronze Age world. Perhaps united and driven by either necessity or opportunism, they would soon be a destructive force that would challenge even the might of Egypt.

The Origin of the Sea Peoples

According to ancient records, the Sea Peoples arrived in waves. They often raided coastal settlements, toppled cities, and disrupted the vast trade networks that had existed for centuries. However, up to this day, the exact origins of these peoples remain one of the most hotly debated topics of the ancient world.

The term "Sea Peoples" came from Egyptian records, particularly the inscriptions found at Medinet Habu. This grand temple was built by the second pharaoh of the Twentieth Dynasty, Ramesses III. Here, scholars discovered inscriptions that detailed dramatic scenes of battles where the Egyptians fought against invaders arriving in ships. These inscriptions tell us of the great struggle the Egyptians were facing, yet they fail to tell us exactly where the Sea Peoples came from. However, scholars and historians agree that the Sea Peoples were not a single unified army but rather a confederation of different groups united by necessity, ambition, or perhaps both.

An inscription at Medinet Habu depicting Ramesses III going against the Sea Peoples at the Battle of the Delta.[13]

One theory suggests that the Sea Peoples came from the Aegean world, particularly from the Mycenaean civilization. They were once the mightiest in the region. Having built grand palace-states in Mycenae, Pylos, and Tiryns, the Mycenaeans controlled a vast trade network that spread across the region. Unfortunately, something went awfully wrong. The civilization found itself in a steep decline by the late 13th century BCE. Centuries of excavations found traces of their fall. Palaces were burned to the ground, trade routes vanished, and the Linear B script (the writing system of the Mycenaean civilization) disappeared. What truly caused the downfall of the Mycenaeans remains a debate, yet we can be sure that when their world collapsed, its people had no other choice but to flee. It is plausible that these displaced Mycenaeans made use of their knowledge of seafaring and maritime trade routes to survive. Of course, they did so not as merchants but as formidable raiders whose targets were vulnerable coastal settlements.

Another theory states that the Sea Peoples came from Anatolia, particularly its western coastal regions like Lukka (ancient Lycia). Due to internal revolts and external threats, the Hittite Empire was struggling during the Late Bronze Age. Records from the capital city of Hattusa described this unrest, indicating that the western provinces, in particular, were unstable. Shifting alliances were normal, and rebellions constantly erupted. Perhaps because of these episodes of hardship, which included economic problems, war, and even famine, the people of these regions eventually chose to leave their homeland. Scholars suggest that they then joined the growing confederation of the Sea Peoples. The Lukka were also mentioned in the Egyptian inscriptions, which possibly links them to the maritime incursions into Egypt by the Sea Peoples.

The Egyptians also mentioned other names of groups of the Sea Peoples. There were the Peleset (possibly the same as the Philistines), the Sherden, the Shekelesh, and the Denyen. According to Ramesses III's inscriptions, these groups were the ones who attacked Egypt on both land and sea. They were portrayed as a fearsome and organized force. However, out of all these groups, the mention of the Sherden opens the door to yet another theory surrounding the Sea Peoples' origins.

The Sherden were described by the ancient Egyptians to be fierce warriors who went into battle wearing horned helmets and armed with round shields. Interestingly and strangely enough, archaeologists found similar helmets in Sardinia. This suggests that the Sea Peoples might have come from the western Mediterranean. However, this finding did not entirely answer the question. Yes, the Sherden might have come from Sardinia, but there is also the possibility that they were simply influenced by the warrior traditions of that region.

Regardless of the answer, it is safe to conclude that the Sea Peoples were a mix of different groups, possibly hailing from different parts of the Mediterranean. The reason behind their unity might have been due to displacement caused by either natural disasters, famine, or societal collapse. These groups possibly shared the same goal, which was to search for new opportunities—or rather survival—amidst the backdrop of the tumultuous Late Bronze Age.

The Sea Peoples vs. the Ancient Egyptians

The Egyptians experienced their first encounter against the Sea Peoples decades before the rise of Ramesses III. Their earliest known confrontation could be traced back to the early 13th century when Pharaoh Merneptah (the successor of Ramesses II) sat on the throne. It was forever immortalized on the Stela of Merneptah (inscribed in 1208 BCE), which recalls an episode where a coalition of Libyan tribes and the Sea Peoples attempted to invade Egypt from the west.

It began when the Libyans had grown desperate due to the periods of drought and famine. With food and water becoming increasingly harder to come by, they had no other choice but to seek better lands. The fertile Nile Valley and its rich resources became their prime target. However, to go against such a powerful kingdom, the Libyans needed help. This was when the Sea Peoples (the groups listed on the Merneptah Stele were the Ekwesh, Shekelesh, Lukka, Sherden, and Teresh) came into play. Together, the Libyans and the Sea Peoples pushed toward the Nile Delta. The sheer size of the coalition, combined with the Sea Peoples' exceptional naval and military expertise, made the invasion a significant threat.

Merneptah wasted no time in responding to the invasion. After amassing his army, the pharaoh met the invaders in battle. According to the stela, the Egyptians were blessed with a resounding victory. Thousands of the Sea Peoples and their Libyan allies were annihilated. Those who were lucky enough to survive ended up captured with no hope of ever tasting freedom again. Of course, it is worth noting that the stela was heavily propagandistic. Yes, Merneptah succeeded in defeating the Sea Peoples, who were already thought to be a major force in the Mediterranean at the time. Yet, the pharaoh's victory only secured Egypt's borders for a temporary period.

The Sea Peoples soon showed their might once more, as they were headstrong in defeating their Egyptian enemies. They launched their most audacious campaigns when Egypt was put under the control of Ramesses III. By 1177 BCE, the Egyptians had begun to increasingly feel the suffering caused by the many raids orchestrated by the Sea Peoples. They launched coordinated assaults by land and sea. They wreaked havoc on multiple cities. Scenes of the Battle of Djahy, fought in the northeastern Levant, and the Battle of the Delta, fought on the eastern Nile Delta, were both recorded in the reliefs carved at the temple of Medinet Habu.

The Battle of Djahy, which was fought on land, was considered the first significant engagement of this big campaign. Due to its location in the northern region of Canaan, Djahy was known to be a critical gateway to Egypt's borders. Therefore, it made sense for the Sea Peoples to shift their focus to this area after successfully devastating several cities across the eastern Mediterranean. They had even succeeded in sacking the Hittite vassal of Amurru, which was located a short distance away from the border of Egypt.

Based on the intricate reliefs at Medinet Habu, the battle was beyond chaotic. Brutality immediately took over as Ramesses III's forces engaged the invaders. However, the Egyptians had an advantage: their knowledge of the terrain. They knew exactly where to establish fortified positions that could slow the enemy's advance. We could say that the Egyptians' morale was through the roof since their own pharaoh was leading them in battle— at least according to the reliefs, which feature the pharaoh at the forefront. The Egyptians, from archers to charioteers to infantry, struck at the Sea Peoples, eventually driving them into disarray. Blood continued to stain the battlefield as the Egyptians advanced.

Once again, the Sea Peoples were defeated. They failed to break through Egypt's northeastern defenses, but they never planned on retreating entirely. With their plan to penetrate the kingdom by land foiled, the Sea Peoples chose to launch a naval assault on the Nile Delta next. Known simply as the Battle of the Delta, this is seen as another one of the most famous clashes to take place during Ramesses III's reign; it was second only to the previous Battle of Djahy.

The reliefs at Medinet Habu portrayed the Sea Peoples' fleet as an imposing force. Perhaps using their expertise to navigate the sea, they could cut swiftly through the treacherous eastern Mediterranean waters. While papyrus-reed boats were commonly used on the Nile, the Sea Peoples were believed to have arrived in vessels with sturdy wooden hulls and high curved prows and stern. This particular design was typically seen on Aegean and Near Eastern ships. They were better suited for navigating rough sea waves, making them well suited for long-distance open-sea voyages. One of the most interesting features of their vessels was the bird-head decorations. Historians and scholars still debate the exact meaning behind this design, but since they bore similarities to Aegean and Mycenaean ship decorations, it might suggest these Sea Peoples had ties to those regions. Aboard these vessels were warriors who were armed with javelins, swords, and round shields. According to the reliefs, some of them also wore helmets adorned with plumes and horns.

Ramesses III was well aware of the Sea Peoples' naval prowess. He was not intimidated by it since the Egyptians had already experienced their fair share of naval battles. Relying on Egyptian intelligence (the pharaoh had scouts, and his people intercepted communications), the Egyptians were able to anticipate the Sea Peoples' movements. To prepare for the impending battle, the pharaoh placed ships—all of which were smaller compared to those of their enemies but still highly maneuverable—along the Nile. The spots were meticulously chosen so that they could gain the full geographical advantage of the river.

When it was time for the confrontation, the Egyptian vessels did not hesitate to ram the Sea Peoples' ships. They splintered their hulls, resulting in the warriors falling into the Nile. Egyptian archers, who were stationed on the decks, unleashed volleys of arrows toward their enemies. This created chaos and undoubtedly affected the morale of the remaining invaders.

The Egyptians were also successful in repelling the Sea Peoples who had managed to disembark. Ramesses III himself was said to have spearheaded the charge. A relief of the pharaoh in his war chariot, bow drawn, can be seen on the wall of his mortuary temple. The Sea Peoples fought with their full might, but their skills were no match for the Egyptians. In the end, many of their warriors were killed or captured. Those who managed to escape made their way back to their shattered ships.

These battles had caused destruction across the lands. Egypt had to use its already draining resources to rebuild its defenses and protect its frontiers. Yet, the kingdom persisted, and it would eventually get back on its feet, flourishing for many centuries to come. However, the same could not be said for other civilizations across the Mediterranean. The Sea Peoples left a path of destruction across the region the moment they disembarked from their ships. They toppled cities, disrupted trade, and, by extension, became the catalyst for the decline of some of the greatest powers of the Late Bronze Age.

Coastal hubs like Ugarit once enjoyed peace and stability, serving as the center of trade and culture on the Mediterranean until the arrival of the Sea Peoples. Letters have been unearthed that give us a glimpse into the city's last days. Ugarit sent desperate pleas to its allies, hoping reinforcements would arrive and repel the invaders, but unfortunately, they were all left unanswered. The city eventually had its defenses overwhelmed by the Sea Peoples, resulting in its complete abandonment later on. Alashiya (modern Cyprus) faced an almost similar fate. Known for its copper production, it is not surprising that Alashiya was included in the Sea Peoples' list of targets. Historians suggest that upon disrupting the kingdom's trade networks, the Sea Peoples laid waste to its many settlements. Even the Hittite Empire was not spared. By the time of the Sea Peoples' emergence, the empire was already struggling because of internal strife and resource shortages. The Sea Peoples were quick to notice this, so they laid attacks on the empire's western territories. Their actions eventually contributed to the downfall of the once mighty empire's capital, Hattusa.

The collapse of these cities not only affected their populations. In fact, it caused a ripple effect across the Mediterranean since the trade networks were disrupted. These networks were the very thing that kept these civilizations connected. Through these networks, the exchange of goods was made possible. Copper and tin (both crucial components of bronze), timber, grain, and other luxury items like gold and ivory flowed through the cities in the region, allowing them to grow and thrive. However, following the raids of the Sea Peoples and their disruption of the trade routes, these cities were unable to obtain the resources they needed. This plunged them into an economic crisis, which, in time, contributed to instability and the displacement of the population.

At a glance, the movements of the Sea Peoples left destruction across the region. However, after looking closely, scholars suggest that their arrival might have contributed to the transition of the Iron Age (c. 1200-1000 BCE). With the disruption of trade networks and the collapse of major cities that produced bronze, such as Hattusa and Ugarit, societies of the region were left with only the choice of turning to iron. Other historians and scholars suggest that the Sea Peoples might have played a role in spreading iron-smelting techniques after adopting them from regions they had previously settled in. This could be seen in Philistine cities, which had early iron artifacts following the arrival of the Sea Peoples.

The Sea Peoples Following Their Defeat against the Egyptians

The Sea Peoples were primarily known for their destruction and invasions. Records of their raids were plentiful, yet none talked about what exactly happened to them in later years. Mentions of the Sea Peoples more or less vanished from the historical records, especially following their final defeat with Egypt. It is safe to assume that they did not all disappear. They likely integrated into local societies.

One of the groups of the Sea Peoples, Peleset, might have settled in Canaan years following the disastrous campaign in Egypt. They soon became known as the Philistines. This theory is further supported by archaeological findings in sites like Ashkelon, Gaza, and Ekron. Here, Mycenaean-style pottery was unearthed, along with unique architectural styles and dietary practices that were fairly similar to those of the Peleset.

Other groups, such as the Sherden and Shekelesh, did not leave a clear trace of what happened to them. It is plausible that they were absorbed into the societies they had once wreaked havoc upon. Scholars suggest that the Sherden mercenaries were integrated into Egypt, where they served the pharaoh as mercenaries. The Lukka might have integrated into smaller, localized communities or other emerging powers. The rest of the groups likely saw their identities dissolve over the generations as they assimilated into the broader cultures of the regions they chose to settle.

As for Egypt, the chaos that came with the Sea Peoples forced them to adapt and evolve. Indeed, they were victorious against the Sea Peoples, but there was always the possibility of more invasions happening, be it by the Sea Peoples or other rising forces. Because of this, the Egyptians began to work on some changes, hoping they would repeat their victory if they were ever faced with another threat.

Despite not being able to emerge unscathed, Egypt's ability to respond quickly and avoid the chaos of the Late Bronze Age from devouring them whole undoubtedly cemented its reputation as one of the most enduring and powerful civilizations of the ancient world.

Chapter 4 – Unveiling the Secrets of Deir el-Medina

The sun had just risen, bringing with it a whole new day. Its rays hit the mudbrick homes of Deir el-Medina, making these structures appear as if they were constructed in gold. This village was nestled between rugged hills and had long been the home of the kingdom's most skilled craftsmen. However, these were no ordinary workers. The inhabitants of Deir el-Medina were the artisans entrusted with building the royal tombs of the Valley of the Kings.

For one particular artisan in the village—let us refer to him as Bakennu—his day began with a ritual. In his humble house, Bakennu had a shrine that was carved into the wall. Before stepping out of his house, the thirty-year-old artisan would pause in front of the shrine, where a small painted figure of Ptah (the ancient Egyptian god of craftsman) stood proudly. He would murmur prayers, hoping the god would grant him safety throughout the day. Bakennu then placed a small offering before the god, usually a piece of bread and water. Only then would the artisan step out of his abode, making his way to work. To Bakennu, it was his duty to finish the construction of the royal tombs, while to others, it was a privilege or a burden.

Although it was still early in the morning, the atmosphere of Deir el-Medina was already alive. The narrow streets were filled with people carrying out their daily activities. Women could be seen carrying baskets of grain, which they would grind into flour. Others wove linens before heading home later in the evening, where they would prepare food for the family. Scribes, holding wooden tablets that they used to take account of the day's work, hastily made their way along the streets. Children ran between houses, their laughter often putting a smile on the faces of the adults. This was a typical scene in the village, which had existed for generations.

What remains of the houses that once belonged to the workers at Deir el-Medina.[18]

As for Bakennu, the artisan was always accompanied by a few other workers who would take the same trek into the valley. All of them carried their tools wrapped in cloth. One was a stonecutter, whose responsibility was to shape the foundations of the tombs and ensure each chamber of the tomb was carved in precise alignment. If he were to mess up even the smallest calculation, the entire structure could crumble in a matter of seconds. Bakennu was a painter. His main task was to bring life to the walls of the tombs. He was exceptionally skilled in painting depictions of the gods and scenes of divine judgment and the pharaoh's own journey into the afterlife.

Once the workers had arrived at the worksite, they immediately gathered around in a shaded alcove. Here, their overseer would be waiting for them. In his hands were a tablet and a reed pen. The overseer, who was also a scribe, recorded everything, from the hours worked to the tools borrowed to which craftsmen were there that day. After the short meeting, Bakennu wasted no time and began to work. He took his place in one of the newly constructed tomb chambers and looked at the undercoat of plaster that had been applied to the smoothened limestone walls just a few days before. To his eyes, this was more than just a wall; it was an empty canvas, waiting to be filled with colorful paintings of the great pharaoh making offerings to Ra, Osiris, and other gods.

The Valley of the Kings.[4]

Bakennu then reached for his reed brush and dipped it into a pot of red ochre. With flair, he began drawing the outline of a figure. He had been painting ever since he could remember, so his hand was very steady. Hours passed by, and the simple outline had transformed into a painting of a pharaoh on his chariot.

Bakennu was not the only painter there. Another, just as talented as him, could be seen working with ground malachite, which he used to add a shade of green to the depiction of the papyrus fields of the afterlife. A few steps away from him was another painter who was crushing lapis lazuli to create the deep blue that would fill the starry ceiling above the burial chamber. These painters knew every detail of their work was essential, especially when these depictions were meant to last an eternity.

Some might say it was quiet work, but at the same time, it was far from silent. Coming from a different tomb from where Bakennu was, faint yet steady sounds of chisels tapping the rock could be heard. The chisels carved away the walls bit by bit as carvers inscribed the hymns from the Book of the Dead. Like the painters, their task was equally crucial; these hymns would guide the deceased pharaohs through the obstacles of the underworld. Without them, it was impossible for the spirit of these pharaohs to unite with the divine.

When the sun hung high in the sky, signaling it was time for lunch, the workers dropped their tools and took their well-earned rest. Sitting under the shade of an overhanging rock, Bakennu and his friends unwrapped the meals prepared by their wives. They enjoyed flatbread, onions, and dried fish. They quenched their thirst with cool water, which was stored in clay jars. Of course, this recess was not only reserved for eating. While enjoying their meals, Bakennu and the others would talk. Some spoke of the pharaoh's recent victories, while others grumbled about their wages and complained about the price of grain.

They continued working afterward, filling the hours with careful brush strokes and precise carvings. It was only when the sun's rays began to fade that they knew the day had almost come to an end. The overseer would give the final call when the sun had dipped behind the rugged cliffs. With the day's work done, Bakennu and the others packed their tools and wrapped them securely in cloth before making the journey back home.

As he stepped into his home, Bakennu was welcomed with a pleasant scent; his wife had been simmering lentils and roasting a goat for dinner. After greeting her husband, Bakennu's wife set out the meal and called for their children. They ate as a family and told each other all the things that had happened in their day. Later that night, Bakennu made sure to perform yet another ritual. He walked to the small temple located at the edge of the village, where he left another offering to the gods. His work on the Valley of the Kings was far from done, so Bakennu knew he would need all the blessings and protection the gods could offer him.

The routine was repeated the following day and the next until the tombs were done and another pharaoh sat on the throne, commissioning yet another grand project. As long as the pharaohs continued to rule Egypt, the inhabitants of Deir-el Medina would always have work to do.

The Early Days of Deir el-Medina

The ancient Egyptians were always known for their belief in life after death. It was important for them to be well prepared for the underworld since the journey was known to be fraught with perils. While the commoners wished to simply be granted peace when they reached the Field of Reeds (similar to the concept of paradise in other religious beliefs), the pharaohs, in particular, sought not just to reign during their lives but also after their deaths.

In order to achieve such a dream, these rulers had to ensure their tombs were filled with goods. And to ensure these goods remained safe from the hands of greedy criminals, their tombs had to be hidden away in the cliffs of Thebes. Later known as the Valley of the Kings, this site of hidden rock-cut tombs was a stark contrast to the burial traditions of the Old and Middle Kingdoms. These two periods saw the construction of massive pyramid tombs out in the open, while the ones in the Valley of the Kings appeared unassuming from the exterior yet extremely lavish on the inside.

Of course, these grand tombs would not build themselves. The pharaohs needed artisans, but not those who were untrained. They required the most skilled craftsmen the kingdom could offer, men who had mastered the art of stonecutting, sculpture, and painting. These men were expected to transform rock into a sacred passage to the afterlife, ensuring their pharaohs could achieve eternal life.

Deir el-Medina began to take shape. This walled village had its initial foundations laid during the early years of the Eighteenth Dynasty, most likely when Thutmose I (c. 1506-1493 BCE)—some suggest it was Thutmose III (1479-1425 BCE)—sat on the throne. Since this was where the permanent workforce would call home, the construction of the village was meticulously planned. Not only was it enclosed by high walls to protect the village from the dangers of the desert, but Deir el-Medina was also positioned far from the bustling city. It was located in a desert valley west of Thebes, right in between the Valley of the Kings and the Valley of the Queens. Despite being secluded, the village was still close enough for regular supplies to reach the inhabitants.

Inside the walls, houses and buildings were laid out in an orderly fashion. There were rows of rectangular houses made from mudbrick and stone. Each house featured the same spaces. There was a small entrance hall, a main living room, a few sleeping quarters, and a kitchen. Most of the houses also had shrines carved in honor of local gods and protective deities. The inhabitants of Deir el-Medina typically worshiped Ptah (the patron deity of craftsmen), Amun (the chief deity of the entire Egyptian pantheon), Hathor (the goddess of the deceased, love, and the afterlife), and Meretseger (the cobra goddess of the necropolis).

Of course, the men in Deir el-Medina were not like the farmers found in agricultural villages that lined the banks of the Nile. Instead of working in the fields to feed the people of Egypt, they worked solely for the dead, focusing only on royal tombs. They were also employed by the state itself and paid in grain, beer, meat, and cloth. It is safe to conclude that Deir el-Medina was a closed society that functioned almost like a guild. This was where skills of tomb building were passed down from father to son.

As for the women of Deir el-Medina, they were far from passive figures despite not having to participate in the construction of the tombs. In fact, they enjoyed relatively elevated statuses compared to those living in other villages of Egypt. Since their husbands spent much of their time working at both the Valley of the Kings and Queens, women were the ones who managed the household. They also played a big role in the community's daily affairs. They were expected to oversee food preparation, weaving, and child-rearing, but they also had other responsibilities on their shoulders that went beyond just domestic duties. Those who married scribes or higher-ranking artisans were literate and involved in economic transactions. They sold goods and managed their property in their husbands' absence.

In contrast to women in many agricultural villages who toiled in the fields alongside their husbands, those in Deir el-Medina benefited from the regular wages their husbands received from the state. Through this financial stability, they were able to own property and inherit wealth. Some women even acted as petitioners before officials, seeking justice in disputes or addressing grievances related to household and inheritance issues.

The First Recorded Strike in History

However, not everything always went smoothly in Deir-el Medina. Believe it or not, this was the location where the first-ever strike occurred. Taking place sometime during the 12th century BCE, the workers of Deir el-Medina suddenly hung up their tools. Those in charge of carving the walls refused to even touch their chisels, and the painters let their paints dry, refusing to paint anymore until they received what was promised to them. It had been too long since they had received grains, and they knew the officials were aware of their discontent. When no action was taken, the workers left their secluded village and marched toward the mortuary temple of Ramesses III. There, they stood before the officials and administrators.

The sight of these workers undoubtedly stunned the officials. Never before had the craftsmen hung their tools for so long. It was their sacred duty to finish building the eternal homes of the pharaohs, so how could they leave the village? Luckily, this was not a violent rebellion. Not once did the workers attack the officials. Instead, they simply sat outside the temple, blocking its entrance so the officials could not complete their tasks. It was clear that they had no intention of leaving until their voices were heard.

The officials could not afford to spare any time. Those royal tombs had to be finished as soon as possible, so the officials scrambled to negotiate. Records suggest that instead of giving the workers their promised payment, they offered only excuses. The officials claimed that the grain had simply not arrived. However, the artisans were no fools. Even though they lived in an area far from the big cities, they were well aware of the state of the kingdom. They knew that the royal treasure was strained by wars and corruption. They knew that someone had mismanaged their rations. The workers refused to accept only words, so they moved from one temple to another, occupying spaces where the government could not ignore them.

Eventually, the authorities relented. They gave the workers what was promised to them. It was only after receiving their overdue wages that the workers returned home. Unfortunately, this was not the only time that the workers failed to get their payments.

Egypt faced yet another period of decline, as the kingdom's resources were stretched thin. The traditional wealth of the state, drawn from conquests and foreign tribute, was dwindling. Tomb robberies became increasingly common. Sadly, it was done not only by outsiders and criminals but also by the very individuals entrusted to guard the necropolis. Perhaps the saying is true: hard times call for desperate measures. As the years passed by, the once-reliable administration that oversaw tomb construction faltered, and payments to the artisans of Deir el-Medina became inconsistent. Delayed rations were the norm, resulting in frequent episodes where workers showed extreme discontent.

Things were getting worse for Egypt by the reign of Ramesses XI (r. 1107–1070 BCE). The kingdom was no longer the great power it had once been. With the emergence of the high priests of Amun in Thebes claiming power over the lands of Upper Egypt, the kingdom was officially fractured. War was constant in the lands, which further drained the state's coffers. With the royal treasure depleted, it was impossible for the kingdom to sustain the workforce at Deir el-Medina.

The village witnessed a gradual abandonment. Seeing no future ahead of them, families left the place they once called home. They either sought work elsewhere or blended into the growing power structures of Thebes. Some might have remained in the region, where they earned a living by working on less grand tomb projects. However, there were many others who managed to find employment with the temple priests. They had grown increasingly wealthy and influential ever since the kingdom fractured. Some people might have also chosen to migrate north, where they planned to build a new life in cities like Memphis or Tanis. Deir el-Medina finally transformed into a complete ghost town by 1070 BCE. Although the tombs that they had built remained, the majority of them were looted.

From here on, Egypt saw a major change in its burial traditions. Fewer royal tombs were commissioned, and if there were any, these tombs were built far simpler and less extravagant. Instead of massive hidden tombs in the cliffs, pharaohs of later periods, including those of the Third Intermediate Period and Late Period (1070–332 BCE), opted for large temple enclosures or burials in the Nile Delta region, where the power had shifted. Although temples continued to dot the vast lands, without the talent and dedication of the workforce at Deir el-Medina, their level of craftsmanship was never again fully replicated.

Deir el-Medina was eventually consumed by the relentless passage of time. For three thousand years, the once lively village lay forgotten beneath the desert sands. It was rediscovered in the 20th century by an Italian archaeologist named Ernesto Schiaparelli. Another set of excavations was carried out between 1922 and 1951. Headed by French Egyptologist Bernard Bruyère, a significant discovery was made during this dig. They unearthed not only artifacts but also the remains of an entire village, which was preserved in astonishing detail.

It was also in 1922 that the famous tomb of Tutankhamun was discovered by British archaeologist Howard Carter. Interestingly, the condition of the young pharaoh's tomb was almost unscathed. It remained intact and completely untouched by looters, unlike many other royal tombs in the Valley of the Kings. Tutankhamun's tomb was hidden beneath debris, which was likely the reason grave robbers had avoided it. Inside, the pharaoh's remains were accompanied by an array of treasures, from golden shrines to intricate chariots, jewelry, and, of course, the golden mask of Tutankhamun.

The interior of one of the chambers in Tutankhamun's tomb.[16]

Aside from the young pharaoh's tomb, the team of archaeologists also unearthed thousands of inscribed ostraca (pottery shards), which contained precious documents like personal letters, complaints, contracts, poems, and even satirical drawings. These findings shed greater light on the lives of the artisans who once lived in the forgotten village. Today, Deir el-Medina is considered one of the best-preserved archaeological sites in Egypt.

Chapter 5 – The Life of Senenmut: A Commoner Turned Royal Advisor

The heat was unrelenting, but the archaeologists were not planning on giving up just yet. For years, they had been excavating Hatshepsut's mortuary temple, brushing off every speck of dust that covered even the smallest inscription on the structure. The excavation and restoration works began in the early 20th century and lasted for nearly a century. It was first led by the Egyptian Antiquities Services until the mantle was passed to the Polish Academy of Sciences in the 1960s. The temple, with its elaborate designs, had suffered a lot over the millennia. However, each time the walls, columns, and statues were restored, a new story of the ancient Egyptians was unlocked, rewarding historians and scholars with more pieces of the puzzle.

The mortuary temple of Hatshepsut.[16]

One of the most intriguing discoveries was a series of statues. While it was completely normal for archaeologists to unearth statues with some of their parts chipped away or perhaps completely broken, these ones appeared rather peculiar. The statues were far from unscathed, but the culprit was neither time nor Mother Nature. Their faces were purposely chiseled off, and the inscriptions were deliberately erased. However, there was one particular statue that caught the attention of the archaeologists. One can only imagine the details of this life-sized figure back in its golden era, but when it was first unearthed by archaeologists, it was nothing more than a shadow of its former self. Although the name inscribed on its base had been erased, faint traces of the hieroglyphs could still be seen. Upon further examination, the archaeologists were able to read the name of the man: Senenmut. For someone who managed to get his own statue carved and placed in Hatshepsut's mortuary temple, Senenmut must have been an important figure who once walked alongside the Egyptian royals. But why was his statue purposely destroyed and its inscriptions chiseled off?

A stone with an inscription of Senenmut's name.[17]

The Obscured Early Life of Senenmut

Under the reign of Thutmose II, the Egyptian kingdom was balancing tradition and transition. Although the pharaoh's rule was quite short (he reigned for only thirteen years, compared to an average of fifteen to thirty years), Thutmose managed to maintain the centralized power of the monarchy. Minor rebellions and conflicts with its neighboring powers still occurred every once in a while, yet the kingdom was relatively at peace. Thebes also flourished during this period. As the spiritual and political heart of the kingdom, the city continued its role as a hub of religious devotion. Temples of Amun were constructed, with their obelisks reaching toward the sky.

Some might consider Senenmut's rise a story of rags to riches. He was thought to have built his life from the ground up, though scholars advise one to take this narrative with a grain of salt. After all, ancient Egyptian autobiographies, especially those authored by officials, were exaggerated and crafted to emphasize the values of loyalty, skills, and divine favor. Claiming that an individual rose from obscurity to a high rank was their way to highlight exceptional merit and curry favor with the gods and future benefactors.

Ancient writings about Senenmut, at least what is left of them, suggest Senenmut's origin was indeed humble. Born in a modest town near

Thebes called Armant, he was the son of Ramose and Hatnofer. His parents had no titles. According to inscriptions uncovered in their tombs, Ramose was simply described as "revered," while Hatnofer was a "lady of the house." Scholars suggest that Ramose did not live long enough to see his son's career take off. Initially, he was buried simply, indicating that Senenmut had not yet obtained wealth from his career. Hatnofer died later on, and in contrast to Ramose, her burial, possibly arranged by Senenmut himself, was more lavish. Perhaps feeling obligated to improve his father's afterlife, Senenmut was said to have reburied Ramose alongside Hatnofer. Their tombs were then filled with the finest grave goods, perhaps in the hopes that his parents could have a comfortable life after death. Senenmut was not their only child. He had at least three brothers and two sisters, although none of them followed his footsteps to the Egyptian high office.

What exactly his earliest position was remains a mystery, but scholars speculate that Senenmut had a military background. This theory came from the paintings in his tomb, which depict Senenmut in a martial setting. However, without further evidence, it is unsure whether this depiction reflected his actual service or was merely symbolic. What we can be sure of is that his first major appointment came when Thutmose II rose to the throne. Senenmut was to serve the royal household. Then, at some point in time, Senenmut was made the tutor to Neferure, the daughter of Thutmose II and his wife, Hatshepsut.

A statue of Senenmut embracing Princess Neferure.[18]

It was an honor to be entrusted with the education and care of a royal child. This appointment showed the pharaoh trusted Senenmut. By constantly being at the side of the royal family, Senenmut began growing his influence. He was probably proud of his role since he frequently referenced his position as Neferure's tutor on his statues and inscriptions. One particular statue—now stored at the British Museum—showed the relationship that Senenmut had with the royal family. The statue depicted him cradling Neferure in a protective embrace, which was extraordinary, especially since the Egyptian royal family was seen as almost divine. Oftentimes, they were depicted standing far above the common people. It was already considered a privilege for a court official to be portrayed kissing the ground before a royal's feet, let alone a mere commoner embracing them in such an intimate manner.

Senenmut rose through the ranks again, reaching new heights after the kingdom witnessed the death of the pharaoh, Thutmose II. Although the late pharaoh left an heir when he departed to the Duat, his son (named Thutmose III) was only an infant. The power to govern Egypt was temporarily passed to Hatshepsut. It was common for an older female family member, especially mothers, to serve as regent until a young king came of age.

Despite Hatshepsut being in her late teens when she assumed the role, she was already ambitious. It was not entirely uncommon for a woman to act as regent, but Hatshepsut's approach was anything but typical. Aside from assisting in state matters until Thutmose III finally grew up, Hatshepsut began to absorb more and more power for herself. In contrast to other women in her position, she never remarried. This way, she could keep other powerful men from taking charge. Over time, Hatshepsut gained enough reputation and influence that she eventually managed to declare herself pharaoh.

This was a bold move. Hatshepsut was the second known female pharaoh, with the first being Sobekneferu, who ruled during the Middle Kingdom. She knew her reign would not be free from obstacles, especially when there were those who were not a fan of the idea that a woman had been placed on top of the hierarchy. In order to make her subjects see her as a legitimate ruler, Hatshepsut began wearing the Egyptian symbols of kingship. Her statues often depicted her wearing a false beard and the nemes headdress (the striped blue and gold crown-like cloth typically worn by male pharaohs).

A statue of Hatshepsut dressed in royal regalia typically worn by male rulers.[19]

Hatshepsut was a capable ruler. Her reign brought the kingdom stability and prosperity. With Egypt's immense wealth, the pharaoh was able to elevate the kingdom's cultural identity and influence. Monumental construction projects took place, and several trade expeditions, particularly to the rich land of Punt, were launched. The pharaoh excelled in her responsibilities with the help of her most trusted advisors, one of which was Senenmut.

Perhaps realizing Senenmut's loyalty and capabilities after observing him as a tutor to her daughter, Neferure, Hatshepsut thought it was high time to promote him to a higher position. Hatshepsut officially assumed the title of pharaoh during her seventh year as Thutmose's regent, and this was also when Senenmut was promoted to steward of Amun. In this new role of his, Senenmut was put in charge of the vast resources and wealth associated with the temple of Amun at Karnak. He was expected to manage the granaries, livestock, and every other resource that kept Egypt's economy alive.

Administration works were only the tip of the iceberg. Since he also held the title of overseer of works, Senenmut was also in charge of overseeing Hatshepsut's architectural projects across the kingdom, including the construction of two colossal obelisks at Aswan. Considered to be symbols of divine connection and political power, these obelisks stood at the gateway to the grand temple of Karnak. However, it was the mortuary temple of Deir el-Bahari (Hatshepsut's mortuary temple, also known as Djeser-Djeseru) that Senenmut was the proudest of.

The temple at Deir el-Bahari.[30]

To this day, this particular temple is considered one of the most remarkable architectural wonders of ancient Egypt. Constructed into the cliffs of Deir el-Bahri on the opposite side of the city Thebes (modern-day Luxor), the temple's main feature was its terraces, which rose in harmonious symmetry. The structure blended seamlessly with the natural backdrop. In every corner of the temple, one could set eyes on the many reliefs depicting Hatshepsut's reign, from her divine birth to a scene of her coronation to, of course, the famed expedition to Punt. When Hatshepsut launched the construction project of this temple, she was not only planning for it to become a funerary monument. It was also meant to stand as a statement of her legitimacy as a ruler, as well as her devotion to the god Amun.

Scholars agree that Senenmut played a role in the construction of Djeser-Djeseru, yet it is still uncertain whether or not he was the chief architect of the project. However, archaeologists found inscriptions of Senenmut with the title of "Overseer of Works of Amun at Djeser-Djeseru," suggesting that he must have played a crucial role in the construction at some point. There also exists another depiction of

Senenmut that symbolizes his contribution to the construction of major buildings dated to this period. Currently housed at the Louvre Museum in Paris, this particular statue shows Senenmut holding a surveyor's rope.

Of course, this is not the only statue that was left behind; excavations have unearthed twenty-five in total. One of them shows Senenmut offering a sacred sistrum (a musical instrument used in religious rituals) to a god, while another depicts him holding a naos (a small shrine housing a statue of a god, typically located in the most sacred chamber of a temple). These depictions broke conventions since they portrayed a non-royal in poses commonly reserved for either the royals or the highest-ranking priests.

The most intriguing depiction of Senenmut was the one found at Hatshepsut's mortuary temple. Inscribed behind a doorjamb in the temple was Senenmut adoring the pharaoh. However, it was the inscription's hidden placement that brought speculation. Some question whether the addition of this inscription was ever approved by Hatshepsut herself, while there are also others who suggest that it symbolized an intimate bond between himself and the pharaoh.

His tombs also provide a little insight into his ambitions and personality. Interestingly, Senenmut commissioned at least two tombs for himself. One was located in Sheikh Abd el-Qurna (part of the Theban necropolis), while another could be found close to Hatshepsut's mortuary temple—the latter was unfinished for unknown reasons.

The entrance of Senenmut's underground tomb.[21]

His tombs, especially the one in Sheikh Abd el-Qurna, were far from modest since both were decorated lavishly with many inscriptions boasting his accomplishments. In ancient Egyptian tombs, it was common to have specific chambers or areas that were reserved for the gods. These chambers were usually where rituals were performed or offerings were left. Symbols of divine connection were also often displayed here. Senenmut had this special chamber built in his unfinished tomb. On its ceiling was a painting of a celestial diagram. While it could simply be viewed as a way to show respect to the gods, some saw it as his attempt to portray himself as someone extraordinary who did not only have a connection to the divine but also a deep knowledge of heavenly matters, such as astronomy.

Archaeologists have also unearthed his sarcophagus. What is interesting, though, is that it was fashioned using the same stone as contemporary royal sarcophagi. Even the decorations painted on it were almost identical to the styles used on those belonging to the royals. However, it was never finished, so scholars believe that it was highly unlikely that Senenmut was ever buried in it.

Senenmut's sarcophagus.[23]

Senenmut and Hatshepsut as Lovers: Fact or a Rumor?

Gossip and rumors have always been a powerful tool in human societies, though it can work in two ways. It can help spread information, but at the same time, it can also cause harm. This tool existed even in ancient times. Gossip was a subtle killer; words could topple even the greatest figures of history.

The famous Greek philosopher Socrates, for instance, had carved his name as the most famous thinker of all time. Yet, he was never free from the dangers of rumors. Word spread, accusing him of corrupting the youth and dishonoring the gods. These rumors eventually led to his trial, where he was sentenced to death. Such tragedies show how rumors—no matter how small they started—could destroy even the most respected people. Whether it was done out of jealousy or fear or created by someone trying to gain power, it was—and still is—one of the most dangerous tools that can ruin lives.

The same thing possibly happened to Senenmut and Hatshepsut. As a commoner who successfully rose to extraordinary heights of influence, it is not surprising that his name became a favorite subject of speculation. Even though scholars suggest that their relationship was forged in trust and mutual ambition, rumors circulated in the royal court speaking of their intimate relationship. This rumor never died down, even after the two died. It survived for millennia and smeared their legacies.

Marriage was important in ancient Egypt. It was not only about forming familial bonds; it was also a way to keep Egyptian society and the economy stable. Men, especially those who held status and wealth, were expected to get married and have children. Therefore, it was highly unusual for Senenmut to remain a bachelor even after obtaining such influence in the kingdom. Combined with his close relationship with Hatshepsut, speculations were born, with the people wondering whether their relationship was indeed more than just being allies.

Although there is no definitive evidence that could confirm a romantic relationship between the two, scholars have found intriguing details that could serve as potential clues. Some suggest that their professional relationship was unusual. Senenmut was trusted by the queen so much that he was given an incredible amount of power and responsibility. Apart from roles where he oversaw various construction projects, Senenmut was also showered with many more titles and honors compared to other royal advisors before him. This subtly suggests that he was very important to Hatshepsut.

Other clues came from his imagery and inscriptions. It is impressive that Senenmut was allowed to create depictions of himself in a manner often reserved for royals. Not only did he have a statue of himself alongside Neferure, but the hidden carving showing himself honoring Hatshepsut was thought to hint at a closer, more private connection with the queen. There is also crude graffiti near the mortuary temple that depicts Hatshepsut with a man in inappropriate positions. The queen never remarried, and the only man close to her was Senenmut, so many believe the man in the graffiti is supposed to be Senenmut. There is no concrete evidence that it is him; while it is plausible that the graffiti reflects a real scandal, it is also highly likely that it was created in an attempt to damage her reputation as a female pharaoh.

It is well known that the ancient Egyptian society was deeply hierarchical. Any sort of breach in royal protocol would have been documented by critics, rivals, or enemies of the pharaoh. Thus, the lack of any explicit contemporary record of their relationship could prove that there was never a scandal to begin with. Furthermore, while women in ancient Egypt did have certain rights compared to other civilizations like the Greeks or the Romans, it was still difficult for a female pharaoh to navigate her reign all alone. Because of this, it made sense for Hatshepsut, who ruled in a male-dominated society, to rely on Senenmut's skills and loyalty. While it is clear that Hatshepsut's decision to not remarry after Thutmose II's death was so that she could avoid her power being diminished, Senenmut's decision to not marry until his death could simply indicate his dedication to his duties.

Senenmut in Later Years

Senenmut continued to be Hatshepsut's most trusted confidant throughout her rule. His career reached its zenith by the sixteenth year of the queen's reign. For a man of non-royal blood, it was beyond impressive that Senenmut was able to gain such authority. Yet, for unknown reasons, shortly after this time, records of his activities ceased abruptly, which signified his decline. Mysteriously, his tomb at Hatshepsut's mortuary temple was left unfinished. His statues and inscriptions faced vandalism, and they were purposely defaced and destroyed. However, what exactly did the royal advisor do for him to earn such a fate?

Of course, the first theory lies in his supposed relationship with Hatshepsut. If the rumors were true, it could very much be possible that their scandal stirred discontent among the court officials. After all, Senenmut had an ordinary background—he belonged neither to the noble nor had royal lineage. For a mere commoner to rise so quickly and earn a soft spot in the eyes of the queen might have led the court officials to turn against him. Another theory, though almost similar to the first one, simply suggests political jealousy. His skills and talent, along with his access to power, likely made him a target of envy among the elites. He had accumulated so many titles and honors. Although he earned them, some may view this as overreach. Egyptian court politics were also notoriously treacherous. Not everyone accepted Hatshepsut as their pharaoh, so it could be plausible that the officials plotted against Senenmut as part of their effort to weaken the queen's position.

Alternatively, Senenmut's sudden fall might have also been the result of Hatshepsut's own decisions. Perhaps she had grown weary of her trusted advisor, who had gained massive influence over her people. As a queen who had successfully navigated male-dominated power structures, Hatshepsut probably found it politically crucial to distance herself from Senenmut and eventually remove him from the court. Meanwhile, there are some historians who propose that Senenmut's decline was Thutmose III's doing. Now that he had come of age, Thutmose desired the throne and was not happy with Hatshepsut denying him his rights. He might have also seen Senenmut as an obstacle to his ascension, especially after witnessing the advisor's close relationship with the queen. Therefore, one of his first steps to reclaim his authority was to silence Senenmut and erase every trace of him.

He might have done this during the later years of Hatshepsut's reign when her power was visibly waning. Perhaps after obtaining the trust of certain factions within the court, Thutmose was able to eliminate Senenmut. With the queen's most powerful supporter gone, his way to the throne was confirmed. Whether it is true that Thutmose was the one responsible for Senenmut's fall remains debatable.

Scholars suspect that the pharaoh might have been the one who ordered the defacement of his statues and inscriptions. When Thutmose finally rose as pharaoh, he worked to erase Hatshepsut's legacy. Anything related to the former queen was destroyed. Since Senenmut was closely associated with her, the advisor also faced the same fate; his memory and evidence of his contributions were condemned to erasure.

Chapter 6 – The Lost Egyptian Labyrinth

Whenever the word "labyrinth" is mentioned, many may immediately conjure an image of the legendary maze in Greek mythology. That intricate structure was believed to have been designed by the Greek architect Daedalus to house the vicious half-man, half-bull known as the Minotaur. According to the ancient myth, King Minos of Crete commissioned the famed labyrinth after receiving the monstrous creature as a punishment from the Olympian gods. The king knew that killing the Minotaur outright would do nothing except invite even more wrath from the gods. The only solution to keep the creature away from mankind was to contain it in a prison so complex that none who entered, including the Minotaur itself, could find their way out. Daedalus succeeded in fulfilling the king's order. The Minotaur was doomed to remain in its prison until the creature eventually died at the hands of the hero Theseus.

The story of this labyrinth is nothing more than a myth. No concrete evidence has ever been unearthed that showed the existence of it. However, the same could not be said about Egypt. As the land of pyramids, sphinxes, and obelisks, it is not surprising that the kingdom also housed a grand labyrinth. Ancient historians claimed it was so colossal that it dwarfed even the grandest structures of its time. It was said to have stood near the shores of Lake Moeris in the region of Faiyum and left its visitors in complete awe, including the famed Greek historian of the ancient world, Herodotus.

The Father of History claimed to have seen the labyrinth with his own eyes during his travels across Egypt. Driven by knowledge and adventure, as well as tales of the past, Herodotus arrived in the Nile Delta sometime in the 5th century BCE. Having grown up in the Greek city of Halicarnassus when it was under the watchful eyes of the Persians, Egypt was a vastly different world from his own. Herodotus might have traveled southward along the Nile in the direction of the famed pyramids of Giza. He had, of course, heard of the magnificent structure, but he was not content with only words. When he finally arrived in Giza, the historian was left speechless. He traced the lines of the limestone blocks and wondered how many hands it had taken to shape such colossal tombs. He listened to priests narrating stories of the construction and the pharaohs who were interred in them. Herodotus took note of all this information, later compiling it in his books.

His next stop was the majestic temple of Amun at Karnak. Greece had intricate columns adorning its architectural wonders, yet the ones he witnessed at Karnak were on another level. The Egyptians constructed the pillars and adorned the walls with vibrant hieroglyphs and inscriptions as if the gods themselves would one day descend to the earth and reside in the temple. Here, Herodotus observed the priests performing their sacred rites and listened to tales of their mighty gods.

Herodotus also spent time in Memphis, where he learned more about the beliefs and religion of the ancient Egyptians. He heard about the sacred bulls of Apis and learned that crocodiles were considered sacred by some Egyptians, especially those who lived near Thebes and Lake Moeris. Each wonder he visited deepened his admiration for the kingdom. Despite describing the Egyptians as starkly different and rather peculiar compared to the Greeks, Herodotus held them in high esteem.

However, out of all the wonders that he had witnessed in the kingdom, none could rival the Labyrinth of Egypt. Some people today may imagine it as a maze, perhaps similar to the ones depicted in paintings or drawings of the famous Greek labyrinth. However, this labyrinth was far from the one told in the myth; the Labyrinth of Egypt did not consist of dark, twisting corridors. Rather, it was a sprawling two-story structure. It was so massive that it housed three thousand rooms. Herodotus told us that half of the rooms were above ground while another half was built beneath the earth. There were also twelve grand patios, built perfectly symmetrical. They were arranged in two rows of six, with each doorway facing its counterpart.

A depiction of the lost Labyrinth of Egypt.[33]

It took Herodotus only a single step into the labyrinth for his eyes to widen. The network of halls, chambers, and passageways before him seemed as if it was endless, stretching into eternity. The historian had Egyptian guides accompanying him. They permitted Herodotus to enter the upper rooms, which were all heavily adorned with elaborate carvings and reliefs. Some of them told stories of the many pharaohs who once ruled the kingdom. Others depicted their mighty gods and the performance of various sacred rites. Herodotus's eyes then darted to the stone ceilings above him and wondered how long it took the Egyptians to craft such intricate wonders. The courtyards were also meticulously designed. Constructed using white marble, each of the courtyards was encircled by a colonnade. The gap between these columns allowed natural light to shine through, giving the courtyard a sense of ethereal beauty.

Herodotus made his way through almost every part of the upper rooms. He walked along the colonnade courtyard, which connected to another intricate room, and then he passed through yet another courtyard, which connected to more rooms, halls, and galleries. Herodotus then noticed another section and was curious to explore the area. However, the Egyptian guides stopped him, claiming that he was forbidden from descending into the lower chambers. When asked why, the guides spoke in hushed tones. They told the historian that the lower chambers were reserved only for the tombs of the kings who built the labyrinth. Herodotus also learned that the underground chambers housed sacred rooms where the Egyptians kept their sacred crocodiles of the Nile. The historian could only imagine these chambers since he was not allowed to lay eyes on them.

A plan of the labyrinth by the 17th-century German Jesuit scholar Athanasius Kircher based on the descriptions provided by Herodotus.[24]

Of course, Herodotus was not the only ancient writer to record and describe the labyrinth's splendor. Two centuries later, the Egyptian priest and historian of the 3rd century BCE documented the architectural wonder. His writings, however, shed more light on the pharaohs who constructed it rather than details of the labyrinth itself. Another Greek historian, Diodorus Siculus, who built his reputation in 1ˢᵗ first century BCE, as well as the Greek geographer Strabo, also included colorful descriptions of the labyrinth. Strabo was one of the few who claimed to have seen the labyrinth with his own eyes. He was especially enthralled by the colossal scale of its courtyards and the seemingly endless chambers.

Word of this famed labyrinth even reached beyond the Aegean and into ancient Rome. Roman author Pliny the Elder left us with his writings, where he described the luxurious sense of the labyrinth's halls and its exquisitely carved stone pillars. The Roman geographer of the 1ˢᵗ century BCE, Pomponius Mela, also briefly mentioned the labyrinth in his writings, though his account was the least detailed compared to the others.

Interestingly, despite being written many years apart, these records contain a high degree of consistency. Each of them mentioned the twelve patios or courtyards, the thousands of chambers and their intricate designs, and the stone ceilings. Some even described a grand temple within the labyrinth that was encircled by forty marble columns. This remarkable consistency, spanning over six centuries from Herodotus to Pomponius Mela, suggests that the labyrinth indeed existed during their time.

The Purpose of the Labyrinth: Was it Ever Intended to Be a Maze?

The main reason behind the construction of this labyrinth has long perplexed scholars, especially when ancient writers provided different explanations in their books. While some suggested that it was initially commissioned as a palace for a ruler named Moteris, others claimed it was a tomb for a certain king named Moeris. There were also those who thought of the labyrinth as a grand temple to honor the sun. The Greek orator Aelius Aristides (117–181 CE), on the other hand, provided a whole different view. He dismissed the idea that the labyrinth had any practical function. Instead, he claimed that it was nothing more than a rhetorical symbol of Egypt's greatness. However, the labyrinth was believed to have been built many centuries before the orator was born, so it could be plausible that the structure had long succumbed to the test of time before Aristides came into the world.

Diodorus Siculus had his own theory regarding the purpose of the labyrinth. He suggested that it was built as a tomb for a certain Egyptian ruler who went by the name of either Mendes or Marrus. This does make sense, given how Egyptian pharaohs tended to construct elaborate burial structures for themselves. The only problem with this is that there are no known pharaohs under that name. Diodorus did not even provide a definitive timeline of Mendes's rule; he only mentioned that he rose many generations before the emergence of the legendary King Minos of Crete.

Some scholars believe that Diodorus might have mistaken Lake Moeris as the name of the ruler who constructed the labyrinth. This theory comes from the similarity between the name "Moeris" and the names "Mendes" or "Marrus." Since Herodotus specifically wrote about the labyrinth's location being near the lake, scholars suggest that there is a possibility that Diodorus misinterpreted the name of the lake as the king who built the wonder. Others argue that the ancient historian was not mistaken. They claim that the name Mendes could be a variation of an actual king who ruled the kingdom long ago. Archaeology professor Joseph MacGillivray, for instance, suggested that Mendes could be the same person as Amenemhat III, the sixth pharaoh of the Twelfth Dynasty.

Regardless of who exactly built the labyrinth, many argue that it would have been impossible for a structure of such scale to be built solely as a tomb. Ancient accounts wrote that it was once used as a political and religious center. Strabo described it as a gathering place for Egypt's regional governors and priests. According to the ancient writer, this was where the Egyptians held religious ceremonies, administrative meetings, and judicial proceedings. The layout of the labyrinth and its numerous chambers and courts lend credence to this theory. The labyrinth might have housed representatives from Egypt's many provinces or nomes. The underground chambers could have served as hidden sanctuaries where secret ceremonies took place.

Herodotus had a different view. In his writings, the historian stated that the twelve courts within the labyrinth were commissioned by the twelve kings who reigned over the kingdom jointly. Each of these courts was designated to a king, reflecting their collective rule. However, many scholars and historians are doubtful about this claim because there are no known historical records that could confirm a time when Egypt was ruled simultaneously by twelve kings. It is plausible that Herodotus mistakenly interpreted the inscriptions on the labyrinth; the twelve courts might have symbolized an administrative system rather than actual co-rulers.

Other scholars suggest that the labyrinth might have been a record-keeping center. If this theory is true, the many chambers in the labyrinth were probably where sacred scrolls and records of administrative, judicial, and economic affairs were stored. The countless passages might have been purposely designed to confuse people. Only those with authority knew the way, thus keeping the records perfectly safe.

Of course, there is also the idea that the labyrinth held a more symbolic meaning. The maze-like nature was probably designed to represent the order and chaos of the cosmos. This mirrored the Egyptian belief in the divine balance of the universe, Ma'at.

The Lost Location of the Labyrinth Unveiled

The labyrinth's exact purpose remains one of its two biggest mysteries, with the second being its location. Whether it was buried beneath the sands of Egypt, dismantled for its stone, or completely lost to the merciless passage of time, no one knows for sure. Ancient writers provided instructions or descriptions of its location, but they were rather vague. However, thanks to these clues, significant discoveries were finally made in the past few decades. The one made by William Flinders Petrie, for instance, shone a better light on the location of the labyrinth.

William Flinders Petrie is a familiar name, especially among Egyptologists, archaeologists, and scholars of the late 19th century. The British archaeologist was considered one of the pioneers of systematic archaeology in Egypt. He earned a reputation for his rigorous fieldwork and contributions that helped us understand the ancient Egyptian civilization. His biggest discovery was at Hawara. Here, Petrie uncovered a massive artificial stone plateau measuring at least three hundred meters by over two hundred meters. After more excavations and studies, Petrie eventually concluded that the stone foundation was the remnants of none other than the legendary labyrinth told by ancient historians.

This conclusion sparked interest, especially among the archaeological community. Some were doubtful that it had once been the site of the lost labyrinth, while others kept an open mind. The dimensions of the foundation, as well as its location close to the pyramid of Amenemhat II, suggest that it could have once supported the colossal labyrinth.

Some also presented the idea that the labyrinth itself was connected to Amenemhat's pyramid. It might have served a religious or funerary purpose. Following more excavations, Petrie later discovered that the structures around the pyramid were much larger and more complex than they previously thought, which led some scholars and historians to speculate that the labyrinth was far from a separate structure but rather a part of Amenemhat's grand construction plans.

The Middle Kingdom (c. 2055-1650 BCE), the period to which Amenemhat III belonged, was described by historians as a time when Egypt achieved political stability, tremendous economic growth, and a flourishing culture. The kingdom had endured the turmoil of the First Intermediate Period, during which time two dynasties vied for power. It was not until the rise of Mentuhotep II of the Eleventh Dynasty that the Egyptians were finally able to rediscover a glimmer of hope for their kingdom. The people saw the expansion of administrative reforms, extensive trade networks, and the start of more impressive architectural projects. While it was typical for pharaohs to cement their reputation through military campaigns, the rulers of the Middle Kingdom were also eager to solidify their legacy through grand construction programs. Pyramids continued to fill the kingdom's map, along with majestic temples and vast mortuary complexes.

Egypt witnessed an even greater period of prosperity and expansion when the throne was passed to Amenemhat III. Reigning over the Nile for nearly forty-five years, his name is often remembered as one of the most famous builders of ancient Egypt. The Faiyum region (also spelled as Fayoum), in particular, experienced rapid upgrades, eventually transforming into a key agricultural and administrative hub. This was largely due to its irrigation improvements and close proximity to Lake Moeris. Perhaps seeing the strategic importance of the region, Amenemhat later chose it as the site for his resting place.

This region was not his first choice, though. The pharaoh had already commissioned the construction of his pyramid at Dahshur. Now famously known as the Black Pyramid, its initial construction was full of structural flaws. It suffered from foundational instability. Cracks were said to have constantly appeared within its corridors and chambers, which made it impossible to house the remains of the pharaoh once the time came. By the fifteenth year of his reign, Amenemhat III had shifted his focus from Dahshur to Hawara, which was a short distance away from the center of Faiyum and Lake Moeris.

The Black Pyramid at Dahshur was not entirely abandoned. Instead of becoming the eternal resting place for the pharaoh, it was repurposed as a burial site reserved for several royal women, especially those who had blood relations to Amenemhat himself. The pharaoh was later interred at Hawara. Unlike the pyramid at Dahshur, his tomb in Hawara featured a more stable design and improved structural integrity.

Approximately twelve kilometers south of his pyramid, archaeologists unearthed another significant structure: the tomb of his daughter, Neferuptah. This adds more weight to the argument that Hawara was an elaborate mortuary complex serving multiple purposes beyond being the eternal home of Amenemhat III alone. Based on the sheer scale of the labyrinth as described by the ancient writers, some scholars proposed that the structure was possibly an essential part of this funerary site.

Many may wonder how the labyrinth disappeared completely despite its colossal size and complex design. Flinders Petrie answered this query by explaining the possibility of the labyrinth being dismantled and its stones reused for other purposes. This theory revolves around Ptolemy II when Egypt was in its Hellenistic period. Scholars suggested that the pharaoh might have used much of the labyrinth's stone to construct the nearby town of Shedet, better known as Crocodilopolis (it was built to honor Ptolemy's wife, Arsinoe). However, the total destruction of such a monumental structure remains a hot subject of debate. Some argue that the dismantling of the labyrinth alone was not enough for the structure to disappear completely; these scholars suggest that natural factors also contributed to its disappearance. The shifting river patterns in the Faiyum regions could have played a role too. Looting might have occurred over the centuries. The only thing left for us today is its stone base.

Another Clue

Although many accepted the conclusion made by Petrie, which suggested the enormous stone slab was the foundation of the long-lost labyrinth, there were those who were not entirely convinced. The most prominent individual to challenge this conclusion was a Belgian researcher named Louis de Cordier.

Cordier revisited Petrie's finding of the enormous stone platform. According to the ancient descriptions written by Herodotus and others, they spoke of a grand structure with an imposing stone ceiling. The roof was so massive that it covered the entire complex beneath it. The mention of this stone ceiling was repeatedly mentioned in multiple sources; one documented how the ceiling seemed like an unbroken stretch of stone, while another highlighted how the entire roof was made of a single solid slab. If these descriptions were true, then what Petrie thought was a foundation could actually be the labyrinth's roof. This means the rest of the structure was never dismantled or lost; rather, it was hidden beneath the earth.

This possibility changed everything. However, Cordier knew that excavating the site would not be easy. Traditional digging methods were definitely out of the question because the massive stone layer was not ordinary rubble or sand but rather a solid—or perhaps artificial, if it were really the roof of the labyrinth—plateau. Any attempt to break through it would cause irreparable damage to the rest of the structure. Furthermore, the labyrinth was believed to have an extensive network of chambers and near-endless passageways. An uncontrolled excavation could negatively impact the delicate architectural features. To avoid these big risks, Cordier and his team chose a non-invasive method: ground penetrating radar.

Known as the Mataha Expedition, Cordier and his team finally received good news after years of planning. In February 2008, the Supreme Council of Antiquities of Egypt granted permission for Cordier to conduct a full-scale geophysical survey on the same site where Petrie had previously explored. Hoping that the mystery of the labyrinth could be uncovered, Cordier brought in a team of specialists from the National Research Institute of Astronomy and Geophysics (NRIAG) to join the mission. Equipped with state-of-the-art radar equipment, their main objective was to scan the site, specifically beneath the stone plateau, without disturbing it.

Anticipation ran high. The team was hoping for even the smallest sign that there were structures hidden below. When positive results came in, Cordier was pleased. It turned out that the radar had detected a massive structure buried beneath the surface, with the depths ranging from eight to twelve meters. What was even more astonishing was that the scans also showed a precise grid pattern, which could possibly be an arrangement of chambers and thick walls, forming an extensive, well-organized complex. The team then discovered that these structures exhibited high resistivity, which meant that there was a presence of stone or possibly granite. This was an astounding discovery since they perfectly matched the ancient descriptions. At this point in time, the world was confident that this physical evidence confirmed the existence of the famed labyrinth.

These positive results were published in the scientific journal of the NRIAG in the fall of 2008. Their discoveries were widely shared at a public lecture at Ghent University in Belgium, which was attended by dozens of scholars and historians. Members of the press were also present since the announcement had sent ripples throughout the archaeological community. This could very well be one of the most significant discoveries of ancient Egypt's grandest wonder.

Unfortunately, hopes were crushed when everything suddenly fell silent. Without warning, the Supreme Council of Antiquities of Egypt imposed an unexpected restriction. Not only were all discussions about the labyrinth halted, but any communication about the findings was also suddenly prohibited. The authorities gave only one reason: Egyptian national security sanctions. Disappointed, some dismissed the result without questions, yet many others, including Cordier himself, thought the decision was strange and unexpected. A few questions linger to this day. Why would such an important historical discovery be suppressed? What was so dangerous about revealing the truth behind the labyrinth?

Cordier waited for two more years, holding on to what was left of his hope. However, by June 2010, it was clear that further examinations would not happen. The mystery would remain unsolved. The labyrinth was left buried not only beneath the sands but also beneath the layers of bureaucratic silence.

Despite the silence, Cordier's expedition breathed new life into the mystery that had puzzled many for centuries. More theories arose from the unanswered questions. While some suggested that the Egyptian government was actually concerned about this renewed attention, fearing that the site might face destruction or even looting, others believe there was a more paranormal reason.

Ancient Egypt has long been associated with curses, especially those involving tombs and sacred sites. The most famous of these is the curse of Tutankhamun's tomb. This curse has already been debunked, yet there are still some who believe in the supernatural consequences of messing with Egyptian tombs. Some speculate the same about the labyrinth; they believe the site also holds a curse.

Regardless of the reason, we can at least be assured that the Labyrinth of Egypt was not just a legend or tale created by ancient writers. It is currently buried beneath the desert, waiting to be unearthed one day.

Chapter 7 – The Nubian Pharaohs: Egypt's Forgotten Dynasty

The Egyptians could do nothing but witness their kingdom slowly descend into a period of weakness, division, and chaos. The last time they had ever seen a capable ruler on the throne was when Ramesses III wore the double crown. Egypt was already in turmoil when the Sea Peoples launched their campaigns, yet the pharaoh succeeded in repelling the invaders. However, his victories came at a heavy cost. The Egyptian treasury, which once had gold flowing like the Nile itself, was now nearly empty following years of conquests and war. Corruption began to seep into the royal court, and the military gradually shrank in both strength and effectiveness.

Then, sometime in 1170 BCE, came the strike at Deir el-Medina. However, this was not the only chaos that Egypt had to endure. By the time Ramesses III was assassinated, Egypt continued to spiral into a state of decline. His successors were weak rulers who failed to hold the empire together. Not only did the kingdom's wealth deteriorate, but Egypt also lost control of a few of its prized territories, such as Canaan and Nubia. It was clear that the kingdom was fracturing.

Soon, another power began to rise that challenged the authority of the pharaoh. For years, Amun had been one of the kingdom's most important deities. Lands and riches were typically granted to the priests of Amun by past rulers, allowing them to grow incredibly wealthy. By the Twentieth Dynasty, the temple of Amun in Karnak was essentially a state within a state. Not only did the temple control the lands, but its priests were also in charge of thousands of workers.

During this time, Egypt was under the rule of Ramesses XI, the last ruler of the Twentieth Dynasty. Despite the pharaoh still sitting on top of the hierarchy, a certain individual suddenly declared himself the ruler of Upper Egypt. His name was Herihor, the high priest of Amun in Thebes. With Ramesses XI's power reduced only to the north and the priests of Amun controlling Upper Egypt (located in the south), the kingdom was officially divided into two. Gone were the times when pharaohs were seen as the almighty ruler, second only to the gods.

The Arrival of the Libyans

Egypt was now vulnerable, especially to ambitious foreigners who wished to claim the land. The Libyans, for instance, held such an ambition. The Libyans did not always see eye to eye with the Egyptians. They once fought against the kingdom until the era of the New Kingdom when pharaohs began hiring them as mercenaries. In return for loyal service, they were granted land and opportunities, allowing them to rise through the ranks. Some earned enough trust from the pharaohs and even became powerful local rulers. Eventually, the Libyans grew so bold that they believed they no longer needed the pharaoh at all.

This could be seen in 945 BCE when a certain Libyan chieftain known as Shoshenq I declared himself the new pharaoh of Egypt. His rule started the Twenty-second Dynasty, marking the first time a foreigner rose to power from within Egypt's own system—unlike the Hyksos kings of the Fifteenth Dynasty, who had taken control through conquest. The pharaohs of this new dynasty ruled from Tanis, a city in the Eastern Delta. They never succeeded in claiming full control over the kingdom since the authority in Upper Egypt belonged to the priests of Amun. The priests refused to acknowledge these Libyan kings as the true rulers of Egypt, which led to the further fragmentation of the kingdom. Many more individuals, often chieftains of the other small territories, soon claimed their right to the throne, worsening the already weakening kingdom.

By the time of the Twenty-third Dynasty (c. 818-730 BCE), Egypt was nearly drowning. There were as many as four or perhaps five different individuals who claimed to be the rightful pharaoh of the kingdom.

Tefnakht Challenged the Priests of Amun

Tefnakht was another powerful individual who sought to see Egypt united again—but of course, it would be under his rule. In order to challenge the Theban priests controlling Upper Egypt, the warlord knew he had to muster every force he could on the Nile Delta. Luckily, Tefnakht was a skilled strategist. Even though he achieved little to no direct conquests, the ruler from Sais succeeded in forging alliances with other rulers of the Delta. With his power and reputation growing each day, Tefnakht began to turn his attention southward. He marched his forces to Middle Egypt and captured the cities that dotted the region.

His advance undoubtedly alerted the priests of Amun. If he were to succeed in entering Thebes, the last stronghold of the priests, Tefnakht would achieve his goal. Once he obtained total domination of both Lower and Middle Egypt, the warlord would be granted a clear pathway to Upper Egypt and even Nubia. The priests of Amun knew they could not rely solely on themselves to defeat the advancing warlord, so they chose to reach for outside help. They turned to Piye, the Nubian king of Kush.

The Rise of the Kushite Kingdom

As early as the Middle Kingdom, the Egyptians valued Nubia. It was thought to be a land of immense wealth. To keep a close eye on the region, the Egyptians began building forts in the area, installing garrisons and trading posts along the Nile in the hopes they could get their hands on the region's resources. When the New Kingdom began, the Nubians began to lose their authority. Pharaohs of the era, particularly Thutmose I and Thutmose III, poured extensive amounts of money to push into the Nubian lands. Eventually, the region was under the complete control of the Egyptians. From there on, Egyptian temples began to fill the region, and their religious practices were imposed on the locals. Nubian rulers, referred to as the viceroys of Kush, were appointed as representatives of the pharaohs.

For centuries, Nubia, also known as Kush, became an extension of the Nile kingdom. The Kushites adopted Egyptian customs and even worshiped the same gods as the Egyptians, particularly Amun. Their arts were also influenced by the Egyptians, as well as their government structure. However, Egypt was not meant to rule over Kush for too long.

When Egypt went into decline by the time of the Third Intermediate Period (c. 1070–664 BCE), its control over Kush had greatly weakened. Seeing an opportunity to break free from the once-mighty kingdom, the Kushites claimed their independence sometime around 1000 BCE. Gone were the days when the viceroys of Kush had to report to the Egyptian pharaohs. Napata, a city near the sacred mountain of Gebel Barkal, was made the beating heart of this blossoming kingdom. Now known as the Kingdom of Kush, it soon turned into a powerful force in the south.

The sacred mountain Gebel Barkal, believed to be the residence of the god Amun.[26]

Regardless of being free from the grasp of the Egyptians, the Kushites still embraced the Egyptian culture. Amun was still greatly worshiped, with temples dedicated to the god constructed in a blend of both Egyptian and Nubian styles. As their influence expanded, the Kushites managed to gain control over the lands that were once under Egypt's control. With these newly obtained territories, the rulers of Kush grew wealthier. With more power in their hands, they grew more ambitious. As a result, the Kushites began to turn their gaze north toward Egypt.

The relationship between these two kingdoms was not always hostile. In fact, the Kushites still maintained close ties with the priests of Amun in Thebes; after all, they shared the reverence of the same god. In many ways, Kush and Upper Egypt became natural allies. They were united in their devotion to Amun, while the rest of Egypt remained divided among warlords and foreign rulers. So, when the priests sent a plea for aid, the reigning Kushite king at the time, Piye, did not hesitate to answer with reinforcements.

Piye rose to the throne in the 8th century BCE. A devout follower of Amun, the Kushite king viewed the fragmentation of Egypt as a violation of divine will. He saw the warlords who had claimed control over Egypt not as legitimate rulers but rather as greedy usurpers who had strayed far from the path of Ma'at. Piye thought it was his sole duty to restore Egypt. With an army of hardened Kushite warriors, exceptionally skilled archers, and his Egyptian allies, who were loyal to the Theban priests, Piye launched his campaign. He marched northward to Upper Egypt.

Thebes was pleased with the arrival of Piye and his forces. He was thought to be its savior. The Thebans welcomed the Kushite king and escorted him to the temple of Amun at Karnak. Here, he was believed to have prayed and made offerings to the god. The priests of Amun then proclaimed him the rightful ruler of Egypt. With the blessings of the gods and the priests, Piye set forth on his divine mission to reunite the vast kingdom. He marched toward the cities of Middle Egypt. Some surrendered willingly after seeing the king was a savior sent by Amun, while others attempted to resist. However, none could rival the might of the Kushite forces. The warlords of Middle Egypt, who had once ruled as independent rulers, eventually bowed down to the Kushite king. Some even sent him gifts, hoping they could get on Piye's good side. The king was not interested in bribes, though; he wanted only their loyalty.

At Sais, Tefnakht was growing wary. He heard news of Piye's advance and the king's success in gaining control of many territories. The warlord quickly formed a coalition of Delta rulers to go against the Kushite king. Among them were Osorkon IV of Tanis, a ruler whose background could be traced back to the Libyan dynasties. Others were powerful rulers from Herakleopolis and Memphis. They were hopeful that, together, they could stop Piye from snatching their crowns.

Nevertheless, their nightmare came true. Piye laid a siege on Herakleopolis. It was considered one of the most important strongholds on the path to Lower Egypt. The exact duration of the siege remains unknown, but according to Piye's victory stela, it was swift. When the city's defenses finally crumbled, its ruler, Peftjauawybast, was left with no other choice but to surrender. This, however, was only the beginning. Following this victory, Piye advanced to the seat of power for Lower Egypt, Memphis. It was crucial for Piye to repeat his success here since Memphis was the stronghold of Tefnakht's coalition. Having the city under his control meant he could easily break the rest of his enemies.

Memphis was well defended; fortified walls protected its subjects at all sides, and the Nile was a natural barrier. The defenders showed their loyalty to Tefnakht by fighting fiercely against the Kushites. Yet, as their resources dwindled, it was only a matter of time before they eventually lost hope and succumbed to their fate. Piye's army, on the other hand, was relentless; the king himself was said to have ordered his men to fight as if there were no tomorrow. The Kushite forces attacked from the river, overwhelming Tefnakht's army. Memphis fell after a few days of intense battle. This victory led the other leaders of the Delta coalition to surrender to Piye.

Tefnakht was hit with the realization that he had lost. However, he refused to face Piye directly. Instead, the warlord fled northward, hoping he could remain safe behind the walls of his capital city, Sais. Piye had all the might and resources to pursue Tefnakht, yet he chose not to. His mission was to restore order, not cause destruction. His key allies had already surrendered and sworn loyalty to the Kushite king. Tefnakht eventually sent messengers to Piye, acknowledging his supreme rule over Egypt. The warlord never appeared before the new pharaoh of Egypt.

With the two lands of Egypt now reunited, Piye's divine task was accomplished. Interestingly, Piye did not remain in Egypt. He never forgot his background; Piye was a Kushite, not Egyptian, king. After vanquishing his enemies and consolidating his power, Piye planned to journey back to his kingdom. He was said to have visited the great temples of Egypt before his departure, where he spent time performing rituals before the great gods. This was to reaffirm his divine right to rule. Then, the new pharaoh of Egypt left, making his way south to the capital of Kush, Napata.

Although Piye was an absent ruler (he ruled from his homeland), Egypt was able to taste a pinch of peace once again. Before leaving, Piye made sure he left a system of governance that ensured stability. Egyptian officials were given a certain degree of autonomy, and the majestic temples in Egypt continued to flourish. Religious traditions, especially those done in honor of Amun, were also revitalized.

Piye's Death, Taharqa's Rise, and the Might of the Assyrians

In contrast to other kings and rulers who often met their fate either on the battlefield or through assassinations, Piye left the world rather peacefully. He died in his homeland of Kush. His remains were buried in a manner similar to the Egyptian tradition. His pyramid, though modest in size compared to the grand pyramids of Giza, can be found in El-Kurru, near Napata.

El-Kurru, located to the south of Jebel Barkal.[36]

Despite his death, Egypt did not immediately descend into another episode of chaos. The Kushite throne was passed to Piye's brother, Shabaka, who was also given the double crown of Egypt. Few sources were left that can lead us through the journey of Shabaka's life, but we do know that the king strengthened the Kushite rule over Egypt. There were no major conflicts that took place during his reign, but another misfortune was brewing. This time, it would come from the east.

During Shabaka's reign, a certain figure was building his reputation. Known as Taharqa, he was the son of the great Piye himself; however, some sources claim that he was actually his nephew. Being raised in the royal court of Napata, it is not a surprise that Taharqa grew up to be an ambitious royal. Sources suggest that Taharqa began his career serving as a military commander, gaining precious experience in warfare. Having spent much of his early life in Egypt, the Kushite prince was well versed in state matters.

Since religious devotion was placed above all else, especially when his name would be on the list of rulers of Kush, it was of the utmost importance that Taharqa commit himself to the spiritual world. He was said to have constantly traveled to Thebes when he was a young man, forming strong ties with the priesthood of Amun.

However, since succession in Kush was based on seniority, Taharqa was not the next in line when Shabaka passed away. Instead, the throne was passed to Shebitku. His relation to both Piye and Shabaka is unclear; some suggest he was either Shabaka's nephew or younger brother. Like his predecessors, Shebitku maintained control over Egypt, continuing the policies of the previous Kushite kings. This was also the time of the greatest test the dynasty faced: the Assyrian Empire.

The Assyrians first rose to power around the 14th century BCE, with their roots tracing back to northern Mesopotamia (modern-day Iraq), but it was not until the 9th century BCE that the empire began to transform into one of the dominant forces of the ancient world. For years, they relentlessly expanded their influence across the Near East, eventually becoming an empire that could rival both Egypt and Kush. The Assyrians were known to be militaristic people. Apart from being famed for their iron weapons, the Assyrians were also exceptionally skilled in siege warfare. Over the years, they successfully conquered a collection of territories from Babylonia to the Levant.

Tensions between Assyria and Egypt became apparent when the Assyrians were under the reign of Sargon II (722-705 BCE). It began when Egypt, which was under the rule of Shabaka, clearly showed support for the anti-Assyrian rebellions that erupted in kingdoms like Judah and Philistia. Even though Sargon managed to quell these rebellions, resistance remained in the Levant, with Egypt continuously supporting them.

Taharqa finally inherited the throne following the passing of Shebitku in 690 BCE. His early reign saw a flourishing of Egyptian culture and military power. He undertook massive building projects, restoring temples and monuments across the land. However, at the same time, the conflict between Assyria and Egypt had already escalated. The Assyrians did not only see Egypt as a distant influence that meddled in Levantine affairs but also as a direct enemy. The Assyrian king was well aware of the land's rich resources and history. However, to get his hands on the land, they first needed to go against the Kushite rulers.

In 674 BCE, the Assyrians, under King Esarhaddon, marched into Egypt. This marked the beginning of their invasion of the kingdom. With his massive army, Esarhaddon trampled through the Levant, crushing anyone who dared to stand in his path. He had a clear goal: break Kushite rule over Egypt and claim the double crown for himself. The mission was far from a piece of cake, though, as Taharqa was not an easy opponent. With haste, the Kushite pharaoh mustered his forces, gathering soldiers who hailed from both Egypt and Nubia.

The two forces eventually clashed. Neither the exact date nor location was ever confirmed due to the lack of records, but Taharqa successfully repelled the Assyrian invasion. This was a major victory for the Egyptians and a humiliation for the Assyrian war machine. Nevertheless, Assyria was not a kingdom that knew how to back down.

Esarhaddon, perhaps fueled by rage, launched a second, much larger invasion in 671 BCE. The preparations were meticulous since the king could not bear to face yet another episode of humiliation. Esarhaddon made sure to use his superior siege tactics to break the fortified walls of Egypt. With his massive army—his numbers were even bigger this time around—the Assyrians overwhelmed the Egyptian defenses. Although Taharqa himself fought bravely, the odds were clearly against him. Memphis, the great city of Lower Egypt, crumbled and fell to the Assyrians. Esarhaddon then pushed south. Taharqa slowly realized there was no easy way out, and he retreated to Upper Egypt and eventually back to Kush.

Again, Egypt witnessed a change of hands in the royal court. This was the beginning of the end of the Kushite rule of Egypt. Esarhaddon installed puppet rulers in the north, which allowed the Assyrians to gain firm control over Lower Egypt. Taharqa attempted to reassert his dominance over the Nile Valley, but the Assyrians were too powerful. It was clear that Egypt was too far out of his reach.

Tantamani, the Last Pharaoh of the Nubian Dynasty

Unless divine intervention happened, it was impossible for the Kushites to reclaim their foothold in Egypt. Following the loss of Lower Egypt to the Assyrians, Taharqa spent the remainder of his life in Napata. He ruled over the Kingdom of Kush and remained a powerful figure in the region. The Kushite king passed away in 664 BCE, possibly due to natural causes. His remains were buried in the royal necropolis of Nuri.

The throne was then passed to his successor, Tantamani. He was either the son or nephew of Taharqa. Tantamani was not planning on sitting still while the Assyrians had their claws in Lower Egypt. During this time, the Assyrians had Necho I acting as their puppet ruler in Lower Egypt.

Tantamani refused to accept the loss of Egypt and soon declared his divine right to rule both Kush and Egypt. Just as Piye before him,

Tantamani also believed that the gods had chosen him to restore Ma'at. He believed that balance and order had been disrupted when Egypt was put under Assyrian rule. Sometime in 663 BCE, Tantamani launched his campaign to retake the kingdom of the Nile. He first had his eyes on Thebes, which had long been a stronghold of Kushite influence. Since the priests of Amun were loyal to the Nubian dynasty, Tantamani was warmly welcomed as the kingdom's rightful ruler.

In Thebes, Tantamani began working on the preparation of his campaign. In order to push north, he had to gather a force; he did so by mustering an army of Kushite warriors and Egyptian supporters. His goal was straightforward: retake Memphis, drive out the Assyrians, and restore Kushite dominance over Egypt. His campaign went well in the beginning. As his forces advanced, many cities fell to his army. Puppet rulers who had been installed by the Assyrians fled for their lives. Even Necho I of Lower Egypt was incapable of stopping the wrath of the Kushite king. Eventually, Tantamani's next target was none other than Memphis, the very city that had fallen to the Assyrians years prior.

Tantamani's Temporary Victory

As soon as he reached Memphis, Tantamani did not hesitate to launch a full-scale assault on the city. His warriors stormed the fortified walls and obliterated those who stood in their way. Fierce and brutal fighting ensued. Necho I was among those who lay lifeless on the ground. Tantamani succeeded in recapturing Memphis, and with this victory, it was not a surprise that other remaining Egyptian warlords came running to submit to his rule.

The Kushite king achieved what his predecessor had failed to accomplish. He had successfully reclaimed Egypt's heartland and drove out the Assyrian-backed rulers. For a brief moment, it seemed as if Amun was on their side. However, this was nothing more than just a temporary victory.

News of Tantamani's success soon reached the ears of the reigning king of Assyria, Ashurbanipal. He was furious and saw the Kushites' campaign as an act of defiance. He refused to see any other outcome; Ashurbanipal wanted Tantamani and the Kushites crushed. In 663 BCE, the Assyrian king wasted no time in launching another massive invasion of Egypt. This time around, the Assyrians refrained from showing even the smallest glint of mercy. They were determined to destroy Kushite rule once and for all.

Along with siege engines and battle-hardened mercenaries obtained from the Levant, the Assyrians marched into Egypt with terrifying speed. It did not take long for them to recapture Memphis. Tantamani's forces, though they fought valiantly, were forced to retreat to Thebes. However, the Assyrians, perhaps driven by their rage, did not sheathe their weapons just yet. They marched to Thebes, and for the first time in history, Egypt's religious capital was completely sacked. Ancient historians recorded the Assyrians' act of plundering the great temples of Amun. They took away the sacred relics and treasure, bringing them back to their capital, Nineveh. Thebes was left in ruins.

Tantamani was forced to leave the Nile kingdom and return to Nubia. Despite continuing to rule his kingdom from Napata, he never set foot on Egyptian soil again. With both Thebes and Memphis securely under Assyrian control, Ashurbanipal's goal was achieved: Kushite rule in Egypt had been wiped out.

To secure their power in Lower Egypt, the Assyrians installed Psamtik I as their new puppet ruler. This, however, was a mistake, as Psamtik I was different from the previous puppet kings. He succeeded in establishing full independence from the Assyrians. Psamtik was the founder of the Twenty-sixth Dynasty, the last great Egyptian dynasty before the Persian conquest. The age of the Kushite pharaohs had come to an end, but with Psamtik I on the throne, the Egyptians could live under the rule of a native pharaoh once more.

Chapter 8 – The Sacred Lake of Karnak

Hatshepsut passed away sometime in 1458 BCE, possibly due to natural causes. The queen reigned for over twenty years, making her one of the longest-reigning and most successful female pharaohs in Egyptian history. Of course, her passing paved the way for Thutmose III to finally claim the crown. The pharaoh inherited a kingdom that was already at its height. Nevertheless, Thutmose never thought of laying low; the pharaoh wished to expand Egypt further and build a reputation for himself that could rival his predecessors.

Also known as the "Napoleon of Egypt" (the term was given by the American Egyptologist James Breasted), the pharaoh was best known for his military campaigns, especially those he launched in the Levant. Through this series of campaigns, Egypt was able to expand its territory, eventually establishing it as a dominant power in the ancient Near East. It was also through these successful conquests that Egypt gained more wealth. Apart from tributes, the kingdom also gained access to valuable resources, including cedar from Lebanon and precious metals from the Sinai Peninsula.

It is safe to say that Thutmose was a good ruler. Not only did he excel on the battlefield, but the pharaoh was also a builder. He was well aware that Egypt's spiritual and cultural identity was intertwined with its religious institutions, particularly the worship of Amun. Thutmose himself was a devout follower of Amun, so it is not surprising that the pharaoh sought any way to glorify the god. Also, in an effort to consolidate his own divine kingship, Thutmose launched dozens of construction projects throughout the years of his reign (he ruled for over fifty years). After all, Egypt had amassed a substantial amount of wealth from its successful military campaigns. Among his many contributions to the architecture of Egypt, the one that stood out the most was his work on the Karnak Temple Complex.

The Karnak Complex

The Karnak Temple Complex was already over five centuries old when Thutmose III came to the throne. Its origins could be traced back to the Middle Kingdom when Pharaoh Senusret I of the Twelfth Dynasty established the site as a sanctuary to honor the chief deity, Amun. The complex was initially filled with modest structures, but it evolved into an impressive site as time went on. Thutmose I, Hatshepsut, and

Amenhotep were a few of the pharaohs who contributed to Karnak's expansion. However, it was under Thutmose III that the complex underwent significant enhancements. It was later transformed into a crucial site that symbolized the divine connection between the gods and the pharaohs.

Karnak was situated on the east bank of the Nile in Thebes (modern-day Luxor). Considered today as one of the largest religious sites ever constructed, this two-hundred-acre sanctuary was built as a dedication to the king of the Egyptian gods, Amun, and his consort Mut and their son Khonsu.

Carved columns at the Hypostyle Hall of Karnak.[38]

Some might agree that one of the most impressive features of Karnak is the Hypostyle Hall, which is described as a forest of columns. There are 134 intricately carved columns in total, with some reaching over 20 meters. These columns were arranged in sixteen rows and adorned with various hieroglyphs and depictions of the pharaohs honoring the gods. The Karnak Temple Complex was also the home to the famed ceremonial pathway known as the Avenue of Sphinxes. Flanked by rows of ram-headed sphinxes, this pathway connected Karnak to the Luxor Temple and played a major role in religious rituals.

Ram-headed sphinxes lined up along the Avenue of Sphinxes.²⁹

Perhaps one of the most notable expansion projects commissioned by Thutmose III was the Akhmenu. Also known as the Festival Hall, this structure could be located in the eastern precinct of the temple complex. It was designed specifically for the Heb-Sed festival, which was a royal jubilee that celebrated the renewal of the pharaoh's power. Besides exquisite carved reliefs that told stories of Thutmose's military successes and offerings to Amun, the Akhmenu also featured a botanical garden. This, however, was not a real garden but a stone-carved relief that depicted exotic plants and animals like giraffes and ibexes brought back from Thutmose's military campaigns in Syria and Nubia.

Akhmenu or the Festival Hall of Thutmose III.[50]

Thutmose III added a few obelisks at Karnak. These towering structures, often gilded to reflect the sunlight, were built in honor of Amun and the sun god, Ra. The pharaoh also played a hand in expanding the temple's boundaries. He added the sixth pylon, which enhanced the grand entrance to the temple of Amun-Ra. Like many other structures and temples at the site, Thutmose's pylon was beautifully adorned with inscriptions and carved reliefs that depicted scenes of his celebrated victories, especially the ones he achieved in the Levant.

However, out of all the expansions he made to the Karnak Temple Complex, the most remarkable was the Sacred Lake. Measuring at least 120 meters by 77 meters, this rectangular lake is considered the largest sacred lake from ancient Egypt. What makes this massive artificial reservoir interesting is the story behind its creation, as it was created as an embodiment of creation itself.

According to Egyptian cosmology, long before the world took its earliest form, before the sky stretched overhead, and before the earth had solidified beneath our feet, there was only Nun. Nun was unlike other important gods of the Egyptian pantheon, like Ra, Osiris, or even Thoth, the god of wisdom. Nun was a being far more ancient. He was infinite and unshaped. Some say he was the eternal flood, while others suggest he was associated with the deep abyss of nothingness and the dark void from which all things would emerge.

It was within this limitless yet silent ocean that the world came to be. From it, a mound of land was born, and it stood alone in the midst of this endless ocean. This sacred mound was known in Egyptian mythology as the benben, and this was where existence began to take shape. Upon it, the first god emerged. This was the self-created ancient god known as Atum. He stood alone on the benben since nothing else existed then.

Later on, from his body, Atum created his children: Shu (the god of air) and Tefnut (the goddess of moisture). From them came Geb (the earth) and Nut (the sky), who, in turn, brought forth the deities known as Osiris, Isis, Set, and Nephthys. These four would be the ones who would shape the destiny of mortals and gods.

As for Nun, he never truly vanished despite the completion of the creation process. Instead, he remained beneath the world. Hidden yet eternal, Nun played a role in nourishing the land just as the Nile's flood brought fortune to the crops every year. This belief inspired the creation of the Sacred Lake; it was meant to be the earthly reflection of the primeval abyss.

The Sacred Lake of Karnak.[81]

The Sacred Lake of Karnak was lined with stone walls and even had stairways that led directly into the water. Surrounding the lake were storerooms and living quarters reserved for the priests. In the morning, before the first rays of Ra emerged from the horizon, the high priests of Amun would go down the stairways into the lake, where they would use the sacred water to purify themselves. This had to be done so that both their bodies and spirits were free from the dust of the mortal world. Only then could the priests enter the temple for other rituals and ceremonial practices. Since the lake was also the home of the sacred geese of Amun (another symbol of creation since the cosmic goose was the one that laid the primordial egg from which creation began), scholars suggest that these priests were also responsible for raising and caring for these creatures. It was important to make sure the geese were in good shape, especially since they would occasionally be used in rituals as living representations of Amun himself.

Interestingly, the lake was said to have never dried up. Besides being used by the priests to purify themselves, the lake was also used in various religious ceremonies and festivals. The waters were used to anoint sacred statues and purify offerings. They were used in ritual processions that celebrated creation, renewal, and divine blessings.

It made sense for later pharaohs who came to the throne after Thutmose III to continue upgrading the lake and its surroundings. The Nubian pharaoh Taharqa, for instance, commissioned the construction of a grand structure on the northern edge of the Sacred Lake. Known by modern scholars as the Edifice of Taharqa, the exact purpose of this structure remains a topic of debate. While some suggest it played a role in religious rituals and royal offerings (especially since Taharqa was known to be extremely devoted to Amun), others claimed it served as temple administration.

Another striking addition near the lake was the sculpture of a scarab (a symbol of the god Khepri) made of granite. It was placed at the northern corner of the lake, a short distance away from the Osirian Temple of Taharqa. This massive scarab, however, was not built on site; it was initially placed in Amenhotep III's mortuary temple, which was located on the west bank of Thebes. Carved entirely in sunk relief, the scarab's pedestal was flattened into the shape of a stela, bearing inscriptions that emphasized the divine renewal of kingship and the eternal cycle of creation. The scarab beetle itself was a sacred emblem of transformation, as the scarab was thought to have rolled the sun across the sky as it emerged from the formless chaos, just as the world had risen from the waters of Nun.

The Osirian Temple of Taharqa.[32]

The Sacred Lake of Karnak was a reminder of the primeval waters of Nun. It was a sacred reservoir where purification was placed above all else. However, like the great temple complex itself, the Sacred Lake was also a portal to something far greater. It was also where the high priests would gather to prepare for one of ancient Egypt's grandest celebrations.

Known as the Festival of Opet, it first gained prominence during the early New Kingdom. This was a time when Egypt had finally gotten free from the Hyksos invaders (they occupied the northern Nile Valley for two centuries). The pharaohs of the rising Eighteenth Dynasty, beginning with Ahmose I, turned Thebes into the political and religious capital of Egypt. The Festival of Opet took place in this city.

Like everything else in Egypt, the timing of the festival was tied to the cycles of the Nile. The festival was celebrated in the second month of Akhet (the season of inundation). During this season, the Egyptians were blessed with the Nile's floodwaters, which deposited rich black silt across the fertile farmlands. As the river replenished the land, Egypt was spiritually renewed through Opet. The Egyptians saw the two as intertwined—the bounty of the flood and the fertility of Amun-Ra (or

Amun-Re), the mightiest of the gods. The festival was held to promote the fertility of Amun and the reigning pharaoh, whom the people saw as Amun's spiritual offspring. The pharaoh himself would be symbolically reborn in sacred rituals.

The great avenue that stretched between the Karnak and Luxor temples, lined with rows of sphinxes and ram-headed statues, was the setting for this festival. For miles, the Egyptians would gather, eager to witness the annual divine event. The festival began with high priests moving through the temple corridors. They had to tend to the golden barque of Amun, which was enshrined in his inner sanctum. It was hidden from common eyes at all times, and this was the only time that Amun's presence would leave the great halls of Karnak and journey into the heart of Thebes.

The Luxor Temple, where the barques of Amun, Mut, and Khonsu would arrive during the festival.[83]

When the grand temple doors were thrown open, the people of the kingdom erupted into cheers. Others sang hymns that praised the gods. The priests, who bore the sacred golden barques of Amun, Mut, and Khonsu atop their shoulders, emerged from the temple. They slowly walked, making sure each of their steps was measured. There was no room for mistake since they were carrying the gods themselves. Lotus petals were thrown to the ground as the procession walked past. Clouds of incense rose into the sky, and the rhythmic beating of drums and cymbals could be heard. Dancers, dressed in flowing linen and adorned with exquisite beads, swayed in hypnotic movements; it was as if their bodies mirrored the rhythm of the Nile.

After carrying the divine barques along the Avenue of Sphinxes, the priests gently placed them onto the sacred boats docked at the banks of the Nile. Here, the gods would embark on the most mystical portion of the journey: a symbolic voyage along the Nile. Once in position, the oarsmen would dip their oars into the river, doing so in perfect unison. Onlookers lined the banks, waving palm fronds and offering prayers to the gods.

By the time the divine vessels reached Luxor Temple, the city was already in full celebration. The Egyptians indulged in a feast while musicians entertained them. While laughter and talking echoed through the city streets, the atmosphere inside the temple was different. In the most secluded chambers, the holiest of ceremonies was about to begin.

At the back of Luxor Temple, one could find the "birth room," a dimly lit space tied to the festival. Here, the pharaoh would stand before Amun's divine presence, getting ready for the ritual marriage between the god and the pharaoh. To the ancient Egyptians, it was common knowledge that their pharaoh was the son—or daughter—of Amun. These rulers were thought to be the living embodiment of the divine's will. In this sacred union, the pharaoh ceremonially merged with the god, reborn through a re-crowning ceremony that emphasized his divine legitimacy. This act was not only a spiritual rebirth but also a powerful political statement. The pharaoh's rule was sanctified, and his bond with Amun was reaffirmed, making his divine right to govern Egypt indisputable.

Now that the sacred rites were completed and the pharaoh's rule reaffirmed, it was high time for Amun, Mut, and Khonsu to return to Karnak. The ceremonial boats were readied once more to carry the golden barques of the gods along the Nile. Priests would cast offerings, such as perfumed oils, lotus flowers, and small golden figurines, into the river. These were considered tokens of gratitude for the gods' presence. As the ceremonial boats floated down the Nile, the celebration in the city continued, with the Egyptians dancing and feasting late into the night.

Once the gods arrived through the gates of Karnak once more, they were carried back to the sanctuary. Once the statues of these gods were placed in their sacred chambers, the temple doors were sealed by the priests, signaling the gods' withdrawal into the realm of the heavens. Despite being hidden throughout the year, their presence lingered. The Egyptians knew that the cycle would begin again, just as the Nile would flow and the sun would return each morning.

The festival lasted for a few days. Under Thutmose III, it was celebrated for eleven days, and by the time Ramesses III came to the throne, it had expanded to an astonishing twenty-four days. The Festival of Opet continued well into the New Kingdom and survived even into the Roman period.

Chapter 9 – Cambyses's Lost Army

Egypt was relatively stable when it was ruled by the early pharaohs of the Twenty-sixth Dynasty (also known as the Saite Dynasty). Especially during the reigns of Psamtik I and Necho II, the kingdom witnessed independence from Assyrian dominance. These rulers also successfully rebuilt Egypt's economy and strengthened its military and infrastructure. Necho II launched ambitious projects across the kingdom. He oversaw the construction of the famed Canal of the Pharaohs (also referred to as Necho's Canal), which was the forerunner of the Suez Canal. The pharaoh also launched successful naval expansion campaigns, which further bolstered Egypt's position as a regional power.

In 589 BCE, the mantle was passed to Apries, who inherited the throne from his father, Psamtik II. The pharaoh began his reign with a strong position, yet his later decisions and external circumstances gradually destabilized Egypt. It all began to spiral when Apries had his eyes completely focused on asserting Egyptian power abroad. He supported rebellions against Babylonian control in the Levant and conducted campaigns in Libya. Apries even sent his Egyptian forces to support Libyan allies against Greek settlers but unfortunately suffered a catastrophic defeat.

From here on, Apries's reputation worsened, especially among his army. A mutiny took place among the Egyptian soldiers, as they had been growing discontent with Apries prioritizing foreign mercenaries over them. Apries sent Amasis, a well-respected and high-ranking military officer, to suppress the mutiny. However, the unexpected happened: the Egyptian troops saw Amasis as a capable leader, and they proclaimed him pharaoh instead. A rebellion, now spearheaded by Amasis, was due.

Apries attempted to suppress Amasis and his followers. A civil war broke out, which eventually culminated in a decisive battle in which Amasis and his predominantly native Egyptian forces emerged victorious. Perhaps out of mercy and hoping to avoid future skirmishes by those still loyal to Apries, Amasis treated the captured Apries with some leniency. Herodotus stated that the former pharaoh lived in relative comfort for a time. However, tensions persisted. It was unsure whether Apries simply became a symbol of rebellion for those loyal to him or if he was involved in an attempt to regain power, but the Egyptians were not planning on forgiving him. They pressured Amasis into punishing Apries the way he deserved. Ancient sources claimed that Amasis eventually placed Apries's fate in the hands of the people, who strangled him to death.

Pharaoh Amasis (also known as Ahmose II) went on to rule Egypt for over forty years. He brought the kingdom stability and prosperity. Egyptian pride and cultural identity were restored. The kingdom also maintained its strong ties with the Greeks, and its economic and political strength in the Mediterranean world continued to grow.

However, chaos returned when the Persians saw the rise of Cambyses II, the son of Cyrus the Great. According to Herodotus, Cambyses initially wished to strengthen ties with Egypt. To do this, he requested that Amasis send him a daughter to marry. The pharaoh was unwilling to give his own daughter, yet he did not want to decline the request entirely. So, he sent Nitetis, the daughter of Apries, to the Persian king, claiming that she was one of his own. Unfortunately for Amasis, Nitetis was not planning on staying quiet; she allegedly revealed the deception to Cambyses. The Persian undoubtedly was enraged by this. Apart from this deception, Herodotus also suggested that Amasis's military and diplomatic efforts to resist Persian influence, such as forging alliances with other states (notably Greek city-states like Cyprus and Samos), also contributed to Cambyses's wrath.

The Persian king launched his ambitious campaign to conquer Egypt in 525 BCE, but by this time, Amasis had already died (he passed away only six months prior to the start of the campaign). However, Cambyses was not a person who backed down; the invasion continued to take place, culminating in the decisive Battle of Pelusium in May 525 BCE, where he went against Amasis's son, Pharaoh Psamtik III.

Pelusium was a fortified city on the eastern edge of the Nile Delta. Due to its strategic location, Pelusium was the first line of defense for the Egyptian kingdom. Its fall would give way for the Persians to advance farther into the kingdom. Cambyses, bolstered by years of military experience, commanded a well-disciplined army. His forces were also numerically superior compared to the Egyptian army led by Psamtik III. The young pharaoh knew there was a huge possibility of them losing the battle, so while preparing his troops at Pelusium, Psamtik also ordered the preparation of his capital, Memphis, to withstand a siege.

Initially, the Egyptians at Pelusium were successful in holding their ground. The fortress of Pelusium was well provisioned and strong, and the pharaoh began to see a glimmer of hope. However, Cambyses was cunning. Herodotus wrote that the Persian king had another trick up his sleeve; instead of relying only on military strategies, Cambyses also employed a peculiar psychological tactic, making use of the Egyptians' sacred regard for cats.

According to ancient Egyptian beliefs, cats were closely associated with the goddess Bastet. Bastet was often depicted with the body of a woman and the head of a cat. She was worshiped as the goddess of cats, fertility, and childbirth. The goddess was also believed to possess the power to protect a household from evil spirits and disease. Being a protector deity, Bastet was highly revered, and cats were considered sacred. Herodotus claims that the Egyptians held the animal in such high regard that if a cat were to get caught in a burning building, the Egyptians would prioritize it before their own lives. Harming a cat was seen as a crime, and those who killed one could be sentenced to death.

Cambyses was well aware of this. He ordered his soldiers to paint images of cats on their shields and carry them into battle. Some accounts claimed that the Persians even brought live cats to the battlefield. When the Egyptians saw this, they hesitated. For a moment, they refused to strike for fear of divine retribution. The Persians took this opportunity to wreak havoc on the Egyptian forces. The battlefield quickly turned into a scene of chaos and bloodshed. The Persians made use of their superior tactics and overwhelmed the Egyptian ranks. Psamtik III's vision had come true. His army was indeed unprepared for the scale of Cambyses's assault, and they were crushed.

The defeat was catastrophic for Egypt. The result of this battle also marked the end of the Saite Dynasty. The prosperous kingdom lost its independence. Although Psamtik was able to retreat to Memphis, the tide of war had turned against him.

A painting depicting the Persians using cats to defeat the Egyptians at the Battle of Pelusium."

Whether Herodotus's writings of the Persians using images of cats to tip the scale of war held any truth at all remains a topic of debate. However, we can safely assume that Cambyses's victory at Pelusium was not achieved solely through his military force. The Persians obtained intelligence provided by defectors. One of them was Phanes of Halicarnassus, a Greek mercenary who served as a tactician and advisor under Amasis. Phanes was well versed in Egyptian defenses, and his betrayal was instrumental in the defeat of Egypt.

With Pelusium secured, Cambyses wasted no time in consolidating his control over Egypt. He knew the Egyptians placed religion and culture above all else. Therefore, one of his first acts was to seek the favor of the goddess Neith, the primordial goddess often associated with creation, wisdom, and warfare. As one of Egypt's most ancient and highly revered deities, her temple in Sais was a focal point of Egyptian spirituality and governance. Cambyses hoped that by paying homage to the goddess, he could portray himself as the rightful ruler of the kingdom who respected its traditions instead of a foreign conqueror.

Then, the Persian king turned his attention to Memphis, the key city to controlling both Upper and Lower Egypt. Just as Psamtik had expected, Cambyses laid siege to it. Their engineering and tactical prowess were remarkable because, despite having time to prepare, the defenders found their hope of success chipped away as the seconds went by. Eventually, Memphis fell, marking a decisive moment in the Persian conquest of Egypt. Psamtik III, who had sought refuge in the city following his defeat at Pelusium, was taken prisoner. He planned a rebellion to overthrow the Persians but achieved no success.

As a result, Psamtik was forced to drink bull's blood. In ancient times, it was believed that drinking bull's blood was lethal or could even drive a person mad. This version of Psamtik's death was narrated in the *Histories* by Herodotus, so this might be more legend than fact. Since bull's blood contains high levels of iron and protein, drinking it in large quantities may result in iron poisoning or hemochromatosis. Other sources suggest that the blood was possibly poisoned to hasten the process. Poisoned or not (and if the story is true), Psamtik likely experienced a daunting episode of nausea and vomiting before going through organ failure, leading to his death.

With Memphis now firmly in his grasp, Cambyses adopted the title of pharaoh and began aligning himself with Egyptian religious practices and traditions. Herodotus claimed that his rule was ruthless, with cities and temples across the kingdom often facing lootings and desecrations. Yet, his records need to be taken with a grain of salt, especially since no contemporary Egyptian sources ever recorded the looting of temples.

From Memphis, Cambyses made his way to the spiritual heart of Upper Egypt: Thebes. This city was known for its temples dedicated to the mighty deity Amun. Here, Cambyses made his desire to be named the legitimate pharaoh of Egypt known. He sought acknowledgment from the priests of the oracle of Amun at the Siwa Oasis. The oracle's recognition would affirm Cambyses's right to rule in the eyes of his new subjects. Being acknowledged by the oracle of Amun would imply that Cambyses had the gods' blessing. This would reinforce his authority, not only in Egypt but also in the broader ancient world, where such divine endorsements carried significant weight.

However, the priests refused to acknowledge him as the kingdom's rightful ruler. Their rejection enraged the Persian king. Cambyses saw their defiance as a direct affront to his authority.

This did not deter the king's ambitions to expand his empire. To further assert dominance over the region, Cambyses launched another bold invasion campaign, this time into Ethiopia. He launched this campaign from Thebes. Yet, the Persian king did not forget about the defiant priests at Siwa. He divided his forces. While he led half of his troops southward into Ethiopian territory, Cambyses also detached a contingent of fifty thousand men toward the Siwa Oasis so that they could punish those who refused to acknowledge him as the rightful ruler.

The journey to Siwa was challenging. Under the scorching desert sun, the troops had to cross treacherous terrain as they navigated the desolate expanses of the Egyptian desert. Modern scholars suggest that the El-Kharga Oasis was their first major stop. Here, the troops must have rested and replenished their water supplies before continuing their grueling march. Their next stop remains a mystery; El-Kharga was the last place that the contingent was last seen.

A relief depicting Persian soldiers during the time of Cambyses.[85]

If we were to take account of Herodotus's writings, the historian claimed that all fifty thousand men faced their demise at the hands of Mother Nature. As they continued their journey, Cambyses's men were eventually met with vast columns of whirling sand driven by powerful desert winds. This brutal sandstorm engulfed each of the soldiers and buried him deep beneath the dunes. As the sandstorm calmed down, it erased all traces of their presence, leaving both historians and archaeologists with only questions about the disappearance of the army.

Theories and Speculations Surrounding the Disappearance of Cambyses's Men

The exact route taken by Cambyses's lost army has long been a subject of debate among historians. Many agree that the soldiers marched southwest from Thebes, traversing through one of the harshest landscapes on Earth toward the Siwa Oasis. Alexander the Great once embarked on a pilgrimage to Siwa. However, this took place two centuries later, and the distance of his chosen route was likely shorter compared to the one taken by Cambyses's men. But despite being shorter in distance, Alexander and his men also went through multiple obstacles. Ancient accounts even suggested that they would not have succeeded if it were not for divine intervention. If the great conqueror faced difficulties traversing the terrain some two centuries later, it is not surprising that Cambyses's men had problems too. Their chosen route, which plunged them directly into the heart of the desert, undoubtedly exposed the troops to unrelenting heat, scarce water supplies, and disorientation.

Of course, logistical challenges might have also played a role in the fate of the lost army. The desert was unforgiving with its searing daytime temperatures and freezing nights. These two brutal differences would have sapped the strength of even the strongest soldiers. Herodotus suggested that the army ran out of provisions rather quickly. As a result, they were left with no choice but to rely on what little they could scavenge. The Greek historian wrote that the army soon grew beyond desperate to the point they ate grass. When no grass could be seen, some of them resorted to cannibalism. Herodotus's accounts are often filled with exaggeration and bias, yet these grim details show the dire conditions faced by the soldiers.

Another theory talks about the army using an incorrect map, which led them to march either in circles or in the direction of an uninhabitable region of the desert. Coupled with the lack of significant landmarks, it made sense that the soldiers wandered aimlessly for an extended period of time. It could also be plausible that because of logistical mismanagement, combined with the natural hazards of the desert, the troops lost their supply wagons. Without enough supplies and equipment, Cambyses's men were left vulnerable in the brutal environment.

Obliterated by an Ambush

While the theory of the army consumed by a relentless sandstorm is considered the most popular to this date, there is another theory that involves an ambush. This particular theory centers around a figure known as Petubastis III. Operating from the remote Dakhla Oasis, Petubastis probably heard the news of Cambyses's men nearing his territory. Leveraging on the isolated location of the oasis and its natural defenses, along with the Persians' lack of knowledge about the region, Petubastis thought he was given a golden opportunity to finally challenge Persian authority. After all, Petubastis was considered a champion of Egyptian independence, and he had the support of local militias who deeply resented Persian control.

The desert had clearly allied with Petubastis and his forces; the vast and arid expanse had already weakened the Persian forces, which were most likely already struggling with logistical challenges. Dehydration, disorientation, and exhaustion might have terrorized the soldiers, leaving them vulnerable despite their superior skills obtained from years of war. Therefore, it would not have been impossible for Petubastis and his forces to gain the upper hand. When they launched an ambush near the Dakhla Oasis, the Egyptians made use of their effective guerilla tactics. The desert was turned into a trap, and the disoriented Persians were almost immediately overwhelmed.

This success benefited Petubastis greatly. This victory opened the gates for Petubastis to declare himself pharaoh in Memphis. However, when Darius I rose to the throne to succeed Cambyses, the new king was said to have worked to suppress this narrative. To avoid telling the world of the Persians' defeat, Darius crafted a tale of a sandstorm that swallowed the army whole.

The Biggest Discovery

Some might agree that the Sahara Desert has long been a graveyard of mysteries. Its vast and continuously shifting sands are capable of swallowing the histories of different civilizations, with Cambyses's lost army being among them. However, in 1996, the mystery began to crack as more archaeological evidence was uncovered. Spearheaded by twin Italian archaeologists named Angelo and Alfredo Castiglioni, the expedition was initially launched to investigate the presence of iron meteorites near the Bahariya Oasis (a small oasis close to Siwa). What they found, however, shed light on one of history's most mysterious disappearances.

As the archaeologists toiled under the relentless sun, they suddenly noticed a strange artifact buried deep beneath the sand. To untrained eyes, this object was nothing but a simple half-buried pot. However, even with a single glance, the brothers knew it was a fragment of a long-forgotten past. Upon further excavation, they soon unearthed more evidence, all of which pointed to that location as a site where an important event occurred. First, they discovered bleached bones and fragments of what might have once been an army. Then, the team of archaeologists uncovered a natural rock formation. Measuring about 114 feet long, close to 6 feet high, and 10 feet deep, its size and shape appeared almost too perfect; it was almost as if it had been used as a refuge for those caught in a sandstorm.

Also beneath this rock formation, the archaeologists found relics of ancient warfare, including a bronze dagger and arrow tips. Less than a mile from the natural shelter were remnants of more treasures, including a silver bracelet, an earring, and spherical trinkets that most likely belonged to a necklace. Interestingly, scientific testing revealed that all of these objects—both the ancient weapons and jewelry—dated to the Achaemenid period, placing them squarely within Cambyses's era.

These findings raised eyebrows. For centuries, scholars and historians held the belief that the army marched along the caravan paths through the Dakhla and Farafra Oases, though no concrete evidence has emerged to fully support this speculation. However, with the findings of the Castiglioni brothers, historians are able to open the door to a whole different theory. It is likely that the army had taken a different southern route. Beginning from El Kargha, they presumably ventured westward to Gilf Kebir. Then, the brothers headed north through Wadi Abd el Melik toward Siwa. The reasons behind the army's decision to use this path instead of the traditional caravan route were probably simple. They could bypass Egyptian-controlled oases, thus minimizing the possibility of them facing resistance or ambush. This way, they could make their way to Siwa undisturbed.

Of course, each theory needs to be supported by concrete evidence, and the Castiglioni brothers were eager to conduct geological surveys along this alternative route. The brothers discovered desiccated water sources and artificial wells constructed from hundreds of water pots buried deep beneath the soft sand. This discovery answered one of the questions surrounding this theory: how did the army sustain themselves while they traversed this longer and harsher terrain? Furthermore, thermoluminescence dating confirmed the pottery's age; they all aligned with Cambyses's time.

The investigations culminated in the year 2002, with the brothers going back to the site of their initial discoveries. They proposed that it could be plausible that the army had used ancient maps that mistakenly placed the temple of Amun in this specific area. The soldiers, thinking that they had arrived at their destination, were then caught off guard, not by mortal enemies but by Mother Nature. The khamsin (a hot, fierce, and unpredictable southeasterly wind) was heading toward them, sweeping everything across the Sahara. Panic undoubtedly terrorized the soldiers. Some might have sought refuge under a natural shelter (like the one discovered by the Castiglioni brothers in the 1990s), while those who managed to escape possibly made their way to Sitra Lake.

Why there were no traces of the survivors remains a mystery. It is possible that since they had failed their mission to reach Siwa, they decided to go incognito, fearing the wrath of their king. After all, ancient armies were often held to strict standards. Failure, especially on such an important—or rather vengeful—mission, could easily result in severe punishment. Apart from this, the lack of evidence could also be a result of the harsh environment of the Sahara. The intense heat and erosion would have made it difficult for any physical remains or artifacts to survive the test of time. It is also worth noting that it was common for historical records to be intentionally altered or omitted to erase any sort of failures.

The brothers heard stories by the Bedouin where they claimed to have seen white bones emerging from the sand during certain wind conditions. Upon further investigations, a mass grave was discovered near the excavation site of the natural shelter, which contained hundreds of skeletons and skulls bleached by centuries of exposure to the harsh desert sun and winds. Persian arrowheads and a horse bit were also unearthed, all of which were identical to depictions in ancient Persian reliefs. A sword was reportedly discovered as well, but unfortunately, it had already been sold to American tourists. With all these findings, it seemed likely that the final resting place of Cambyses's famed lost army had been discovered, buried beneath over sixteen feet of sand.

Nevertheless, the mystery never got its official ending. The Castiglioni brothers reported their findings and handed over the artifacts to the Geological Survey of Egypt. However, they never heard back. Even so, the brothers were certain that they had successfully come closer than anyone to solving the disappearance.

Conclusion

Some describe ancient Egypt as a treasure trove of mysteries, while others picture it as an endless labyrinth of forgotten stories, hidden tombs, and unanswered questions. It is indeed one of the most intriguing civilizations. For many centuries, it has fascinated not only historians, scholars, and archaeologists but also avid history enthusiasts, curious readers, and mystery lovers. With its grand structures, cryptic texts, supposed curses, and secrets, this civilization attracts the attention of even those who have very little interest in history.

Despite many traces of the civilization having been unearthed, from the remnants of the pyramids and temples to the houses of the artisans and papyrus full of spells and hymns, there is still so much that remains buried deep beneath the sands. One can only wonder what else lies in the tombs that have yet to be discovered. What other secrets do the ancient hieroglyphs hold? Which cities are still under the desert, doing nothing but remaining silent until they are discovered once more? Every discovery gives us new questions to ponder and brings forth another piece of the puzzle.

It is safe to say that Egypt remains an unfinished story. There are still missing chapters waiting to see the light once more. But perhaps this is why Egypt continues to capture the imagination of so many. With every excavation, every deciphered text, and every newly uncovered relic, new details emerge, new mysteries unfold, and new perspectives reshape what we think we know.

Part 2: Ancient Greece

Discovering Lost Stories from Greek History

Introduction

Ancient Greece has long captured the imagination of many, be it historians, scholars, or casual readers. Its history is brimming with tales and legends that speak of great conflicts like the Battle of Thermopylae, stunning architectural wonders like the Parthenon and the many open-air theaters, and a pantheon of mighty gods and heroes who continue to inspire modern fiction. From Leonidas's bravery against the Persians to Homer's beautiful musings, ancient Greece often feels like the birthplace of everything we value—philosophy, democracy, drama, and even the Olympics. However, despite its fame, there is a side to this celebrated ancient civilization that remains hidden or rather overlooked that, when uncovered, could surprise even the most avid history buffs.

Sure, many may be very familiar with Herodotus and his extensive documentation of the Persians; few may be aware of Pytheas, the Greek merchant and explorer who dared to sail beyond the known world. The Greeks were experts in trade, war, and colonization, but they never ventured far beyond their familiar map. Pytheas was among the earliest to have set his sights on something far more ambitious. His voyage led him to the edges of the known world, allowing him to witness various natural phenomena the Greeks initially thought to be nothing more than just stuff of legends. Yet, his story is often overshadowed by the more famous exploits of generals and kings.

Images of the Spartans, clad in their bronze armor and marching with spears, often appear in our minds whenever we think of ancient Greece. Some may have even heard of the city-state's law of discarding infants they deemed unworthy off Mount Taygetus. This grim narrative endured for centuries, but is it even true? The Spartans were certainly merciless, but their history and daily life were far more nuanced—and perhaps even more intriguing. For a city-state famous for its military discipline, the realities of life and death reveal a society that was both brutal and deeply misunderstood.

Apart from their wondrous architecture, the Greeks also had a peculiar obsession with tragedy. Interestingly, this obsession was not only limited to their plays but also to their lives in general. Ancient Greece gave birth to a myriad of figures with the greatest minds, yet so many of them often met ironic or downright bizarre ends. The Stoic philosopher Chrysippus contributed many of his ideas to the ancient civilization, particularly in the realm of physics and ethics. His ironic death, however, soon became a topic of discussion, overshadowing his contributions. An Olympic athlete once won a wrestling match despite dying in the match. These peculiar episodes prove that even death wasn't free from the dramatic flair that shaped so much of their culture.

It is sufficient to say that ancient Greece was more than just feats of gods, monuments, wars, and conquests. The history of civilization is a patchwork of ideas, innovations, and contradictions. This book's purpose is not to revisit the well-trodden paths of Greek history. Instead, it offers a window for those curious enough to take a peek into the overlooked corners, of the stories that remind us that, even in antiquity, humanity was wonderfully complex.

Chapter 1 – The Strange Case of the Athenian Plague

It was 480 BCE, and Xerxes I had been defeated at Salamis, his great ships rammed to pieces by the Greek triremes commanded by Themistocles. This was the day that the Greeks had been waiting for. After years of seeing their lands overrun by the Persians, this victory allowed them to regain the upper hand. Many Greeks were confident that they would never be forced to bow down to the Persians anymore—except for the Athenians.

Athens was worried that it would only be a matter of time before the Persians regrouped and attempted another invasion. So, Athens spearheaded the formation of the Delian League, which comprised key member states such as Chios, Lesbos, Rhodes, Delos, Samos, Naxos, and Thasos. This coalition of Greek city-states was united under a banner of collective defense. The league's aim was to maintain a force formidable enough to meet any Persian resurgence. Member states often contribute ships and immeasurable funds in the name of this goal. These riches were stored in a treasury located in Delos, a sacred island where the league's meetings were held.

However, as the years passed by, it became clear that the Persians were not capable of launching more invasions into Greek territory. The Delian League began to evolve into something altogether different. As tribute from member states flowed into the league's treasury, Athens began to utilize it, turning the riches into a tool for the city's own prestige. Even the treasury was moved from Delos to Athens. This presented a clear message to the member states. Athens was not just a self-proclaimed leader of the alliance; it was, in fact, a hegemon.

Athens entered its golden age because of the funds of the Delian League. Pericles, the city's charismatic leader and statesman, went on an ambitious program of public works to uplift Athens' status. Dozens of monuments were erected, and multiple other construction projects were commissioned. From the Parthenon to the famous Long Walls and the Erechtheion dedicated to both Athena and Poseidon to the sprawling Agora, Athens soon rose as the region's most glorious center of art, philosophy, and, of course, democracy.

However, it is safe to say that this flowering of Athenian culture came at a cost. To the other Greek city-states, Athens' transformation into an empire was not seen as an inspiration. Rather, it alarmed them. Sparta, in particular, was concerned about Athens' growing naval and economic influence; it feared a challenge to its own supremacy in Greece. Sparta was also a staunch supporter of the oligarchy, which differed from Athens' advocacy of democracy. Because of this, as well as a few other factors, a civil war brewed on the horizon where Greeks would fight against Greeks.

What began as nothing more than a skirmish over Corcyra and Potidaea eventually escalated into a full-scale conflict known as the Second Peloponnesian War (also referred to simply as the Peloponnesian War). The war erupted across the Aegean in 431 BCE and was fought between the Delian League, led by Athens, and the Peloponnesian League, which was commanded by Sparta.

The Beginning of Terror

The second year of the war began with the sound of Spartan boots trampling through the plains of Attica. Fertile fields that had once been abundant with olive trees and wheat were torched. The blue skies turned gray as the smoke rose. However, the Spartans, under the command of King Archidamus, were not planning on simply breaching Athens' walls. They knew very well that the Athenians were exceptional architects and that their fortifications were pretty much impenetrable. The mighty Spartans sought another way. They decided to force the city into submission through starvation.

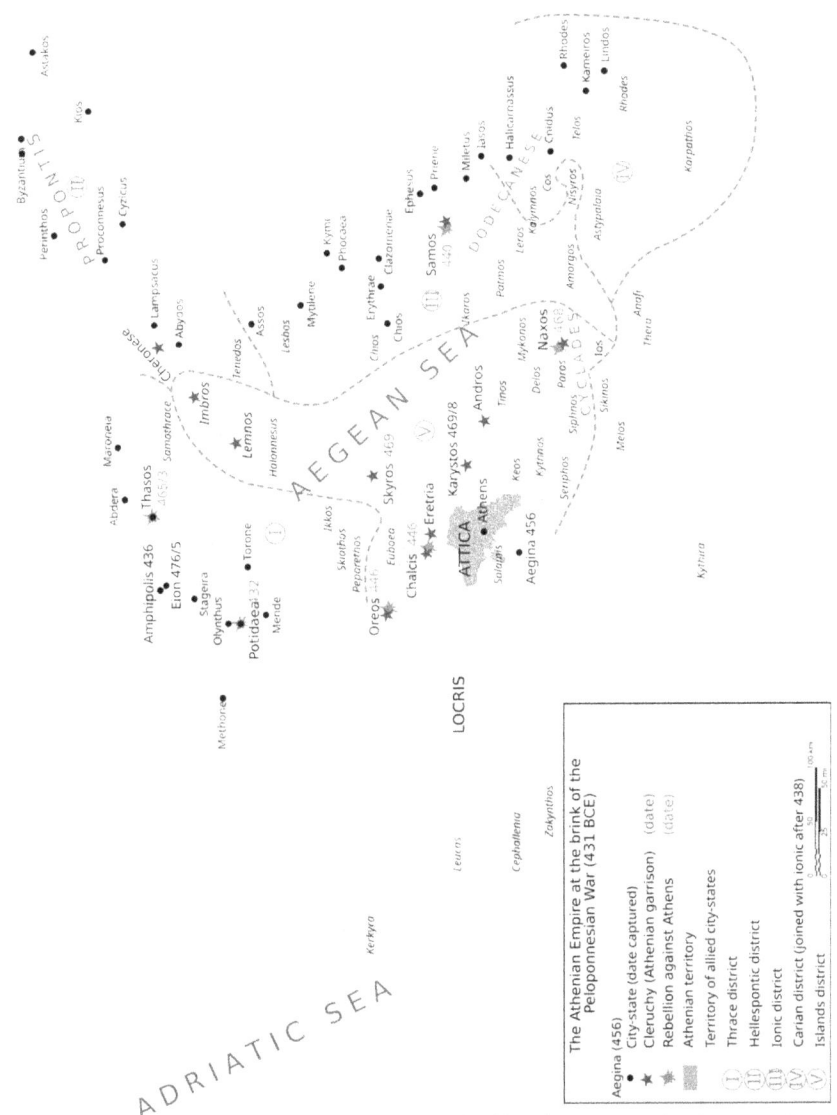

The Athenian Empire by the time the Peloponnesian War erupted.[86]

Pericles had anticipated this move. He ordered the rural populace to abandon their farms and make their way behind the walls of Athens. The Long Walls provided safety. Since the walls stretched to the port of Piraeus four miles away, Athens was able to maintain its naval lifeline. However, the influx of refugees from the countryside strained the city's capacity. This eventually gave way to something far worse than war.

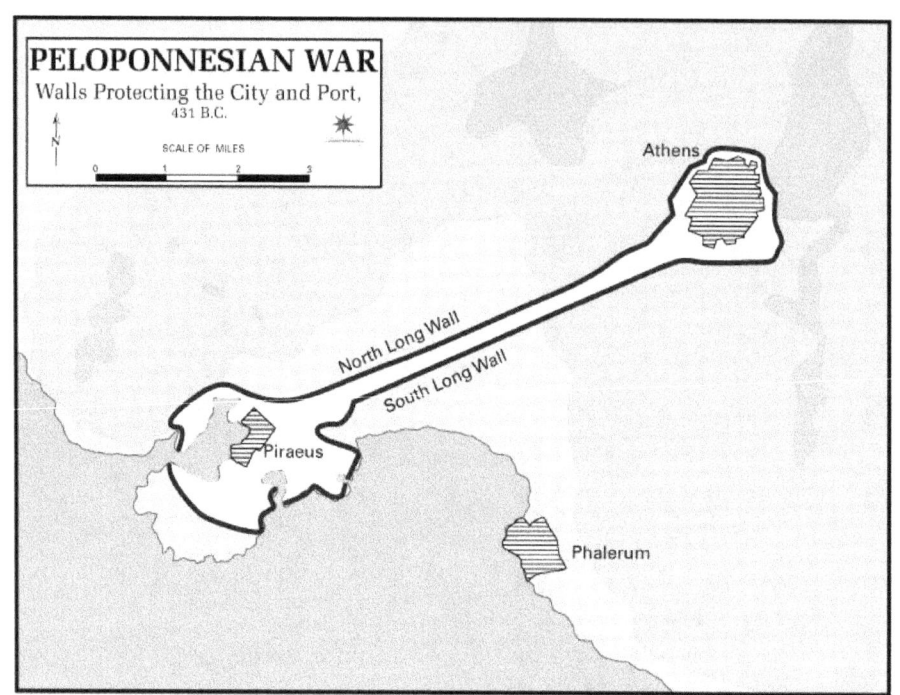

PELOPONNESIAN WAR
Walls Protecting the City and Port,
431 B.C.

N

SCALE OF MILES

0   1   2   3

Athens

North Long Wall

South Long Wall

Piraeus

Phalerum

Ancient Athens protected by its Long Walls.[37]

Among the citizens of Athens was a man who was part of the military. Just weeks prior, he had been fighting alongside his comrades. He was used to wounds and scars from the battlefield, but a sudden throng of pain made him worried for his life. At first, he felt a searing pain in his head. It was as though his entire skull was set aflame. His throat then grew extremely parched as fever suddenly terrorized his body. His stomach constantly churned, often emptying itself in violent convulsions. When his body could not take it anymore, the man collapsed.

He was not the only one to have contracted this unknown disease. Almost everyone around him showed the same symptoms: raging fevers, inflamed eyes, diarrhea, ulcerated throats, and extreme thirst. Many succumbed to the disease within days. Despite the man's suffering, he survived. Perhaps as a warning or a guide should the mysterious disease break out again in the future, the man decided to record the nightmare that struck Athens. His name was Thucydides, and in his book *History of the Peloponnesian War*, he described everything in meticulous detail, from the early symptoms of the sickness to the signs of death and even the state of Athens and its populace amidst the plague.

It was believed that the plague arrived via sailors and merchants at the bustling port of Piraeus. The sickness itself, however, was thought to have originated beyond the Greek world. Thucydides claimed that it came from Ethiopia and had made its way to Egypt and Libya before it began ravaging the Athenians.

Thucydides wrote that symptoms typically began in the head. Those who contracted the disease would feel as if their heads were on fire. Their eyes would turn red and inflamed as fever began to make its appearance. The first internal symptoms were equally harrowing: throats turned raw and bloody, tongues swelled, and breaths turned rancid. This, however, was only the beginning of the suffering. From here on, the illness would work its way down. Sneezing was common, and people's throats would become so hoarse that their voices were reduced to rasping gasps. The sickness would then attack the chest. Victims would let out hacking coughs that racked their entire bodies, often leaving them desperately gasping for air.

The heart was not spared from the terror of the disease. Once the sickness seized control of the organ, it induced agonizing convulsions that lasted hours. The victim's body would expel bile in different colors and shades, such as green, yellow, and even black. Those who lasted to this point had to endure episodes of empty retching.

The plague also changed the skin of its victims. Pustules and ulcers would typically emerge, their fiery red color contrasting with the patient's flushed complexion. Their bodies usually did not feel hot to the touch, but the internal burning was indescribable. Oftentimes, those who contracted the disease could not even bear wearing even the thinnest of linen garments; they were so desperate for the cool relief of air or water that they would tear up their clothes or be naked. Ancient records claimed that many hurled themselves into wells or plunged into cold baths in the hopes they could escape from the burning ravaging their body.

The disease also terrorized their instincts. Thirst became an insatiable torment, driving the infected to swing between extremes. Some drank only sparingly, while others gorged themselves on water. Sleep became an unfamiliar term; the patients knew they needed it, but the continuous agony kept them wide awake. Their bodies craved rest, yet their minds would not allow them to sleep; they were trapped in a relentless cycle of exhaustion and despair. The internal burning would eventually reach its boiling point on the seventh or ninth day. From here on, the patients would be free from their suffering as they stepped into a whole different realm: the land of the dead.

As for those lucky enough to survive all of this, the plague delivered a final test—or rather, a final devastating blow. Victims would feel the disease shifting its focus to the belly. Ulcers erupted inside, followed by unforgiving diarrhea. Thucydides noted that this was the worst stage since it drained even the strongest of survivors of their remaining strength. Death came to some, but instead of a sudden strike, it came creeping in slowly.

As more Athenians contracted the disease, many tried to make sense of the origin of the plague. However, fear bred speculation. Whispers soon turned into wild accusations. Since they could not completely fathom why or how such a calamity could strike their great city, many Athenians believed that the Spartans were the ones who caused it. Rumors spread across the dying city that the Spartans spread the disease by poisoning the wells of Piraeus. They thought the plague was an act of war. This suspicion undoubtedly deepened the already bitter relationship between the two city-states.

An illustration of Athens during the plague.[38]

The Spartans continued their campaigns after learning what had happened to Athens. However, they were cautious enough to avoid direct confrontation with the city. The Peloponnesian War, now in its second year, did not stop with the plague. But for the Athenians at that time, the Spartan army was no longer the immediate enemy—the invisible disease was.

For days, Athens witnessed the increasing death of its population. Even the city's physicians, who were highly regarded for their expertise, were left speechless. They found themselves powerless, as their knowledge and remedies proved to be futile. Ironically, their dedication to studying more about their patients and the plague often led to their own demise. The more frequently they interacted with the infected, the more likely they were to contract the plague and succumb to its horrifying symptoms. With no treatment in sight, the Athenians became hopeless.

As the epidemic worsened, fewer and fewer were willing to approach the sick and tend to their condition. This resulted in hundreds dying in isolation, abandoned entirely by their families, friends, and neighbors. The city's air was thick with the stench of decay as bodies were left to rot in the streets and alleyways. The huge number of dead made it impossible for the Athenians to conduct proper burials. Thucydides himself provided a grim picture of Athens during this time, stating that corpses were piled atop one another in public spaces. These bodies were then thrown into mass graves with little to no ceremony. This account is supported by modern archaeology. Excavations near the Kerameikos cemetery revealed a mass grave that contained nearly a thousand skeletons dating between 430 and 426 BCE.

What remains of the Kerameikos cemetery today.[39]

Perhaps because there was no more land to bury the dead, those tasked with removing the bodies often added them to funeral pyres that were still burning from previous cremations. Once done, they would quickly step back, afraid that the plague would latch onto them next. Thucydides described that even animals refrained from going near the contaminated remains.

Those fortunate enough to have survived the plague were able to let out a small sigh of relief. Not only were they free from the agonizing fever, headache, and diarrhea, but the survivors also seemed to have developed immunity. Thucydides said that these survivors became the caretakers for the sick. Some believed that the gods had given them a second chance, while others simply fostered a deep empathy for the suffering of others.

It is safe to say that the Athenians were deeply religious. Religion was embedded in their culture for as long as they could remember. Yet, as the plague continued to terrorize the city, the Athenians' faith in their gods began to crumble. They began to doubt their religious beliefs. Since the disease struck without exception, sparing neither the devoted nor the impious, many questioned the purpose of their prayers and sacrifices. The same question lingered in their minds as they battled the sickness. If the gods would not protect their devoted subjects, then what was the point in worshiping them?

The temples of Athens experienced a great change. Once filled with various food or objects of offerings and the scent of burning incense, these temples turned into sites of great suffering. Refugees from the countryside, who had been brought into the city to avoid the Spartan invasion, sought shelter wherever they could, including temples. So, the very places where the Athenians had once communed with the heavens became choked with the stench of decay and the echoing howls of the sick.

While they were religious, the Athenians were also highly superstitious, like most Greeks of their time. Some believed that the plague was not an act of war ignited by the Spartans but a divine punishment. There was an oracle who predicted that Apollo himself—the god of prophecy, healing, and diseases—would side with Sparta if the Athenians chose to fight them with all their might. Because of this, many thought that the divine favored their enemies and that the plague was a manifestation of Apollo's wrath.

Of course, not everyone in the city was willing to accept such explanations. Thucydides, for one, approached this claim with skepticism. In contrast to his other contemporaries, Thucydides dismissed the idea that the divine had any hand in unleashing the plague. Instead, he chose to hold strong to the medical theories of his day, particularly those stemming from the school of Hippocrates (a group of ancient Greek physicians and scholars). Led by Hippocrates, the Greek physician who laid the foundation for modern medicine, the school highlighted that diseases arose from natural causes rather than divine intervention. The Hippocratic school also emphasized the balance of bodily humors (blood, phlegm, yellow bile, and black bile). Imbalances in these humors, rather than supernatural causes, were believed to cause illness.

Thucydides preferred to approach the plague with a rational and almost clinical eye. He strove to document its symptoms and progressions through careful observation. He even noted the strange absence of carrion-eating birds and animals in the city when the plague was at its height. He expected these creatures to feast on the unburied corpses scattered throughout the streets of Athens. Yet, he did not see any. This led Thucydides to deduce that they either died after consuming the infected bodies or, driven by instinct, avoided getting near them entirely.

The Athenian Plague in the Eyes of Modern Medicine Practitioners

Despite Thucydides's vivid description of the plague, the Athenian Plague remains both a subject of fascination and debate among historians and medical researchers. Even today, the precise nature of the disease remains unknown, even though scholars have spent centuries trying to uncover its cause. At first, researchers deduced that the illness was an outbreak of the bubonic plague, which was famously known to be the culprit that devastated many populations across Europe and Asia in the medieval age. Yet, after a closer analysis of Thucydides's writings and more research conducted on the outbreak's patterns, new theories emerged.

One of the earliest alternative suggestions made by modern researchers was typhus, a type of bacterial infection typically transmitted by lice. This disease features symptoms that align to some extent with Thucydides's account, such as high fevers, chills, and a characteristic rash. Typus can also spread rapidly, especially in overcrowded and unsanitary locations. This theory, however, is not accepted by everyone. Some doubt this hypothesis due to the absence of certain symptoms, such as the distinctive "rose spots" associated with typhus.

Some scholars and researchers have also drawn similarities between the Athenian Plague and smallpox. Also known for a high fever, smallpox causes pustular rashes and severe internal symptoms, all of which were once experienced by the unfortunate Athenians. However, the rashes from smallpox typically leave survivors with almost permanent scars—a detail missing from Thucydides's account. Measles could also be a contender. This viral disease has a high contagion rate and usually includes symptoms like fever, cough, conjunctivitis, and widespread rash. The only challenge to this theory is the absence of the internal ailments that Thucydides noted in his writings. Severe diarrhea, intense thirst, and bile evacuations are not associated with measles, making it an imperfect fit.

In recent years, scholars have come up with yet another suggestion: viral hemorrhagic fevers such as Ebola or a related pathogen. Thucydides's description of the plague surprisingly bears striking similarities to the symptoms of Ebola, from high fever to severe diarrhea, constant vomiting, and internal bleeding. What made researchers even more confident is that according to Thucydides's notes, the Athenian Plague might have been traced to Africa, specifically Ethiopia, before it spread through Egypt, Libya, and eventually Athens. This geographic origin aligns with the historical prevalence of viral hemorrhagic fevers in sub-Saharan Africa.

The recent outbreaks of Ebola in Africa have shown how the disease can ravage populations in densely packed areas. When the plague struck Athens, the city and its surrounding regions were home to around 250,000 to 300,000 people. The densely packed urban centre itself was home to 140,000 residents, many of whom had fled from the countryside due to the war. Thucydides also noted the absence of scavenger animals during the outbreak, which aligns with observations of modern Ebola outbreaks where animals often stay away from infected bodies and carcasses. There is no definitive evidence that could firmly link the Athenian Plague to Ebola. Without access to ancient DNA or more definitive archaeological evidence, we can only guess. However, the similarities are striking and compelling enough to make it one of the most plausible theories.

What Became of Athens Following the Plague

It is sufficient to say that the Athenian Plague was catastrophic. It left a mark on the city's history. The plague killed around 25 percent of its population, amounting to somewhere between 75,000 and 100,000 people. Other than the staggering death toll, the disease also deeply affected the Athenians' social and moral life. Chaos and despair replaced order and unity, two of the city's greatest virtues.

The plague lasted for three years, likely ending because of the eventual development of herd immunity among survivors and the natural waning of the outbreak over time. However, Thucydides wrote that it took Athens fifteen years to recover its population.

Pericles himself fell victim to the plague. As a figure who had guided Athens through its golden age, his passing was a turning point for the city. Just a year before his passing, Pericles delivered the Funeral Oration. Delivered during the funeral of the fallen soldiers of the Peloponnesian War, the famed speech was intended to inspire both hope and unity among the Athenians during the war. According to Thucydides, in his speech, Pericles praised the valor of Athenian democracy and emphasized the strength of its people. He talked about the ideals of freedom and civic duty while instilling positivity. Yet, even as he spoke, the plague loomed on the horizon, mocking his very optimism.

Pericles's funeral oration.[40]

The political stability in Athens crumbled as the city saw the death of its leader. The Athenians never again saw a leader who could match Pericles's intellect, charisma, and exceptional ability to navigate the complexities of war and internal governance. Athenian politics turned into factionalism, where rival leaders vied for control. Athens became increasingly divided as a result.

Before the sickness arrived and took away Athens' glory, the city was known for its powerful military. Athens had shown its naval might during the First Peloponnesian War (460–445 BCE). The city's fierce fleet of triremes was known throughout the Aegean, and its influence spread across the Mediterranean.

Of course, the city's military strength was not only focused on its navy. Athens was also known for its disciplined hoplites. This unit of heavily armed infantrymen was composed of citizen soldiers. They usually marched into battles wearing linen armor (linothorax) or muscle cuirass, greaves, and the striking Corinthian or Phrygian helmet. Typically armed with a round shield, an eight-foot-long spear, and a two-foot double-edged sword for close combat, the hoplites were instrumental in forming the phalanx formation. This tightly packed formation consisted of rows of soldiers standing shoulder to shoulder. Once in position, the hoplites would then hold their shields so that they overlapped one another. This served as protection for incoming projectiles. They also pointed their spear outward. This formation was especially effective against enemy cavalry and less organized infantry.

Unfortunately for Athens, the plague disrupted its military might. By the time the Second Peloponnesian War erupted in 431 BCE, the city still had its well-trained hoplites and navy. But the moment the plague made its appearance, it ravaged Athens' military power, just as it did the civilian population.

With the disease claiming the lives of many seasoned veterans and newly trained soldiers, it was impossible for the military to maintain its discipline. With fewer able-bodied men to defend the great city, Athens became more reliant on mercenaries and its allies. Mercenaries fought for pay rather than loyalty to Athens, while allies could shift their stance, especially when Athens was in the midst of chaos.

The naval crews, who were once the backbone of Athenian power, also fell victim to the disease. The triremes that had once patrolled the Aegean were left idle at the harbors. Since Athens also relied heavily on the navy to avoid direct land battles with Sparta (the Greek city-state was traditionally dominant on land), the city had no choice but to witness it crumble.

Athens was unable to mount decisive offensives following the plague, which allowed Sparta to gain the upper hand. In 404 BCE, about twenty-seven years following the start of the Second Peloponnesian War, Athens surrendered to Sparta, marking the end of its golden age. The Spartans imposed harsh terms on Athens. They diminished the city's fleet, reducing it to only a few ships, and the Long Walls were torn down. The Athenian Empire was dissolved, and an oligarchic regime was installed. Known as the Thirty Tyrants, the regime was established to govern Athens and the former members of the Delian League.

However, this was not the complete end of Athens. A democratic uprising took place in 403 BCE, which successfully overthrew the Thirty Tyrants. From here on, Athens was able to regain its independence, though the city never succeeded in returning to its former glory.

The Greek world, on the other hand, entered a tumultuous period, with Sparta briefly asserting hegemony over the others. This would change when the Greeks saw the rise of Thebes and, later, Macedon under Philip II and Alexander the Great.

Chapter 2 – The Alexander Conspiracy Theory

Alexander the Great knew no boundaries when it came to war and conquest. As he surveyed the battlefield, he noticed that his army was acting differently. Weary from years of unrelenting campaigns, they were about to face yet another formidable foe—the massive forces of King Porus. When the Battle of Hydaspes commenced in 326 BCE, it immediately became known as one of the fiercest encounters the Macedonians had ever faced. The Macedonian phalanx had to survive not only volleys of arrows and slashes of enemy swords, but it also had to hold its ground against the Indian king's war elephants.

Victory eventually belonged to Alexander and his mighty army, yet it came at a tremendous cost. They faced huge casualties, and combined with fatigue that came after years of endless combat, the soldiers began to fracture. Their morale and fighting spirit were not what they had been at the start of the campaign. The campaign had finally reached its end, not because of external forces but because of issues from within.

Despite winning at Hydaspes, Alexander's men mutinied. Longing for their home, the soldiers refused to march any farther into the Indian subcontinent. Alexander gave a speech to his soldiers, persuading them to continue, but he eventually changed his mind. Claiming that the omens were unfavorable for further advancement into India, the conqueror announced that the campaign was done and that their next stop was home.

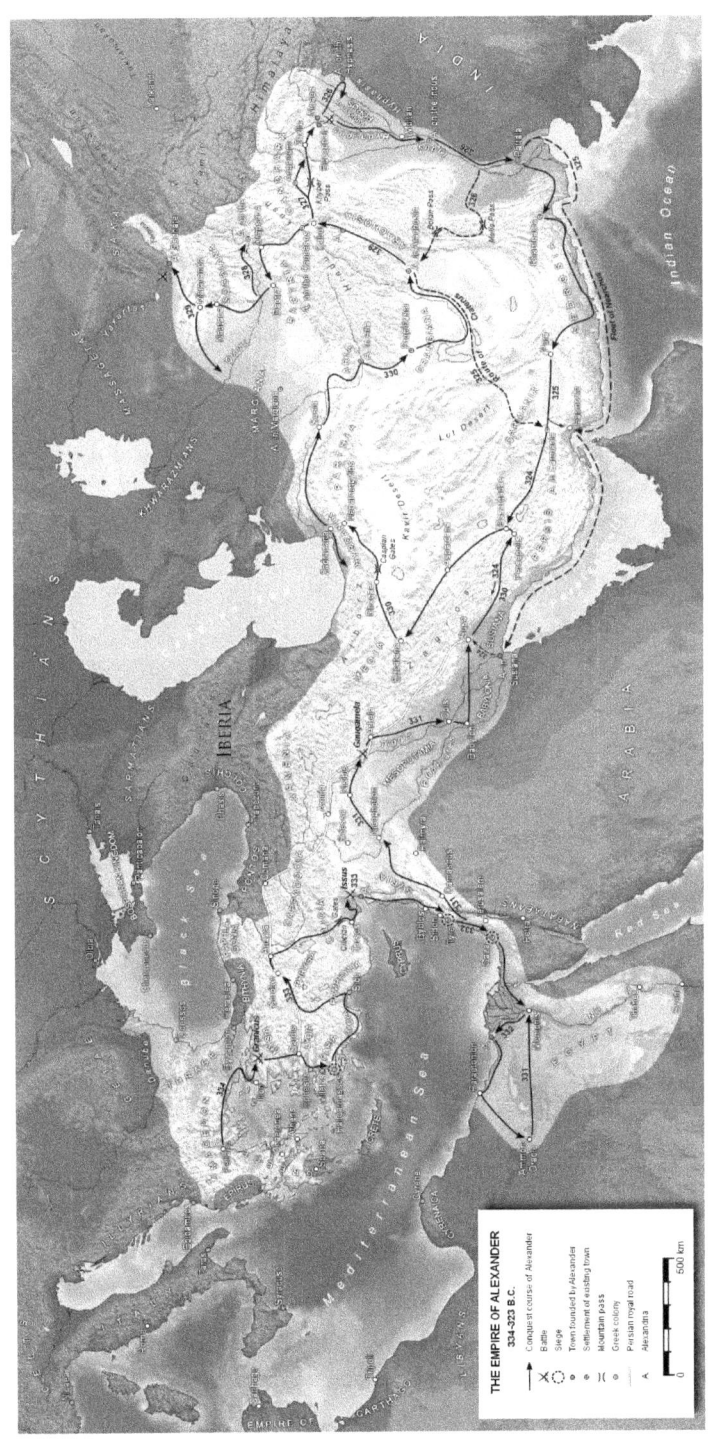

Map detailing Alexander the Great's empire.[41]

However, the march back home was no walk in the park. Alexander's troops had to endure skirmishes, treacherous terrain, deadly sickness, and the punishing weather. They finally reached Babylon in 323 BCE, where the city welcomed its king with celebrations. Some viewed the mighty conqueror as a living god or a man who brought glory to the Macedonian Empire. Others saw him as an unpredictable conqueror whose ambition knew no bounds. Alexander's time in Babylon was full of grand celebrations and more planning for future conquests. But beneath the surface, Alexander was actually a man burdened by loss.

The previous year, Alexander had lost his closest companion and confidant, Hephaestion. Raised together in Macedon and sharing an education under Aristotle, the two were nearly inseparable. Hephaestion was not just a general in Alexander's army; he was also the other half of his soul. There were even whispers that the two were entangled in a romantic relationship. Hephaestion was Alexander's adviser and his mirror; he was the only person who truly saw the complexities of the man who sought to conquer the world.

Alexander and Hephaestion (dressed in red cloak) at the Battle of the Hydaspes.⁴⁸

When Hephaestion died, possibly from typhoid or another illness he contracted during their campaigns, Alexander was plunged into a deep depression. His grief was indescribable. He saw to it that Hephaestion was honored with extravagant funerary rites and declared that his friend would be worshiped as a hero. There was also a shrine dedicated to Hephaestion in Babylon. Alexander even went as far as to petition the oracle at Siwa to deify Hephaestion.

Alexander was said to have withdrawn from his court and those surrounding him. He refused to eat for days. Ancient sources recorded that the mighty conqueror was so consumed by sorrow that he would lie on Hephaestion's bed, often weeping inconsolably. At this point, those around him were sure that Hephaestion's death had left a void inside the conqueror that no amount of glory or conquest could ever fill. As the months passed, Alexander began to feel his health deteriorating.

The Fall of the Great Conqueror

In the spring of 323 BCE, Alexander hosted a grand banquet. It was a celebration held for his admiral, Nearchus, who had successfully explored the Indian Ocean and returned with tales of its marvels and riches. The feast was unsurprisingly extravagant; it was hosted by the conqueror of the known world. There was music and wine as Alexander's closest generals and loyal companions mingled. However, this night of revelry would soon turn into a tragedy.

Although accounts vary, many ancient sources suggest that Alexander drank excessively that night. The Greek historian Plutarch, for one, wrote that Alexander even joined a drinking contest where he consumed enormous amounts of unmixed wine. The consequences of this were severe. Alexander woke up the next day with sharp abdominal pains that continued to worsen as the hours passed. It was said that the stabbing pain was so intense that the conqueror, who had survived through the harshest of wars, howled in agony. His attendants could only watch helplessly as he clutched his stomach, screaming for the pain to subside.

Days later, his condition had become even worse. A fever soon took hold of him, absorbing whatever strength Alexander had left. Eventually, the Macedonian king became bedridden, unable to rise, let alone oversee his vast empire. His attendants, physicians, and generals took turns crowding him over the days. They were desperate to ease his suffering, yet their efforts were all in vain.

His inability to speak in his final days left many puzzled. However, it is possible that it stemmed from an old injury that he sustained during the siege of Cyropolis years earlier. During the siege, Alexander was struck in the neck by an enemy projectile. Although not fatal at the time, the effect was perhaps delayed; it could have left lingering damage that compromised his ability to speak under extreme stress or illness. Nevertheless, as the fever ravaged his body, his vocal cords gave up.

Alexander was acquainted with paranoia in the days before his death. The conqueror had always been a man who believed in omens and divine signs. Plutarch described an omen that foretold the misfortune that was about to befall the Macedonian king. He told stories of a flock of ravens circling over the palace in Babylon before falling dead at Alexander's feet.

Another story involved Alexander's prized lion, who was inexplicably kicked to death by a mule, a creature often associated with sterility and bad luck.

There was also another prophecy that talked about Alexander's impending doom, though Alexander likely never realized this until his death. Known as the prophecy of Calanus, it involved an Indian sage who accompanied Alexander's campaign in India. According to ancient records, Calanus chose to voluntarily self-immolate (an act of setting oneself on fire) upon discovering that he was ill. The sage claimed that he would prefer to die with dignity rather than be a nuisance. However, before he departed, Calanus was said to have cryptically told Alexander, "We shall meet in Babylon." His words were dismissed at the time. However, as Alexander's health worsened following his return to Babylon, the prophecy took on a chilling significance.

Alexander was more or less a living corpse by the ninth day of his illness. He could no longer move. The once mighty conqueror only lay in his bed, barely conscious, while surrounded by his grieving generals and loyal companions. His fever reached its peak on the tenth day. Alexander finally breathed his last. It was believed that his generals remained by his side, perhaps waiting for a sign of recovery. It never happened.

Interestingly, ancient sources wrote that Alexander's body did not decay for six days following his passing. Plutarch, ever superstitious, and other historians suggest this was strong evidence of his divine lineage.

The Poisoning of Alexander

It is not surprising that the idea of divine retribution captivated several ancient writers. Although Alexander was a man of superstition, he could not refrain from doing actions that were considered an affront to the heavens. His claim of divine ancestry, his deification, and his disregard for sacred customs, including the burning of the palace at Persepolis and adopting Persian practices, were thought by some to be acts of arrogance that invited divine retribution. While this concept of divine wrath gave a rather poetic explanation to the mighty conqueror's mysterious death, other scholars and historians suggest a more earthly culprit: poison.

Poisoning was one of the most effective methods of eliminating powerful rivals in the ancient world. Since it often left little trace, this subtle weapon often became the choice of those seeking to seize power in the court. As for Alexander, his sudden illness and death happened during a time when his empire was fraught with tension, both political and familial. One suspect that might have played a role in his death was Antipater, one of Alexander's former allies.

Antipater once served as regent of Macedon when Alexander was away campaigning in Asia. With the king's absence, it was up to Antipater to oversee Macedon. He was a trusted figure at first, but his relationship with Alexander began to take a negative turn in the later years of the campaign. Alexander, despite clashing with the Persians day and night during his campaign, surprisingly grew fond of their culture. When he began adopting Persian customs, the conqueror made an enemy out of Antipater, whose loyalty to the Macedonian aristocracy was unmatched. These two became increasingly estranged.

Tensions soon reached a boiling point when Antipater's son, Cassander, visited the Macedonian king's court in Babylon, acting as a representative of his father. Cassander was said to have expressed dissatisfaction over Alexander's adoption of the Persian practice of *proskynesis* (the act of bowing or prostrating oneself before the king). Enraged, Alexander grabbed Cassander by his hair and slammed him against the wall. This humiliation undoubtedly broadened the rift between the king and his Macedonian elites, particularly Cassander and Antipater.

Some claim that Antipater, having seen the conqueror growing erratic as the days went by, began to see Alexander's death as the only way to secure his influence. His reputation was smeared in 324 BCE when Alexander dismissed him as regent, passing the position to Craterus, another one of Alexander's most trusted generals and companions. Through another one of his sons, Iollas, who served as Alexander's cupbearer, Antipater poisoned the Macedonian king while he was at the grand banquet held for Nearchus.

However, the exact poison used (if he was indeed killed by poison) remains a subject of speculation. Some suggest it contained hemlock since it was a well-known and readily available poison in the ancient world; this was the very same poison drunk by the famous Greek philosopher Socrates. Although hemlock can cause paralysis and respiratory failure, its effects are usually immediate. It took Alexander ten days to die, so hemlock seems unlikely. Others have suggested that the poison was made from ergot, a toxic fungus that grows on cereals. This poison causes high fevers, vomiting, and death in severe cases. However, while ergotism might explain some symptoms, such as fever, it does not account for Alexander's sharp abdominal pain or the gradual loss of motor functions.

Strychnine, a rare but potent poison, is another possibility. Since it could have been easily masked in wine, it would have been very difficult for Alexander or his attendant to detect it. However, its effects are completely different from what the king experienced. Instead of causing a high fever, the poison typically leads to convulsions. The white hellebore might be a better candidate. While the plant was known among the Greeks for both its medicinal and toxic properties, those who consumed it in large quantities could experience severe abdominal pain, vomiting, diarrhea, and fever—all of which matched the symptoms of Alexander before he passed away. Hellebore poisoning also aligns with the timeline of his decline, as it often leads to a protracted and painful death. White hellebore does not cause a loss of speech or motor functions, but scholars answered this mystery by suggesting that these symptoms were exacerbated by his previous injuries, particularly the neck wound sustained during the Siege of Cyropolis.

Plausible Diseases That Killed the Conqueror

Although speculation of foul play surrounds Alexander's death, it is plausible that the Macedonian king did not depart the world as a result of political intrigue. Alexander lived a life full of relentless military campaigns, which often rewarded him with immense physical and emotional stress. All those years of marching through hostile environments might have eventually weakened his immune system. The Indian campaign that he launched during the last few years of his life had pushed not only his army to its limits but also his own body. Coupled with the loss of Hephaestion, which added another layer of emotional strain, it could be possible that the conqueror succumbed to death because of an illness.

Scholars and historians have pointed to several diseases as likely candidates for Alexander's death. One of them is the West Nile virus. If this virus really was the culprit, then Plutarch's account about birds dying in Babylon around the time Alexander's death was near—a story that has long been interpreted as a dramatic embellishment—might actually reflect a real event. Birds are known to be the carriers of the West Nile virus. Their deaths could indicate the presence of the disease in Babylon at the time. The virus is typically transmitted to humans through mosquito bites. Babylon was surrounded by marshlands and abundant mosquitoes. Thus, we could assume that Alexander might have been infected by the virus during his stay in the city.

The only problem with this hypothesis is that many aspects of Alexander's symptoms did not align with the virus. While fever is a common sign of the West Nile virus, the virus can also cause delirium or confusion. No historical accounts ever suggest that the Macedonian king experienced such symptoms. Paralysis and coma are rather rare symptoms, even in fatal West Nile virus cases.

Another possible candidate is malaria, which was endemic to Mesopotamia. Since the Euphrates River flowed through Babylon, it could be plausible that the city was a prime breeding ground for malaria-carrying mosquitoes. Alexander could have contracted the disease when he was in the city or perhaps even earlier in his campaign, with the infection growing fatal later on. Alexander started off with a fever, which fits one of the symptoms of malaria. If the disease gets severe, malaria can also cause neurological complications, which would explain Alexander's gradual loss of motor functions and his eventual coma before his death. However, malaria never causes sharp abdominal pains.

The ancient world was also familiar with typhoid fever, another fatal disease that often ravaged the lives of many. Since this disease is spread through contaminated food and water, typhoid became a constant threat, especially in densely populated cities like Babylon. Alexander's severe fever, abdominal pain, and eventual loss of key bodily functions align with the symptoms of a typhoid infection. Alexander's neurological decline could have been the result of encephalitis (inflammation of the brain), which is one of the complications of typhoid.

This theory is accepted by many since typhoid is known to have the ability to cause intestinal perforation, which would explain the sudden onset of sharp abdominal pain that Alexander suffered from. A ruptured bowel would have caused immense pain and rapidly worsened his condition, eventually leading to his demise. The only challenge to this theory is that a perforated bowel usually happens in later stages of a typhoid infection; Alexander experienced this much earlier.

Alexander as a Prisoner of His Own Body

There is another theory surrounding his death, which is far more unsettling than the rest. Some scholars suggest that the mighty conqueror did not actually die when those around him pronounced him dead. Instead, he was afflicted with a rare and severe neurological disorder known to us today as Guillain-Barré syndrome (GBS). If this theory holds any truth at all, the implications are rather chilling. Alexander the Great might have been alive the entire time but trapped in his own body. He could do nothing as the world mourned him and made preparations for his burial.

GBS is a condition in which the body's immune system mistakenly attacks the nervous system, causing progressive neurological damage. One would feel extreme weakness taking over their body or tingling in the limbs that eventually escalates to severe paralysis. As the disease goes on, GBS will typically impair breathing, speech, and even movement. In the end, the patient will be rendered almost completely immobile. Although they cannot move a muscle or even let out the faintest whisper to communicate their plight, those suffering from GBS are actually fully conscious and aware. GBS can also develop after certain infections, including typhoid fever and acute necrotizing pancreatitis, both of which have been suggested as possible causes of Alexander's illness.

This theory also explains a certain detail recorded in ancient accounts. According to these sources, Alexander's body did not decompose for several days after his death. While some believed this was because of his almost divine status, scholars suggest this was because Alexander was never dead to begin with. In the ancient world, death was not determined by checking for a pulse or brain activity; instead, it was determined by the cessation of breathing. If Alexander had GBS, the condition would have caused near-total paralysis, including a slowing of his breathing to the point where it became imperceptible to those around him. The paralysis would have reduced his body's need for oxygen. This would have made his minimal breathing appear even less noticeable. Alexander might have appeared lifeless to those at his "deathbed." They could not see the conqueror's chest rising and falling, but in reality, he was still breathing, albeit very slowly. His heart never stopped beating, and his organs were still functioning, preventing any sort of body decomposition.

This theory reveals a deeply disturbing possibility. Alexander the Great, the mighty ruler who conquered the known world, was helpless in his final moments. He was aware that his coffin was being made. He heard his attendants and loyal companions weeping for his fate, yet the once unstoppable, almost divine conqueror could not even open his eyes or give the smallest signal as physicians prematurely declared him dead. He might have been a prisoner of his own failing body, treated as a corpse while his mind remained intact. The king, whose voice had commanded thousands of armies and whose actions had shaped the course of history, could do nothing in the end except wait for his eventual death, perhaps days after he was declared dead.

Chapter 3 – The Legendary Battle of Marathon

Under the reign of King Darius I, the Persian Empire rose to become one of the most powerful forces to ever exist in the ancient world. Its territories stretched from the edges of India to the shores of the Aegean, with each region guarded by a fierce army that was once feared by many. Yet, the Persians were rarely free from challenges, especially on the western fringes of their empire. By the late 5th century BCE, the spark of defiance was clearly in the air, leading to a conflict that would soon alter the course of history: the Ionian Revolt.

The Ionian Greeks inhabited the areas along the western coast of Anatolia. Ever since Cyrus the Great's successful conquest of the Kingdom of Lydia (sometime in 547 BCE), the Ionians were put under Persian rule. The Ionians were allowed a degree of autonomy, but they were also forced to pay tribute to the Persians. Tensions began to simmer beneath the surface. Eventually, these tensions began to reach a boiling point. Desiring independence, the Ionians, led by the city of Miletus, rose in rebellion against the Persians in 499 BCE. One of their earliest acts of defiance included the burning of the Persian regional capital at Sardis, which undoubtedly enraged Darius I.

However, the Ionians knew that in order to fully go against the mighty Persians, they needed a stronger force. So, they sought aid from mainland Greece. Without hesitation, Athens and Eretria responded to their call. The two city-states sent ships and troops to support the Ionians, further drawing the ire of the Persian king.

Unfortunately, the revolt ended in failure by 494 BCE. The Persians decisively defeated the rebels at the Battle of Lade. As a result, Miletus, the heart of the revolt, was destroyed. Its once-thriving harbor became nothing more than a thing of the past. Its people were forced to face their nightmare as they were taken into slavery. However, the consequences of the revolt were not limited to the lands of Ionia. Darius was furious at the Greeks' interference, particularly the Athenians and the Eretrians, and wanted to punish them. According to Herodotus, Darius's anger toward the Athenians was so great that he ordered one of his servants to say "Master, remember the Athenians," three times before his dinner every day.

This anger resulted in the first Persian invasion of Greece. Apart from being an act of punishment for both Athens and Eretria, Darius was also determined to expand Persian dominance over the entire Greek mainland, sending a clear message to those who dared to challenge him. Without wasting too much time, Darius sent a preliminary expedition in 492 BCE, which sought to secure the northern regions of Greece and establish a foothold for a larger campaign. Led by Mardonius, the expedition achieved some success before misfortune struck. Perhaps sent by Poseidon himself, storms arrived near Mount Athos, ravaging the Persian fleet.

Never known to back down that easily, Darius launched another campaign two years later. This time around, the campaign was spearheaded by Datis and Artaphernes. The Persian fleet sailed across the Aegean, hoping they could avoid the wrath of the Greek god of the sea. As if luck was on their side, the Persians were able to capture a few islands and establish garrisons along the way. Eretria fell swiftly to the Persian advance. Not planning on showing mercy, especially with its involvement in aiding Ionia, the Persians sacked the city. Temples were burned, and the population was enslaved.

With Eretria subjugated, the Persians turned to their main target: Athens. The Persians marched toward the city, displaying both the empire's vast resources and organizational might. The army commanded by Datis and Artaphernes was said to have numbered about twenty-five thousand infantry, supported by seasoned cavalry and another fleet of hundreds of ships. In contrast, the Athenians only had roughly ten thousand hoplites to spare, each armed with spears and shields.

The sheer size of the Persian army, combined with its reputation for annihilating its enemies, made the coming confrontation seem like a hopeless endeavor to the Athenians. However, the Athenians were not dissuaded. Like the Ionians, the Athenians knew that they needed not just strategy but also reinforcements to defeat such a colossal army. And so, the Athenian generals turned to their most powerful ally, Sparta. The Spartans were, after all, formidable soldiers, and with their support, Athens could have a chance at tipping the scales in their favor.

Since the two Greek city-states were over 130 miles apart, the Athenian military had to dispatch a *hemerodromos*, a type of courier, to deliver their request for aid to the Spartans. They chose a man named Philippides for this task. He was thought to have been the best among the *hemerodromoi* (plural for *hemerodromos*). Not only did he have experience traversing the rugged terrain of ancient Greece, but Philippides also had unmatched stamina and endurance, allowing him to cover hundreds of miles in a matter of days.

Philippides's task was rather straightforward: run to Sparta, deliver the message, and return to Athens with their answer. However, the journey was grueling. He had to run through rocky trails and make his way through sun-scorched plains and dense forests. Fatigue undoubtedly weighed heavily on his body as the miles wore on. Yet, Philippides knew that Athens' fate rested on his shoulders. And so, he pushed forward. Suddenly, a faint voice came out of the dense forest, calling out his name. Philippides halted, but his heart continued to race.

The *hemerodromos* was left speechless when he realized that the voice came from the god Pan, who stood before him. Pan, with his goat-like legs and horns, was the Greek god of the wilderness, shepherds, and hunters. Unlike the Olympian gods who ruled from Mount Olympus, Pan called the wilderness his domain since he was, more or less, the embodiment of the untamed forces of nature. His presence was also believed by the Greeks to have the ability to instill terror; the term "panic" was derived from the god's name.

"The Athenians once worshiped me as they do the Olympians," Pan said to Philippides. "But tell me, Philippides, why did they stop when I have aided them in the past?"

After finding the courage to finally speak, Philippides responded to the god. Knowing that the Athenians needed all the help they could muster—both mortal and divine—he reassured Pan that the Athenians would soon honor the god with shrines and temples again. He then expressed his hope for the god to aid Athens should the time come.

"Very well," Pan responded. "You may go now. I will lend my hand to the Athenians as I have before."

This legendary encounter was recorded by the ancient historian Herodotus. Although Herodotus is widely known today as the "Father of History," his accounts often blended fact with myth and oral tradition. This was a common practice among many writers of his time.

Philippides then continued his journey, eventually reaching Sparta. Without wasting a second, the *hemerodromos* made his way to the Spartan officials and delivered Athens' plea. He explained the imminent threat that loomed over Greece and Athens' dire need for Spartan warriors to join them at Marathon. Although the Spartans agreed to lend their spears, there was a problem. The battle was about to begin at the same time as the Carneia festival, a sacred period during which Spartan law prohibited military action until the full moon. Sparta was also in the midst of internal unrest. There was news of a potential revolt brewing among the Messenians. So, despite being willing to fight the Persians alongside the Athenians, the Spartans could not send their army at that moment. They did, however, promise to march after the festival's conclusion. The Spartans ended up arriving a day after the battle took place.

A 17th-century drawing of Pan, currently held at the National Gallery of Art, Washington, DC.[48]

Although disappointed with the answer, Philippides hurried back to Athens so that he could deliver Sparta's response to the officials. Once safe behind the walls of the city, Philippides recounted his experiences to the Athenian generals. He told them all about Sparta's decision and his encounter with the god Pan. The Athenians believed every one of his words. In their eyes, his encounter with the god was a sign of divine favor. The Athenians worked to honor the god. Shrines and temples were constructed in Pan's name, and rituals were performed to worship him.

The Battle Commenced

The Persians reached the plains of Marathon in early September 490 BCE. To them, the location of the battlefield was strategic. The flat land was spread between the mountains and the sea. The Persians could use it to their advantage by deploying their fierce cavalry to overwhelm their enemies. For days following their arrival, the Persians raided nearby villages. Datis and Artaphernes spent day and night preparing their forces and waited patiently for the Athenians to respond.

Meanwhile, in Athens, the population braced itself for the clash. The Athenian army, which numbered only ten thousand, was put under the command of generals Callimachus and Miltiades, both of whom were extremely experienced in the art of war. Despite the fact that they were greatly outnumbered by the Persians, the Athenians were able to remain hopeful due to their knowledge of the terrain—and perhaps the divine favor of the gods.

After ensuring everything was prepared, the Athenian army began marching to Marathon. Miltiades played a key role in the battle, not only because he was a seasoned general but also because he had once served under the Persians themselves. He even accompanied the Persian army during Darius I's campaign against the Scythians in 513 BCE. All those years fighting with the enemy allowed him to understand the Persians' strengths and weaknesses. Miltiades devised a bold strategy to counter the Persians' numerical advantage. Relying on the discipline and superior training of the famous Greek phalanx, the Athenians focused on strengthening their flanks.

An illustration of the Greek hoplites marching in phalanx formation."

This deliberately thinned the center of their formation, but it was a calculated risk. Miltiades anticipated that the Persians, confident in their numerical superiority, would exploit the weakened center and push forward aggressively. By drawing the Persian forces into the center, the Athenians could envelop them with their stronger flanks. The disciplined Greek hoplites on the wings would hold firm and then pivot inward, creating a pincer movement to trap the Persians in a double envelopment. This maneuver would make use of the Greeks' strength in close combat, as the well-trained hoplites could easily overwhelm the lighter Persian infantry. The plan was bold and ambitious. If it was executed correctly, Athens could live to see another day.

The battle began at dawn, with the Athenian hoplites charging down the slopes. Clad in bronze armor and armed with spears and shields, they attacked the Persians as if there would be no tomorrow. After all, the Athenians had to win the battle, or Athens might crumble entirely since the city had no more soldiers to spare should the Persians decide to attack the city itself. The Persians did not hold back; they launched volleys of arrows as the Athenians advanced. This, however, failed to disrupt the Athenians' momentum since the Greek hoplites were covered in heavy armor.

The Athenian troops charging into the Battle of Marathon.“

Legend has it that the god Pan was present the entire time. The god observed the battle from a cave near the field. Perhaps true to his promise to Philippides earlier, Pan was believed to have eventually intervened in the battle, lending his divine assistance to the Athenians. But at the beginning, he lay low, waiting for the right moment to strike fear into the hearts of the ambitious invaders.

The battle raged for hours, and for a moment, the Athenian center started to falter under the relentless assault of the Persians. With their superior numbers, the Persians pressed hard, hoping they could break the Greek lines entirely. The Greeks, refusing to back down, were holding their ground when they suddenly noticed a figure emerging on the battlefield out of nowhere. According to ancient records by Herodotus and Pausanias, this mysterious figure was Echetlaeus (Hero of the Plowshare).

Pausanias claimed that Echetlaeus had an archaic and otherworldly demeanor. Instead of wearing heavy armor and a helmet similar to the hoplites, his clothes were rather simple and rustic. He looked like a farmer but had the frame of a bodybuilder. The mysterious warrior also wielded an *echetlon* or a plowshare, which he swung around with a precision that bordered on the supernatural. Each strike was precise; Pausanias recorded that Echetlaeus cut down the Persians without difficulty as he swiftly moved through the chaotic battlefield.

Herodotus added a haunting detail to the tale. On the battlefield was an Athenian soldier who went by the name Epizelus. He fought bravely on the front lines, but something extraordinary occurred that changed his fate. Herodotus claimed that Epizelus suddenly turned blind even though he had never been struck by a weapon. The last thing he saw was a mysterious muscular man—neither an Athenian nor a Persian soldier—with a beard so long that it covered his entire shield. It was believed that the cause of his sudden blindness was the result of divine energy that came from Echetlaeus striking down a Persian soldier next to him.

Seeing that the gods were on their side on the battlefield, the Athenians pushed on and executed Miltiades's brilliant strategy. While the center steadied and held its ground, the stronger wings of the Athenian formation enveloped the Persian sides. This was the moment when the Athenians successfully broke through the enemy's ranks, driving them into disarray. The Persian soldiers, now hemmed in on all sides, began to fear that they might not leave the battlefield alive.

As if there was some kind of cue, the god of wilderness, Pan, was believed to have taken the chance to intervene. He sent waves of panic through the Persian ranks. Some even claim that the god himself appeared before the Persians, his wild eyes and goat-like legs and horns instilling fear into the hearts of the invaders to the point where they broke formation and scrambled toward their ships in desperation. It was a chaotic scene, with the panicked Persians trampling one another, desperate to leave the battlefield.

And so, victory belonged to the Athenians. While the Athenians only lost 192 soldiers, the Persians left behind a far more staggering number of casualties. Herodotus, who was prone to exaggeration, recorded that the Persians lost about 6,400 men in total.

Upon seeing the Persian forces retreat, the Athenians thought it would be good to spread the news of their victory to the rest of the city-states. Philippides was summoned once more and tasked with delivering the message to Athens. Exhilarated by the triumph, Philippides immediately set off on yet another grueling journey. He ran for nearly twenty-six miles from Marathon to Athens. Upon reaching the city-state, Philippides was said to have burst into the assembly and proclaimed "Χαίρετε, νικῶμεν" (*Chairete, nikomen*—"Hail, we win!") before collapsing to the ground and dying of exhaustion.

A depiction of a runner, possibly Philippides, arriving in Athens to announce the victory at Marathon."

Celebrations were in order for the great victory, yet the Athenian soldiers could not help but think about the mysterious figure who had appeared on the battlefield to assist them in turning the tide against the mighty Persians. Despite their efforts to look for Echetlaeus, the Athenians failed to find him; it was as if he had vanished into thin air. Perplexed, the Athenians turned to the Oracle of Delphi. As the most sacred authoritative source of divine wisdom in Greece, the oracle must have some answers about the mysterious figure. However, when asked about Echetlaeus's identity and whereabouts, the oracle simply replied that it was the will of the gods that the Athenians honor him as a hero. The Athenians did not question any further. Eager to fulfill the gods' will, they erected marble monuments to commemorate the mysterious warrior. His depiction can be seen today in the Stoa Poikile (Painted Portico) in Athens, where his image was carved alongside other heroes of Marathon.

Although the Athenians were satisfied with the oracle's answer, the mystery surrounding Echetlaeus captivated many others, especially historians and mythologists. Research and theories have emerged to uncover the truth behind who the muscular hero who fought at Marathon really was. His name offered the first clues. Derived from the Greek word *echetlon*, which means "plowshare," the name Echetlaeus literally translates to "he of the plowshare." This association with a farming tool led many to believe that Echetlaeus symbolized the agrarian roots of Greek society; he represented the strength of the common people who toiled the land and defended their homeland.

Of course, many also came to the conclusion that Echetlaeus was not a mortal warrior. Some ancient accounts suggest that he was a divine being sent by none other than Pan, who had given his word to Philippides that he would help the Athenians. Although Pan was known for his unpredictable nature and power to cause panic in his enemies, some suggest that the god might have taken a physical form on the battlefield to fulfill his promise.

A depiction of Echetlaeus fighting with his plow carved onto an Etruscan funerary urn.⁴⁷

Others associated Echetlaeus with the goddess Demeter and Persephone, both of whom were considered central figures in Greek mythology. While Demeter was the goddess of agriculture and the harvest—fitting the appearance of Echetlaeus, who looked like a farmer—Persephone was the queen of the underworld. In this interpretation, the mysterious warrior was seen as a manifestation of their divine influence, a protector of the land and its people in a battle fought on the soil they deeply respected. Some even suggested that the plowshare symbolized Demeter's dominion over the earth and the idea of renewal after destruction.

Unfortunately, despite these theories, the true nature of Echetlaeus remains a mystery. We will likely never be sure whether he was just a farmer inspired to fight and defend his homeland, a strong hero whose deeds were mythologized, or even a divine emissary sent by the gods, but we can safely say that Echetlaeus represents the enduring Greek belief in the intertwining of the mortal and the divine.

As for the Persians, the Battle of Marathon was not their last clash with the Greeks. A decade later, in 480 BCE, the Persians, under Darius's son, Xerxes I, would embark on a larger campaign in Greece. These episodes of war brought forth another set of new heroes and legendary battles, including the popular stand of Leonidas and his three hundred Spartans at Thermopylae, as well as Themistocles's outstanding naval strategy at Salamis.

Chapter 4 – Spartan Myths, Misconceptions, and Untold Stories

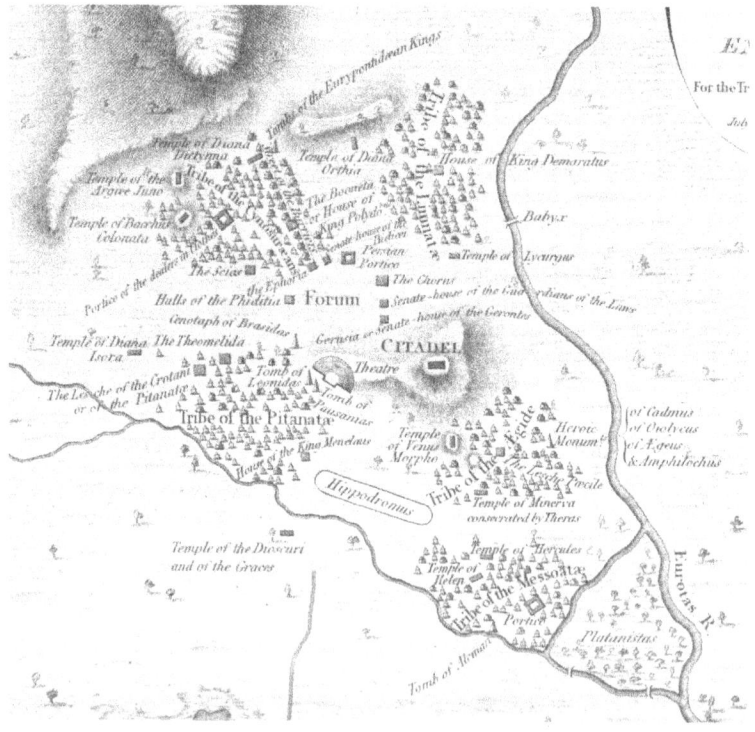

An old map of classical Sparta.[48]

The silence of dusk was shattered with the sudden cry of a newborn. Born into a modest Spartan family, the child was cradled by his dear mother, who held him close to her chest. The baby soon calmed down. He cooed softly, eventually drifting into a deep sleep. The mother smiled but only for a moment, as she could not ignore the tension that had been hanging heavy in the room. Sparta had a law where every child must be judged for their worthiness to live.

The father carefully took the boy into his arms. Nodding to his wife as if to tell her everything would be fine, he walked out of their humble home and set out toward the Lesche. Other than being a public gathering place typically used by elders, citizens, and philosophers for discussions, storytelling, and making civic or political decisions, the Lesche was also where Spartan elders would gather to determine the fate of newborns.

The father was hesitant as he made his way through the village, his heart beating even faster the moment he laid eyes on Mount Taygetus looming in the distance. According to ancient tales, the mountain's peak, also known as Taleton, was a place of reverence. It was dedicated to Zeus and the god of the sun, Helios. The peak was once a place of sacred rituals, where horses were sacrificed in the name of the gods. However, for many Spartans, the mountain was significant for another reason; it was believed to be a site where unworthy infants were left to die at a chasm down below.

When the father arrived at the Lesche, he immediately saw the elders. The Spartans lived by the belief that the city's survival depended on the physical and moral excellence of its people. Thus, it was of the utmost importance for the elders to examine the baby thoroughly. They checked for signs of sickness, deformity, and frailty. The father could only watch as the elders did this. The father could not help but think of his neighbor's unfortunate child. Just a week earlier, the elders had deemed the child unworthy. His neighbor was ordered to discard his newborn at the chasm of Mount Taygetus.

The father was brought back to reality when one of the elders called his name. They announced that his son was indeed strong and healthy, showing potential that he could one day serve the city.

"You must raise him well," one of the elders said.

The father, forever thankful to the gods, could finally let out a huge sigh of relief. He took his son into his arms, eager to return home and deliver the good news to his dear wife.

However, one question remains. Did the Spartans really practice this? Or was it nothing more than a myth told by ancient sources or enemies of the city-state to exaggerate Sparta's image as a cold and calculating society?

Archaeologists have uncovered forty-six human remains at the foot of Mount Taygetus. But interestingly, none of them belonged to infants. All of the bones that were discovered, which were dated to the 6th and 5th centuries BCE, actually belonged to individuals over the age of eighteen. This physical evidence contradicts the stories of how the Spartans left their unworthy babies in the chasm. Scholars suggest that instead of infants, the Spartans might have thrown criminals and prisoners off the mountain as a form of punishment. After all, Sparta was known to have dealt with criminals harshly, so the use of the mountain for such a purpose fits more closely with what is known about their justice system.

An 18th-century painting depicting a scene where infants were being judged by the Spartan elders.⁹

While the story is most likely a myth that stems from the cultural perception of Sparta as a militaristic state—they valued physical perfection above all else—infant exposure was not unfamiliar in the ancient world. In certain Greek city-states, it was practiced, albeit only occasionally. Although it was by no means the norm, the Greeks resorted to this in response to severe deformities or extreme poverty. Athens, for one, allowed fathers to leave their unwanted infants, especially illegitimate or severely deformed children, in public spaces. Some sources claim that these infants were first put into jars or a clay pot before being left on the roadway. Babies who were lucky enough would be saved by passersby, while the rest would have to face their demise slowly.

Mount Taygetus as seen from Sparta.[50]

This practice of exposing a child to the elements or outright killing a child was not only limited to Greece; it also happened in other parts of the ancient world. At times, it was done as part of a religious practice or for population control. The Carthaginians, for instance, were said—or rather accused since there is no concrete evidence to prove it—to have sacrificed children in the name of their gods. Ancient China and India also participated in infanticide, though it was usually done for females. In ancient China, these unfortunate female babies were typically drowned, suffocated, or starved to death. There were also cases where they were placed in baskets and hung on trees, where they would die from the elements or starve to death.

However, despite the existence of these practices, the idea that Sparta systematically discarded infants who they deemed unworthy seems to be an exaggeration of Spartan culture. This claim might have been crafted by their enemies to paint a harsh picture of the Spartans.

The Krypteia

Meanwhile, far in the Spartan countryside, an episode of murder would take place. It began with a laborer who was perhaps walking home after a long day's work. It was obvious that the weight of exhaustion slowed his steps as he trudged along the dirt path between the fields. Suddenly, he caught a sight of something ominous. Squinting into the shadows, the laborer could see a figure slumped against a gnarled olive tree. He looked at the figure for a few seconds, yet there were no signs of any movement. With his heart pounding, the laborer crept closer, letting his curiosity take over him.

It was a lifeless body. The laborer had seen the dead man before. He was one of the helots (the enslaved class) and was known to be a leader among the Messenian rebels. Beneath the body was a pool of blood, and as the laborer's eyes moved up, he noticed that the poor helot had his throat slashed. The laborer quickly took a step back. He knew very well that this was the work of the Krypteia. Not wanting to meddle in their affairs, the laborer made haste to his home, hoping he could erase the image of the dead helot from his mind.

The Krypteia worked silently in the shadows, yet everyone in Sparta knew of them. They did not target random civilians or laborers—only helots. This was the subjugated class who toiled on the fields and fed the Spartan war machine. Without them to work on the fields, the Spartan society would crumble. But why were the helots treated as if they were criminals? In the eyes of the Spartans, the helots were a threat to the fragile balance that kept Sparta intact.

The Spartans had a hierarchy. At the top were the Spartiates, the full male citizens who had gone through the military training known as the agoge. Next in the hierarchy were the Perioeci. These were the free men who lived in neighboring cities and villages under the governance of Sparta. They lived their lives working as craftsmen and traders and produced various other goods. They handled much of the economic activity that the Spartiates themselves avoided. The Perioeci, however, only had political rights in their own cities. They did not hold any in the state of Sparta itself; these rights were reserved exclusively for the Spartiates. At the bottom of the pyramid were the helots. These people, who often hailed from Messenia and Laconia, had been conquered by Sparta.

Of course, these people had not always been slaves. Before they had been captured, they were free. They could work their lands without fear and live a normal life. It all changed when Sparta came during the Messenian Wars. After conquering the region, the Spartans, as typical as it may sound, reduced them to servitude. They bound them to the land as agricultural laborers. These people were forced to grow crops for their Spartan overlords. Some say that the Messenians and Laconians were once proud people. So, it was not a surprise that resentment simmered over time. When Sparta was struggling during a massive earthquake in

464 BCE, the helots took this as an opportunity to strike. Unfortunately, the Spartans proved to be mightier; the uprising was unsuccessful.

The Spartans decided to make their cruelty to the helots even clearer. Plutarch described a scene where the Spartans forced the helots to drink excessive amounts of wine until they were drunk. They were then paraded during public messes, known as syssitia—an event where Spartiates would gather every day to share meals in communal dining halls. This was said to serve as examples of the disgraceful effects of excessive drinking and drunkenness. The helots were also often forced to sing and dance in degrading ways during banquets and other public events.

The Roman historian Livy provided a more daunting account of Spartan oppression. According to his writings, helots who were accused of desertion were usually subjected to public whippings. However, their punishment did not end there. After the whippings, they were immediately put to death. There was also an episode where two thousand helots mysteriously disappeared. Some believe that they were victims of a mass killing.

In order to instill fear in the helots, the Spartans established the Krypteia. Although its exact origins are debated, some historians suggest that the Krypteia's roots trace back to the Dorian invasion of the Peloponnesian Peninsula. It was initially created as a guerrilla force tasked with suppressing resistance among conquered peoples before evolving into a more formalized institution. Other scholars claim that Krypteia's origins did not stretch that far back. Instead, they suggest that it was developed in the 6th century BCE when Sparta was heavily focused on consolidating its power.

While its origin is still unclear, we can be sure that the Krypteia drew its members from the agoge. This infamous Spartan education and training system was designed to transform Spartan boys into warriors capable of upholding the city-state's military supremacy. Training was compulsory for all male Spartiates, beginning when boys reached the age of seven. They were removed from their families and lived communally with each other. These boys had to go through years of relentless physical and mental challenges. They were expected to come out of the program exceptionally disciplined, obedient, and, of course, masters of martial skill—both with weapons and in unarmed combat. Spartan men typically graduated from the agoge at the age of thirty; this was also when they were allowed to marry and start a family.

Candidates for the Krypteia were chosen from this highly disciplined pool of young men. It is safe to assume that the selection criteria were stringent. Only those who showed signs of exceptional leadership, combat prowess, and a knack for stealth were selected. Once their names were listed to join the Krypteia, these young men would undergo additional training. Although details of this stage of training remain shrouded in secrecy, it likely involved advanced training in survival, espionage, and assassinations, which were all necessary for their future missions.

The Krypteia's main goal seemed straightforward: its members had to identify and eliminate potential helot leaders or agitators before they could fuel a rebellion. Oftentimes, the Krypteia worked under the cover of darkness; this was when they infiltrated helot communities. Usually working alone or in small groups, the Krypteia members were armed lightly. They carried only a dagger and minimal supplies that were enough for them to survive. Secrecy was their utmost priority. The Krypteia members had to conceal their true identities. Precision was also important when it came to assassinations; the Krypteia had to ensure that they eliminated their targets without leaving any traceable evidence.

Despite operating in secret, the Krypteia succeeded in creating an atmosphere of constant fear among the helots. With the removal of so many helot leaders, successful rebellions were considered almost impossible. Perhaps consumed by fear of getting slaughtered by the Krypteia, some helots refrained from even listening to early plans of revolt. Instead of facing the Spartan secret service's wrath, they chose to obey their masters.

The Krypteia also played a role during wartime, with its members often engaged in espionage and reconnaissance. They focused on gathering intelligence that proved invaluable to Spartan military campaigns. Scholars suggest that the Krypteia likely played a key role in the Greco-Persian Wars. During this chaotic period of war, the members of the Krypteia were the ones responsible for conducting covert operations, which eventually contributed to the Spartan victory at the Battle of Plataea in 479 BCE. The same could also be said during the Peloponnesian War, where the Krypteia, again, were instrumental in counter-espionage operations against Athens.

Of course, everything had its ending. The Krypteia saw its influence gradually wane when Sparta faced a series of catastrophic defeats and political issues. However, it was the Battle of Leuctra in 371 BCE that marked the turning point. When the Thebans decisively defeated the mighty Spartans, the Messenian helots were liberated. This was undoubtedly bad news for Sparta since the people had long relied on helot labor to sustain both its economy and lifestyle.

With the loss of Messenia and its agricultural wealth, Sparta was plunged into an episode of economic and social crisis. Due to years of warfare and strict citizenship requirements, the population of the Spartiate class dwindled to only a thousand adult males. Sparta could no longer sustain its warrior culture. These major changes eventually rendered the Krypteia irrelevant.

The Battle of Tegyra

When speaking of Sparta, one could not help but think of its military prowess. The Spartans forged their reputation by emerging victorious in countless battles, even those where the Spartans were greatly outnumbered. The famous Leonidas, for one, went down in history as one of the greatest Spartan kings. With only three hundred Spartans to spare, he successfully held off a massive Persian force, though victory in the famed Battle of Thermopylae eventually belonged to the Persians. Despite this reputation as an invincible force, there was a moment when this myth was broken. This time around, it was not the Persians but the Thebans who proved that Spartan steel could definitely be bent and broken despite their strong numbers.

Thebes had a rather complicated history with Sparta. It was once a key member of the Boeotian League, which was formed in 550 BCE. However, when Thebes fell under Spartan control in 382 BCE, many Theban leaders fled to Athens. Unwilling to bow down to the Spartans, they bided their time, waiting for the golden opportunity to reclaim their city. That moment came in 378 BCE under the command of Pelopidas. A daring leader, Pelopidas led 300 exiled Thebans back to their homeland and launched a nighttime assault on the Spartan garrison of 1,500 soldiers. Following this, Thebes was free from Spartan claws once more.

The Spartan kings, Agesilaus II and Cleombrotus, were quick to acknowledge the danger posed by Thebes. They launched several campaigns to retake the city and reestablish Spartan control over Boeotia. This, however, failed, leading to other Boeotian cities like Tanagra, Haliartus, Lebadea, and Coronea to make a bold move—they expelled their own Spartan garrisons. By 375 BCE, these cities had announced their allegiance to Thebes. The Boeotian League was reborn. Seeking to secure their influence and power, the Thebans—now led by Pelopidas and his close ally Epaminondas—set their sights on Orchomenus, the last Boeotian city under Spartan influence.

When word reached Pelopidas that a large Spartan garrison had left Orchomenus for a battle in Locris, he immediately planned his strategy. Since the city was left undefended, Pelopidas rode to the city. Ancient sources wrote that he took with him three hundred members of the Sacred Band. As an elite Theban infantry unit, the Sacred Band was popular for its extreme bravery and cohesion. The unit was composed of 150 pairs of soldiers, each bound by ties of friendship and love. This made them fiercely loyal and almost unbeatable in battle.

Upon nearing Orchomenus, Pelopidas learned that the city was far from defenseless; additional Spartan reinforcements had arrived to protect the city. The Thebans lacked siege weapons at the time, and coupled with insufficient manpower to take an entire city by force, Pelopidas ordered a retreat. Perhaps hoping to avoid direct contact with the Spartans, Pelopidas led his men north of Lake Copais.

However, in a twist of fate, Pelopidas received a messenger who carried bad news. The Spartan army knew the Thebans were just miles away from them and were marching straight toward them. Knowing that retreat was no longer viable, Pelopidas chose to fight.

Since both sides were caught off guard by the encounter, it is safe to assume that they had little time to plan. The Spartans were led by the polemarchs (commanders) Gorgoleon and Theopompus. They numbered between 1,200 and 1,800 troops compared to the Thebans, who only had 500 men at most. The Spartans were confident. Not only were they well trained and had experience from countless battles, but they also greatly outnumbered their enemy. However, Pelopidas had the strength of the Sacred Band.

The armies clashed. Details of the encounter are scarce, but some accounts described that the Theban cavalry managed to harass the Spartan flanks long enough until the Sacred Band was in position to strike. With precision and speed, the elite Theban infantry attacked the Spartan right flank, eventually killing the polemarchs. The Spartans were now on the battlefield without their commanders. It did not take long for them to falter, giving way for Pelopidas and the Thebans to gain the upper hand.

In another version of the battle, records narrate that instead of attacking the Spartan flanks, Pelopidas had his forces focus on the Spartan center. Using tactics almost similar to those employed by the Theban general Pagondas at the Battle of Delium (424 BCE), the Sacred Band successfully drove a wedge through the Spartan ranks. This broke their formation, thus leaving the flanks completely vulnerable for the Theban cavalry to wreak havoc on the Spartans.

Regardless of the exact strategy, the outcome of the battle was the same. The Spartans, despite their numerical superiority, were defeated by the Thebans. Those who survived managed to flee the battlefield and regroup with the garrison at Orchomenus. Nevertheless, the Thebans succeeded in proving to the world that the Spartans were far from invincible. This victory at Tegyra was only the beginning. Thebes would continue to challenge Spartan dominance, eventually reshaping the balance of power in the ancient Greek world.

Gylippus of Sparta

It was 415 BCE, and Athens had just launched one of its most ambitious campaigns: the Sicilian expedition. The Athenians had suffered the plague, and the Peloponnesian War was not going well for them. They believed that by securing Syracuse, a city of immense resources, Athens could once again tip the balance of the ongoing chaos in their favor.

The invasion of Sicily was spearheaded by a few Athenian generals, including Nicias, Alcibiades, and Lamachus. The campaign itself was beset by obstacles in the beginning, such as disagreements between the generals and logistical problems, but with a fleet of over 130 triremes and thousands of soldiers, Athens achieved some success in the early stage of the expedition. However, Syracuse was not ready to back down that easily. The people mounted a fierce resistance against the Athenians. Nevertheless, perhaps believing in their superior naval power and resources, the Athenians pressed on, hoping that they would eventually defeat the Sicilian defenders and claim the city for themselves.

Finally realizing the gravity of their situation, Syracuse requested help from its allies, especially Sparta. The Spartans were well aware of the strategic importance of Sicily. If Athens succeeded, the city-state would have no difficulties securing a foothold in the western Mediterranean, which would threaten Sparta even more.

In the meantime, Athenian General Alcibiades had been recalled to Athens. Upon learning that he was charged with sacrilege—the controversial general was said to have mutilated and mocked the sacred statues of the Eleusinian Mysteries—Alcibiades made the decision to defect to Athens' enemy, Sparta. He then advised the Spartans on how to stop the Athenian campaign in Sicily, which was by appointing a certain general named Gylippus.

Gylippus was not an ordinary Spartan. His family had a rather bad reputation—his father had been exiled for accepting bribes—but Gylippus managed to create a name of his own through years of military experience. When the seasoned general was appointed as the leader of Syracuse's defense, Sparta was a step closer to ensuring Athens suffered a massive defeat.

With only a small contingent of troops, Gylippus's arrival almost immediately boosted the morale of the Syracusans who had been trapped in the city. The Spartan commander's first priority was simple: break the Athenian siege of Syracuse. Gylippus began working right away. Upon surveying the battlefield, the seasoned general found the Athenians' key weakness: their reliance on maintaining control over their siege works. Without wasting more time, Gylippus launched his troops—composed of infantry and cavalry—to harass the Athenian forces. The plan was to disrupt the Athenians' efforts to complete their encirclement of the city. Gylippus also paid attention to Syracuse's fortifications. He oversaw the construction of counter-walls that could render the Athenian siege lines ineffective.

Gylippus soon witnessed the Athenians falter. The Athenian forces did not lose just one but two of their leaders. Alcibiades had defected shortly after the expedition began, and Lamachus died during one of the skirmishes that took place outside the city walls. Morale was depleting. Disease soon wreaked havoc throughout the Athenian camp, further diminishing their numbers. With their supplies running terribly low and reinforcements arriving late, the Athenians began to lose hope.

Gylippus made use of every one of the Athenians' weaknesses. After successfully coordinating with Spartan allies and Corinthian forces, they agreed to send reinforcements and ships to improve Syracuse's defense. With these additional resources in hand, Gylippus made the decision to fight the Athenian navy. Under his command, the Syracusan fleet engaged the Athenian fleet in the Great Harbor of Syracuse. Athens suffered terribly during this series of brutal naval battles. The Athenian fleet had once been known as one of the ancient world's greatest naval powers; what remained of the Athenian fleet was only splintered hulls and desperate crews.

Nicias attempted to withdraw his forces, but Gylippus was not planning to show mercy. Knowing that victory was near, he ordered multiple blockades on the escape routes, both by land and sea. The Athenians, realizing there was no way out, launched one final assault. It ended in catastrophe. Those who attempted to flee overland were hunted down and captured by Gylippus's men. As for Nicias and his commander, Demosthenes, they were both taken prisoner. Gylippus was said to have sought ways to spare the Athenian commanders, but he was overruled. Nicias and Demosthenes were executed.

The Athenians had set sail for Sicily with tens of thousands of soldiers and crews. Yet, only a handful of them managed to return home. Those who had been captured were either killed or enslaved. Gylippus returned to Sparta a hero. However, his later life contrasted with his military achievements.

Shortly after the end of the Peloponnesian War, Gylippus was accused of embezzlement. Sparta had received funds from Persia throughout the war—the empire sided with Sparta so that Athens would fall—and these resources were entrusted to Gylippus. According to ancient records, Gylippus was said to have tampered with the money bags. He secretly took some of the funds and resealed the bags, making them appear as if nothing had been taken.

Unfortunately for Gylippus, his tricks were discovered. He was forced to go into exile, a fate mirroring that of his father's.

Chapter 5 – The Story of Neaira

Women in ancient Greece, especially in Athens, lived a life that was largely confined to the home. They were restricted from meddling in public affairs. Their daily lives basically revolved around managing the household and caring for their children. While men could carve their life achievements by participating in politics, war, and philosophy, Greek women, for the most part, had little independence or opportunity to leave their names in history. Public roles for women were very rare, and most of them were limited to religious duties, such as serving as priestesses.

It is safe to say that, even compared to Rome, Greece was more restrictive when it came to women's visibility in history. Yes, women were also treated unequally in Roman society, but history remembers women like Livia Drusilla and Agrippina the Younger, both of whom have been recognized as two of the most influential figures in the imperial court. In Greece, however, only men could debate and make decisions in the Agora; women could not even comment on state affairs, let alone participate in them.

Helen of Troy, Medea, and Penelope are some of the names that likely come to mind whenever we think of female figures from ancient Greece, yet these are (more than likely) mythological figures. Some may recall the name Aspasia of Miletus, but many often remember her largely due to her association with her husband, Pericles, rather than for her own intellect or influence. More often than not, her reputation in ancient sources was rather controversial; it was common for the wife or partner of ancient leaders to be subject to criticism.

As for Neaira, her story is almost like a whisper. Few have heard of her name. However, it is this silence that makes her story so unique. We know parts of Neaira's life primarily because of a speech made by Apollodorus of Acharnae, an Athenian politician. However, his accounts of her were far from positive. In his speech, which was preserved in the Demosthenic corpus—a collection of speeches used in law courts, political debates, or other public forums—Apollodorus talked about her early life as a courtesan and her struggles. Yet, they were talked about not to offer a glimpse into her life but to tarnish her reputation and convince the jury to side with him.

Neaira's story began in the ancient city of Corinth. Although it once thrived as a bustling hub of commerce and culture, Corinth was infamous for its indulgence and vice. In contrast to Athens, where the lives of women were restricted, Corinth offered some freedom to women, especially those who chose to be courtesans. Although courtesans were often exploited for their beauty and charm, some chose this path so that they could at least gain some kind of public visibility and influence rather than being forever confined to domestic life and excluded from all public affairs.

As for Neaira, however, she did not choose to be a courtesan. We know nothing about her childhood and family except the fact that she was sold into slavery at a very young age. Her journey as a courtesan started when she was bought by a woman named Nikarete. It was said that Nikarete was once a slave, but after gaining her freedom, she began to shape her influence and wealth by becoming a madam. She could often be seen at the Corinth slave market, where she would buy young girls to be trained as *hetaerae*, the celebrated courtesans who mingled with the elite. Unlike common prostitutes who were confined to brothels, *hetaerae* enjoyed a level of social mobility and independence. *Hetaerae* accompanied the men who paid for them to symposia (drinking parties common in ancient Greece) and games. Neaira once accompanied a young aristocrat named Simus of Thessaly to the Great Panathenaea (a Greek festival) of 378 in Athens.

Many claimed Nikarete to have had a good pair of eyes. She could see the potential of young girls just by looking at them. The madam was also adept at creating the illusion of respectability. She bought the girls from the slave market, but she would often claim that she adopted them. Nikarete often referred to the girls as her daughters. This way, she could increase their value and attract influential customers. It was more likely for wealthy patrons to pay a premium price for the company of young women they viewed as "untarnished" and "refined" rather than a simple slave from the market who had been sold for only a few drachmae.

Neaira became one of the madam's most prized daughters. She was groomed well. Other than training in the art of engaging conversation, she was also taught music and dance. Combined with her beauty and charm, Neaira quickly became one of Nikarete's most sought-after protégés alongside two others, Metaneira and Anteia. Apollodorus himself claimed that Neaira was highly sought after by wealthy men to the point where they were all willing to pay outrageous amounts of money for her company.

A Greek *hetaira* attending to her client.[51]

But still, Neaira's life was far from secure. Her life was under the control of Nikarete, and all of her movements were dictated by the demands of her patrons. Every drachma that she earned from her work did not flow into her own coffers but straight into Nikarete's pockets. However, things were about to change when Nikarete decided that she had had enough of profiting from Neaira's beauty and charm. Nikarete decided to sell Neaira. This was commonly practiced by Corinthian madams, especially when the *hetaera* had passed their prime years. However, instead of landing in the slave market yet again, Neaira was instead sold to two men who were once frequent patrons. Known as Timanoridas and Eukrates, the two had grown extremely fond of her and did not think twice about taking her off Nikarete's hands. They bought Neaira for 3,000 drachmae (equivalent to somewhere between $25,000 and $175,000 in today's time), which was undoubtedly an extraordinary amount for purchasing a person.

Of course, Timanoridas and Eukrates eventually planned on building their own family. They had met their soulmates and wished to marry them. They knew that keeping Neaira as a companion could only bring problems. However, the two were so fond of her that they did not have the heart to cast her aside. So, they chose a middle path. Timanoridas and Eukrates offered her freedom but on one condition. Neaira had to buy her way out of servitude. Despite appearing better than outright abandonment, Neaira was thrown into a moment of desperation. She could see freedom in front of her, but she had to pay for it using money she did not have.

Not known for giving up, Neaira chose to turn to her former patrons. Leveraging on their lingering affections for her and perhaps a pinch of their generosity, Neaira sought funds from them. One of the men she contacted was a wealthy Athenian named Phrynion. Along with several others who had once been enamored with her, they each contributed a portion of their wealth until Neaira could finally meet the price demanded by Timanoridas and Eukrates. And so, with enough money, Neaira was finally free after years of servitude.

Perhaps eager to turn a new chapter, Neaira chose to leave Corinth for Athens. However, she did not go to the city alone. Neaira went with Phrynion, one of the men who helped buy her freedom. At first, Phrynion appeared like a benefactor, but as she spent week after week with him, Neaira began to see his darker side. It is easy to assume that Phrynion did not see Neaira as a partner but rather as a possession.

Apollodorus described a harrowing incident that befell her. Phrynion had been invited to attend a grand feast hosted by the Athenian general Chabrias. He accepted the invitation and brought Neaira with him. Since the general was celebrating his recent victory at the Pythian Games, the feast was very opulent. Influential men were mingling, and wine flowed endlessly into their goblets. Neaira, having spent most of her early years as a *hetaera*, was well accustomed to such events, so she mingled with the guests as she always had. At one point, Neaira, who was also intoxicated from all that wine, fell asleep. This was when the night took a darker turn. While unconscious, she was assaulted by both guests of the feast and a few slaves. Phrynion was present when this all happened, yet he did nothing.

This was only one of the many mistreatments and humiliations that Neaira had to go through under Phrynion's roof. It was clear that the man saw her as nothing more than a trophy to flaunt. He cared very little for her dignity and well-being. So, around 372 BCE (possibly only a year after she arrived in Athens), Neaira decided enough was enough. She packed everything she could carry—her clothing, jewelry, and a few other items that belonged to Phrynion—and left Athens. She was also said to have brought along two maids.

Neaira's next chapter of her life brought her to Megara. While the city looked like it could finally offer her peace and a sense of autonomy, Neaira could not help but think of the risk she faced for leaving Phrynion. As a woman without any influential familial ties, Neaira was exposed to challenges that could drag her into the confines of slavery once more. But at least in Megara, there was a distance between her and the abuses of Phrynion.

Here, Neaira found herself working in an industry with which she was familiar. She became a *hetaera* once more to sustain herself. However, times were harsh since Greece was deeply embroiled in war. Neaira began to think of Athens again. Although the city-state was also involved in the war, Athens remained better off economically compared to Megara. However, returning to the city meant there was a possibility she would face Phrynion once again. Despite the man not having legal claim over her as her master—technically, Neaira had purchased her own freedom—Phrynion could easily accuse her of so many things, such as stealing, and those around him would believe every word he said. In the Greek world, once accused, even if baseless, one's life would be ruined. Neaira knew that in order to set foot in Athens again, she had to find protection.

Perhaps the Olympian gods heard her plea. Protection eventually reached her in the form of Stephanos. Hailing from Athens, Stephanos had come to Megara and stayed with Neaira for a time. It was unknown what the two discussed, but Stephanos was said to have laid out a solution to Neaira's problem. Neaira could return to Athens with Stephanos and live in his household. She was not obligated to accept this option. She was, after all, free and no longer confined to any masters or madams. Neaira could choose to remain in Megara, but her decision to follow Stephanos suggests that she believed in him. She probably saw a better future in Athens. Whether it was security or companionship, Neaira soon set off to Athens and shared a roof with Stephanos.

As she had foreseen, Phrynion soon discovered she had returned to the city. He was headstrong about taking her back into his household. Stephanos, however, was not planning on letting him do so easily. He resisted and argued that Neaira had never been his property but was instead a free woman. Enraged, Phrynion was said to have planned on challenging this claim in court. He was determined that he could prove Neaira had no right to claim independence. What followed is obscure, yet Apollodorus told us that an agreement was eventually reached through arbitration. It was decided that Neaira was indeed her own mistress or kyria (Greek: κυρία). However, the arbitrators did compel her to split her time between Stephanos and Phrynion. So, despite being acknowledged as a free woman, Neaira was somehow neither free nor entirely bound. Her own desires were never considered in the arrangement. Neaira obeyed the arrangement, though at some point, Phyrnion's name went off the record. The reasons behind this remain unknown, but it is possible that he simply died.

We will likely never be entirely sure about the details of her life following this. However, we do know that Neaira was forced to face yet another obstacle when she entered her fifties. Neaira was brought to trial. This was when Apollodorus delivered his speech. It is also worth noting that Apollodorus knew Stephanos from a couple of incidents that took place years earlier. In 348 BCE, for instance, Stephanos had publicly accused Apollodorus of sponsoring an illegal policy. As a result, Apollodorus was ordered to pay a hefty fine. As if this did not already tarnish his reputation, Apollodorus was also said to have been accused by Stephanos again in 346 BCE. This time, Stephanos claimed he had murdered an enslaved woman. Unlike his previous accusation, this one was dismissed due to conflicting testimonies. We will never know whether the accusation was true, but it is safe to assume that Apollodorus saw Stephanos as a massive thorn in his side.

Sometime between 343 and 340 BCE, Apollodorus decided to point the finger back at Stephanos and, of course, Neaira. Since it was known that Stephanos and Neaira lived together, Apollodorus accused them of having married illegally. Under Athenian law, this was a serious offense.

Marriages between Athenian citizens and foreigners were strictly prohibited. This law, enacted sometime in 450 BCE, sought to preserve the exclusivity of the citizen body and protect its citizenship. It was also enacted so that the Athenians could protect their access to political rights and inheritance.

Interestingly, Neaira was said to have arrived in court with two men and a woman. They were believed to have been her children, and they all lived with Stephanos in Athens. The uncertainty of whether they were the product of her union with Stephanos or not became the foundation of Apollodorus's case.

An 18⁰⁰-century painting depicting a different *hetaira* (possibly Phryne) on trial.⁶²

However, the claim that the children were in fact Neaira's raises doubts among many. Neaira began her profession as a *hetaera* under Nikarete ever since she was a young girl. It was highly unlikely that Nikarete would keep her if pregnancy ever occurred. Such a condition could have definitely jeopardized her marketability and physical appearance, diminishing her value as a courtesan. Even if she had become pregnant, it would be more realistic for her to abandon her child through the practice of exposure. She was, after all, penniless since every coin paid for her service went straight to Nikarete. Some might suggest that they were her children with Phrynion, but it is hard to imagine that Stephanos would have willingly supported children who brought them no benefit.

Apollodorus drew upon the arrangement that Stephanos and Neaira had agreed on when they were in Megara years prior. Apollodorus claimed that through this pact, Neaira managed to persuade Stephanos to raise her children as Athenian citizens. In return, Neaira would remain with Stephanos under the same roof. This arrangement set in motion their illegal marriage. Apollodorus had nothing to support this claim other than his words. He was not even present when Stephanos and Neaira met in Megara, so how could he know what their arrangements were? Many questioned the credibility of his account.

Since there was no evidence that the two were ever married—there was no such thing as written contracts or official ceremonies when it came to marriage in Athens—Apollodorus could only claim it by highlighting how Stephanos treated the children. In ancient Greece, it was common for sons from legal marriages to be introduced to their father's *phratry* (kinship group). They were then registered as citizens when they became adults. Daughters, on the other hand, were typically married to citizen husbands. Apollodorus claimed that Stephanos had done all of the above for the children. Phano, the only daughter, was even married twice, with dowries provided each time. To Apollodorus, this was clear evidence that Stephanos and Neaira had indeed entered into an illegal marriage.

However, it is weird that no one ever raised objections in the decades after Neaira's return to Athens. If the children were the offspring of Neaira, why did no one in Stephanos's phratry ever question it? This led some to conclude that the children were, in fact, not Neaira's but rather Stephanos's children from his previous marriage with an Athenian woman. Even Apollodorus was ready to acknowledge this possibility and drop the case—if Stephanos could prove it. It was said that Apollodorus proposed torturing two of Neaira's slaves, the ones she brought from Phrynion's household. He was certain that the slaves would tell the truth. Stephanos, however, refused to do so. Whether it was an act of compassion since the slaves had been through so much with Neaira, an action to protect the truth, or perhaps just a choice to avoid them giving out false information—most people would say anything if they were desperate—we can never be certain.

This was not the only claim Apollodorus made to support his case. Another sensational allegation made by the Athenian politician was that Neaira never stopped working as a *hetaera*. Apollodorus claimed that Stephanos worked together with her. While Neaira's main task was to lure men, Stephanos would orchestrate schemes to extort her clients. As per usual, these were nothing more than baseless accusations; no witnesses were ever presented to support this.

Again, Apollodorus turned his attention to the daughter, Phano. He condemned Phano's participation in major religious rites in Athens. In his eyes, Phano was Neaira's daughter, so her status as a non-citizen of Athens restricted her from taking part in such activities. This was considered sacrilegious under Athenian law. Apollodorus's strategy was simple: he hoped to inflame the jury's outrage by narrating how this family flagrantly violated societal norms. Yet, the question remains. If Phano had never been a citizen, why had the religious authorities remained quiet all that time? This silence, much like the lack of objections to the children's citizenship, raises doubts about Apollodorus's version of events.

Unfortunately, without Stephano's defense speech, we can never uncover the full picture of his and Neaira's lives. It is indeed frustrating that we will likely never know the trial's resolution. It is plausible that, due to Apollodorus's lack of concrete evidence, Neaira was allowed to return to her life, with this trial being the last obstacle she had to endure. However, it is also hard to dismiss the possibility of Apollodorus succeeding in swaying the jury, especially if he played on their prejudice and fears.

Chapter 6 – The Daunting Fall of Influential Greek Figures

Aside from its architectural wonders, epic battles, and myths that made it into books and movies, ancient Greece also had a long list of big personalities. From war generals to philosophers, thinkers, poets, and kings, they all left their mark on history in the most unforgettable ways. However, despite their brilliance and ambition, not all of them were bestowed with the glorious ending they might have imagined. Some of them met their demise rather ironically, adding an unexpected twist to their legends and stories. Take the Ionian mathematician Pythagoras, for instance. His life was all about numbers, philosophy, and harmony. But his death? That is a whole different story.

The Death of the Great Pythagoras

By the 5th century BCE, Pythagoras was considered the most influential philosopher in Croton, a Greek city in southern Italy. He and his followers, referred to as the Pythagoreans, were best known for their esoteric teachings that blended mathematics, music, and spirituality. Interestingly, the Pythagoreans operated almost like a secret society. However, their secretive practices and growing influence over local politics eventually alienated the wider populace. According to ancient sources, this was where the chaos began. A violent uprising erupted in 510 BCE when the citizens of Croton targeted Pythagoras and his followers. The angry mob was said to have cornered them in a temple. What happened afterward, however, remains debated, as ancient records were often written with a blend of both facts and myths.

Pythagoras teaching a class of women.[58]

One version talked about how the Croton citizens burned the meeting place of the Pythagorean schools. While some claimed Pythagoras was absent during the time—he was said to have been on the island Delos—others narrate a scene where he and his small group of followers narrowly escaped the blaze. They fled to the city of Locris, where they pleaded for sanctuary. Unfortunately, their request was denied, so they made their way to Metapontum. Here, Pythagoras and his followers found refuge in the Temple of the Muses. Starvation struck the Pythagoreans, but rather than desecrating the sacred site for food, they chose to die.

Another version of the story, recorded by the philosopher Porphyry, claimed that Pythagoras died by his own hand. Failing to find an escape route as the flames consumed their meeting place, the Pythagoreans chose to lie down on the ground, forming a safe path for their master to escape. Pythagoras managed to escape to safety, but as he turned around to see the bodies of his followers, the mathematician was immediately overwhelmed by grief. Unable to bear the loss, Pythagoras took his own life.

However, the most popular tale of his death revolved around fava beans. This story suggests that Pythagoras managed to escape from the burning of his meeting place. The angry mob was not planning on letting him live, though, so they pursued him relentlessly. Pythagoras ran but halted when he came upon a field of fava beans. Long believed that these beans held the souls of the dead, Pythagoras refused to continue his escape, afraid that he would trample upon the poor beans. When the angry mob caught up with him, they did not think twice about killing the philosopher.

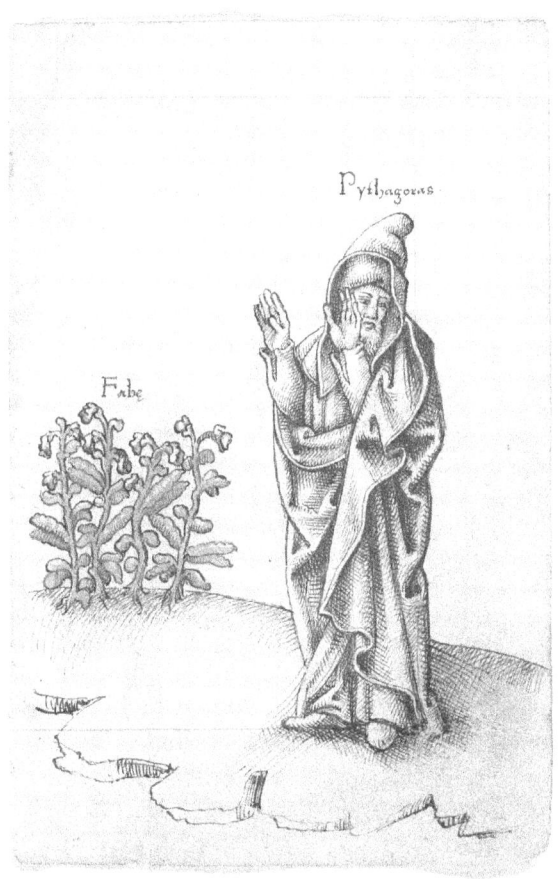

A 16ᵗʰ-century drawing of Pythagoras turning his face away from the fava beans.⁵⁴

To this date, his demise remains unsolved; no one has been able to uncover the real cause of his death. Regardless, it is safe to assume that he did not die peacefully. Some said it was an ironic end for the man who sought to unveil the universe's secret harmony.

Alcibiades, an Athenian Commander Hailed Both as a Hero and a Traitor

Alcibiades could sense that his end was near. He had taken refuge in a modest home in the heart of Phrygia (located in west-central Anatolia). Alcibiades was once the darling of Athens. A charismatic general gifted with both looks and brilliance, he had led the city-state to victory in many conflicts. But now he was a man in exile, hunted and despised.

Alcibiades (left) and his mentor, Socrates.⁶⁶

What seemed to be a normal day in 404 BCE quickly took a turn for the worse with the arrival of assassins near his house. These assassins were thought to have been sent by Pharnabazus, the Persian satrap of Phrygia. Pharnabazus initially welcomed Alcibiades when he arrived to seek protection in Phrygia. However, things changed when he was pressured by Lysander, a Spartan admiral who feared that Alcibiades would regain influence in the fragile balance of power in Greece. Lysander persuaded the Persian satrap into thinking that Alcibiades was nothing more than a liability. So, the assassins were sent, tasked to return only when Alcibiades's body had touched the ground.

The assassins set Alcibiades's quarters ablaze, yet the Athenian managed to escape the fire. Armed with only a dagger—or a sword according to some sources—and his cloak wrapped around his arm, acting as a shield, Alcibiades rushed toward his attackers. The assassins were caught off guard by his sudden emergence from the fire and fled at first before standing their ground upon finding a safe distance. They then unleashed a flurry of arrows, which pierced the Athenian's torso. Alcibiades's corpse was left on the very spot he fell until his mistress, Timandra, found him and buried his remains.

Alcibiades's life was not always filled with obstacles; he had not always been an outcast. He had actually been a respected military leader and statesman. Born into a wealthy and influential family in Athens, it was not a surprise that he had been groomed for greatness from a young age. Yet, his insatiable ambition and tendency to place self-interest above loyalty became his undoing. Thucydides claimed that he was over ambitious when he proposed the ill-fated Sicilian expedition, which he proved to be right about since the campaign ended in a catastrophic defeat. However, before the expedition reached its end, Alcibiades had already switched sides. Fleeing Athens after being charged with sacrilege, the Athenian commander offered his services to Sparta.

Alcibiades assassinated by Persian soldiers.[56]

Alcibiades enjoyed his time in Sparta at first. He advised the Spartans on strategies to counter Athens; he was said to have been credited with so much honor that some Spartan soldiers grew discontent. When rumors of his affair with the Spartan king's wife began to surface, Alcibiades was forced to flee once more.

This time around, he defected to the Persians, serving as the adviser to the satrap Tissaphernes. At the same time, he was also negotiating his return to Athens. He promised the city-state that he could secure Persian support for Athens. His political maneuvering eventually impressed the Athenian oligarchs who controlled the fleet at Samos. They recalled him in 411 BCE, hoping that his aid could help them turn the tide of war. Indeed, once back in his homeland, Alcibiades led a series of successful campaigns, thus restoring his reputation. However, his success would not linger for long. Later on, the rival Athenians turned against him, and he was exiled yet again.

Alcibiades then made his way to Thrace. Once more, he tried to help his fellow Athenians by warning them about an incoming Spartan attack. Yet, his words were ignored, and the Athenians were decimated. By this time, he knew Thrace was no longer safe for him. This was when he took refuge in Phrygia, which, little did he know, would be the last location he would ever set his eyes on.

Themistocles

The Battle of Salamis had just begun, and Themistocles stood on the prow of his trireme, commanding his men to strike at the enemy. The narrow straits had purposely been chosen by the hero for their strategic advantage. He knew the Persians would find it difficult to steer the ships. Making use of both speed and their knowledge of the region, the Greeks soon outmaneuvered the Persian vessels. They rammed the Persian fleet and sank the ships. Others were boarded by the Greeks. In the end, the Greeks succeeded in sinking over four hundred of the Persian ships while losing only forty of their own.

An illustration of Greek triremes at the Battle of Salamis.[67]

Following the battle, Xerxes postponed his campaigns into Greece, giving the city-states more time to unite. Themistocles returned to Athens as the savior of Greece.

Unlike Alcibiades, who had been born into an already influential family, Themistocles was raised by a rather modest family. Themistocles's political savvy and knack for appealing to the common people allowed him to climb the challenging political ladder in Athens, which was typically dominated by aristocrats. Even as a young politician, Themistocles felt the growing threat that the Persians posed to his homeland, so he wasted no time in proposing the strengthening of Athens' navy. Upon hearing news of the newly discovered silver mines at Laurium, Themistocles persuaded the city to use a portion of its wealth to invest in a stronger fleet of triremes, which ultimately played a decisive role in the Greek victory at Salamis.

However, not everyone was fond of the great general. Some said it was also Themistocles's growing arrogance and penchant for self-promotion that caused him to be alienated by several leaders of Athens. He was eventually accused of corruption; he was believed to have accepted bribes from Greek allies, extorting funds under the guise of Athenian protection, and manipulated the Oracle of Delphi to sway political decisions in his favor. After losing more support, Themistocles was ostracized (a practice in Athens where citizens were given a chance to vote an individual into exile).

An illustration of Themistocles.[8]

Forced to flee Athens, Themistocles sought refuge among those he had once defeated: the Persians. The Persian king, Artaxerxes I, surprisingly welcomed the Greek hero with open arms, perhaps knowing the value of Themistocles's experience. The Persian king held him in such high regard that Themistocles was given the governorship over Magnesia. Things, however, changed when Artaxerxes put him in a precarious position. The Persian king allegedly ordered the Greek hero to lead a Persian campaign against his own people.

Themistocles did not have the heart to betray the land he had once called home. So, the Greek hero chose death over dishonor. According to the narratives from ancient sources, Themistocles staged a somber yet ritualistic sacrifice. He sacrificed a bull on an altar in the name of the gods. He then filled a cup with its blood and drank it to his death. This was viewed as his ultimate refusal to turn against his people, even those who had previously ostracized him.

While this account gave the hero a rather dramatic end, other historians claim that after years of enduring strain, Themistocles eventually died of natural causes. Whether it was sickness that robbed his life or foul play involving jealous Persian courtiers, Themistocles never got to redeem himself to the Athenians. While he was branded a traitor by the Athenians, the Spartans remembered his contributions at Salamis and viewed him as a hero.

Cleomenes I, the Spartan King Who Slashed Himself to Death

Cleomenes came to power in the 6th century BCE when the Greek world was in the midst of great instability. His reign left a mark on Sparta. He introduced several reforms and foreign policies that managed to elevate the city's influence. One of his greatest military achievements was the Battle of Sepeia, where the Spartans defeated their longtime rival, the Argives.

Off the battlefield, Cleomenes knew how to navigate the realms of diplomacy and politics. His decision to support Persian King Darius I secured Sparta's position in the larger geopolitical landscape. However, Cleomenes could also be unpredictable. He soon betrayed the Persian alliance, which undoubtedly contributed to the decline of Sparta's foreign relations. Cleomenes was also infamously known to have bribed the Oracle of Delphi so that she would influence decisions in his favor.

Yes, Cleomenes enjoyed many successes in his early years. But as time went on, cracks in his rule began to become apparent. His controversial policies and erratic behavior alienated many of his companions and peers. According to ancient records, the king gradually became mad. Rumors of his instability spread to the civilians. One day, as he walked along the streets of Sparta's agora, the king was said to have hit anyone he encountered with his staff. Each day, his behavior grew increasingly unpredictable, which eventually forced the Spartan ephors (a board of five magistrates in ancient Sparta in charge of the city-state's judicial, religious, legislative, and military decisions) to act.

Cleomenes was arrested in the name of protecting the king himself and, in extension, Sparta. While he was in custody, Cleomenes managed to persuade a helot guard to hand him a knife. With this small weapon, the king was said to have mutilated himself to death. The Spartans claimed he slashed not only his belly but also his shins and thighs. To many, this brutal act of suicide was thought to be the result of his madness, but historians claim otherwise. They suspect his madness was nothing more than a fabrication to discredit him posthumously.

There are modern theories that explain his death. Some argue that Cleomenes did not kill himself. Instead, he was a victim of political assassination orchestrated by his half-brother, Leonidas. Others, however, claimed that his gruesome death was a staged spectacle. Cleomenes had broken taboos before, especially when it was discovered that he had bribed the Oracle of Delphi. The Spartans might have staged his self-mutilation so that his death could serve as a cautionary tale against breaking Spartan customs and laws. Another theory is related to his deteriorating mental state. Contemporary sources describe him as erratic, with behaviors that suggest he might have suffered from alcoholism or a neurological disorder. If this theory holds any truth, it lends some credibility to the idea of suicide, though perhaps not in the grotesque form described by Spartan accounts.

Thales of Miletus, the Father of Philosophy Who Fell into a Well

Thales of Miletus was one of the Seven Sages of Greece (a title given to influential philosophers of archaic Greece). Also considered by many to be the father of philosophy, Thales dedicated his life to understanding the natural world through reason rather than mythology alone. He declared that water was the fundamental substance of all things; he claimed that water was the First Cause of all things and the basic substance of the universe, a view that was later discarded by philosophers.

Thales of Miletus listening to Urania, the Muse of Astronomy, revealing to him the secrets of the skies.[59]

According to Herodotus, Thales once accurately predicted a solar eclipse during a battle between the Lydians and the Medes around 585 BCE. When it happened, the sudden darkening of the sky was said to have abruptly stopped the battle. The Lydians and the Medes thought the occurrence was a sign from the divine to stop fighting. So, they sheathed their weapons and negotiated for peace instead.

However, despite being one of the ancient world's greatest minds, even Thales himself could not escape the hands of mortality. Plato mentioned a story of a Thracian servant girl who witnessed Thales falling into a well. However, instead of worrying about him, the girl laughed at the incident. She remarked that he was so focused on learning more about the sky that he failed to see what was in front of him. This might only serve as an allegory rather than a historical account; it was probably nothing more than an ancient warning about spending too much time philosophizing without caring about earthly matters.

It is highly likely that Thales met his demise sometime between 550 and 548 BCE. According to the biographer of the Greek philosophers, Diogenes Laërtius, Thales, who was around seventy-eight years old at the time, was attending the fifty-eighth Olympiad Games when he suddenly collapsed. Historians claimed the culprit behind his demise was a combination of old age and heatstroke.

Pyrrhus of Epirus: The Warrior King Who Died from a Roof Tile

Pyrrhus of Epirus was another one of ancient Greece's most accomplished kings and

A statue of Pyrrhus in Ioannina, Greece.[60]

military leaders. As the second cousin of Alexander the Great, Pyrrhus was said to have modeled himself after his famous relative. He spent his life pursuing conquests across not only Greece but also Macedonia and Italy. Many agree that his campaigns against Rome forever immortalized his name in the records of history.

In 279 BCE, Pyrrhus emerged victorious against the Romans in the Battle of Asculum. However, the cost of achieving the victory was immense. While he successfully defeated the entire force of the Roman commander Publius Decius Mus, Pyrrhus's army suffered devastating losses to the point where he was unable to continue the broader war effectively. Ancient sources talked about his famous remark when he was congratulated for his victory: "If we are victorious in one more battle with the Romans, we shall be utterly ruined." The outcome of this battle also led to the term Pyrrhic victory. This term describes a triumph so devastating that it feels more like a defeat.

The death of Pyrrhus.[61]

In 272 BCE, Pyrrhus found himself involved in chaotic street fighting. Eager to seize the city of Argos, the king showcased his best military skills as he made his way through the narrow alleyways. Ancient accounts recalled a scene where an old lady who sat on a rooftop observed his fight with an Argive man. Many believed the lady to be the mother of the Argive soldier, and upon seeing his son almost defeated by the king, she quickly intervened. The old lady threw a piece of roof tile toward Pyrrhus, which knocked him off his horse. The mighty Greek king, with a part of his spine broken, could no longer move; his injury had left him paralyzed. While some said he died simply because of the impact, other ancient writers, such as Plutarch, claimed his death was assured when a Macedonian soldier named Zopyrus stumbled upon the unconscious king and beheaded him.

Aristomenes of Messene

Aristomenes of Messene is best known for his fierce resistance against Spartan domination during the Second Messenian War (c. 685–668 BCE). His status as a king of Messenia was further elevated when he achieved major early victories, including the one at "The Boar's Barrow" in the plain of Stenyclarus. His success, however, did not last too long. When the Arcadian king, Aristocrates II, suddenly withdrew his forces, Aristomenes and his people were left with no choice but to face a catastrophic defeat at the battle of the Great Trench. They were forced to retreat. They managed to fortify themselves in the mountain stronghold of Eira, but the Spartans were relentless. They laid attacks on the Messenians there for eleven years.

Nevertheless, Aristomenes never planned on surrendering to the Spartans. Over the years, he led multiple raids. In one encounter, the king and fifty of his companions were captured by the Spartans. They were then thrown into the chasm on Mount Taygetus. Although his companions died, Aristomenes was said to have survived. Legend has it he was saved by an eagle who cushioned his fall. He then made his way to safety by following a fox, which appeared before him to guide his way.

However, there is another account that narrates his escape differently. In this version, Aristomenes was captured during a truce by Cretan auxiliaries of the Spartans. He was then freed because of the devotion of a Messenian girl, who later became his daughter-in-law.

Aristomenes saved by a Messenian girl.[63]

Even though Aristomenes managed to escape his fate, the hero was unable to turn the tide of the war. By 668 BCE, it was clear that the war had turned against the Messenians. According to the ancient geographer Pausanias, it all went to chaos for the Messenians when Eira was successfully breached by the Spartans. A heavy resistance ensued, which Aristomenes led. Yet, the Messenians were forced to evacuate. Leaving their homeland, they continued their journey and eventually found refuge with their Arcadian allies. Some said the former king of Messenia never stopped searching for ways to reclaim his domain. He was believed to have planned a journey to Sardis and Ecbatana, where he hoped to get aid from the Lydian and Median kings. Yet, fate had already caught up with him, and there was no escape this time around. Aristomenes died in Rhodes.

Chapter 7 – Ancient Greek Technology Revealed

It is common knowledge that the ancient Greeks were master builders. However, what's truly fascinating is how they managed to create structures that still amaze us today without the help of modern tools or machinery. There were no electric cranes, power tools, or even laser-guided measurements. Instead, they crafted their works using a combination of ingenuity, teamwork, and a deep understanding of mathematics and physics.

Cranes and pulleys, for instance, played an important role in the construction of many structures across ancient Greece. They were used to lift massive blocks of stone, allowing workers to assemble mighty columns and walls that could withstand some natural disasters and also the test of time. These ancient devices, albeit simple in design, were highly effective. The Parthenon is a great example, as it is well known for its grandeur. However, its true brilliance lies in the details. The temple, which dominated the Athenian Acropolis, once had subtle features that reveal the Greeks' extraordinary understanding of perception, artistry, and mathematics.

What remains of the wondrous Parthenon.[68]

Constructed in the 5th century BCE in honor of the goddess Athena, the temple's most fascinating aspect is its connection to the Fibonacci sequence. This mathematical pattern is often associated with natural harmony and beauty. This sequence, where each number is the sum of the two preceding ones (1, 1, 2, 3, 5, 8, etc.), appears frequently in nature, from the spirals of shells to the arrangement of leaves. This sequence can be seen in the Parthenon, especially in the dimensions of its columns and the number of steps on its base. The ratio of the Parthenon's length to its width is also close to the golden ratio, a proportion associated with the Fibonacci sequence.

This may suggest that the architects of the temple (Ictinus and Callicrates, who also worked under the supervision of the talented sculptor Phidias) incorporated this principle to achieve some sort of visual balance and proportionality, making the temple appear harmonious and naturally beautiful even if viewers are not consciously aware of it.

The Parthenon also had other fascinating details besides its mathematical precision. The columns, for instance, were never perfectly vertical. Instead, they were purposely constructed to lean slightly inward. If they extended upward, their axes would converge nearly a mile above the temple. This subtle tilt, combined with the curvature of the base and the tapering of the columns, gave way to an optical illusion; even if one focused their gaze on it from any angle, the structure appeared perfectly straight and balanced. Interestingly, even the spaces between the columns were not uniform. They were arranged with slight variations that enhanced the building's overall harmony.

Phidias showing his work on the Parthenon friezes to his friends.⁴⁴

At the heart of the grand temple's artistic achievements is the work done by the master sculptor Phidias. Aside from the intricate carvings and friezes that beautifully adorn the Parthenon, Phidias was also responsible for creating the temple's crowning masterpiece: the colossal statue of Athena Parthenos. The statue was twelve meters tall and depicted the goddess of wisdom in gold and ivory. She could also be seen holding a smaller statue of Nike (the goddess of victory) in one hand and a shield in the other. The massive statue was then put atop a base that featured intricate reliefs that told the story of Pandora's birth.

Since myths and legends were deeply embedded in the Greek civilization, Phidias made sure to adorn other parts of the Parthenon with artistic carvings depicting scenes from various Greek myths and Athenian history. The east pediment, for instance, had carvings that narrated the birth of Athena herself from the head of Zeus. The west pediment told the story of the famous contest between Athena and Poseidon, who once vied for the patronage of Athens. Meanwhile, the frieze that ran along the inner colonnade showed scenes of the Panathenaic procession, a grand festival honoring the goddess.

A small model of the Athena Parthenos.[65]

The Greeks are often celebrated for their construction of temples and theaters, but it is also hard to dismiss their mastery of water management. Since water is one of the most precious resources, the Greeks developed ingenious solutions to ensure its availability and utility. The aqueducts are the greatest example of this; this marvel of engineering is considered to be one of the earliest systems ever designed to transport water over long distances. The Greeks began constructing aqueducts as early as the 6th century BCE. Perhaps the most remarkable example of Greek aqueducts is the Tunnel of Eupalinos on the island of Samos. Over one thousand meters long, it was used to supply the city of Samos with water from the mountains.

To ensure smooth and steady water flow, the Greek aqueducts relied heavily on a combination of gravity and carefully engineered channels. The Greeks incorporated open channels, underground pipes, and clay pipelines in their aqueducts. This ensured the water was transported efficiently, supplying various other public structures in their cities, from public fountains to bathhouses to even private homes.

While it is true that Greeks pioneered many aspects of the aqueduct design, the Romans expanded on these concepts centuries later. Using the ideas born from the Greeks, the Romans went on to create massive aqueduct systems that became iconic symbols of their engineering prowess. Roman aqueducts like the Pont du Gard and the Aqua Appia were both built on Greek principles. The Romans used large-scale arches and elevated structures to transport water over vast distances.

It is also worth noting that Greek aqueducts were not only functional but also reflected a harmonious balance between practicality and aesthetics. These structures often blended in seamlessly with their natural surroundings, mirroring the Greeks' broader architectural philosophy by emphasizing utility without sacrificing beauty.

When it came to hydraulic engineering, the Greeks showcased their prowess by inventing the clepsydra, or water clock. Just as its name suggests, this device was designed to measure time. The Greeks did so by regulating the flow of water through the

Two outflow water clocks from the Museum of the Ancient Agora in Athens.[66]

narrow opening into or out of a container. The early models of the clepsydra seem rather simple. The Greeks would simply use a container with a hole at the bottom. While this hole allowed water to flow out at a consistent rate, the markings on the inside indicated the passage of time. However, as the years passed by, models became more sophisticated, allowing the Greeks to measure time with greater accuracy.

The clepsydra was also used in courtrooms. The Greeks used this device to time speeches. This allowed them to be fair, giving each speaker an equal amount of time to deliver their statements. Aside from courtrooms, public meetings and assemblies also made use of the device to manage discussions efficiently. The clepsydra held scientific significance as well; it provided a reliable means of measuring time for experiments and astronomical observations.

Of course, the usage of this device was not limited only to the Greek world. The Romans and even early Islamic civilizations adopted the idea and improved its design to suit their needs.

The Antikythera Mechanism: An Ancient Computer

The Antikythera mechanism was once lost. It was not until the early 20th century that the device was finally discovered, left untouched in a shipwreck off the Greek island of Antikythera. Dating to around 150 to 100 BCE, the device is now considered a symbol of ancient Greece's engineering complexity.

The Antikythera mechanism was a compact bronze device encased in a wooden frame. It contained over thirty interlocking gears that allowed the device to perform precise calculations of celestial movements. On its front, the mechanism featured dials that scholars believe to have been used to track the sun, moon, and planets according to ancient Greek cosmology. There was another separate dial that displayed the different phases of the moon. On the back of the device, one could find two spiraling scales. One was used to track the Metonic cycle—a nineteen-year period of aligning the lunar and solar calendars—while the other showed the Saros cycle, which was used to predict eclipses.

A fragment of the Antikythera mechanism.[67]

It is safe to say that this level of precision required a great understanding of astronomy and mechanical engineering. Scholars praise the ancient Greeks for their ability to create gear teeth that were small and consistent enough for the mechanism to perform smoothly. Since the mechanism used a complex system of gears to perform precise calculations, the Antikythera mechanism is considered by many to be a prototype of modern analog computing devices. By turning a hand crank, the device could simulate the natural movements of celestial bodies. This made it a mechanical tool for understanding and tracking the patterns of the heavens, such as predicting eclipses and planetary positions. Its design is similar to later mechanical calculators, showing how physical parts can be used to solve real-world problems, much like early computers.

The Aeolipile (Hero's Engine)

The aeolipile, also known as the Hero's engine, was invented by the 1st-century CE engineer Hero of Alexandria. Regarded as the world's first steam engine, the aeolipile demonstrated the principles of steam propulsion centuries before such technologies would be widely utilized. Although the device itself appeared to be relatively simple, scholars agree that it was brilliantly effective. The aeolipile featured a hollow, spherical vessel mounted on a pivot. Protruding from its surface were two bent nozzles. When water was heated beneath the sphere, the steam that was produced would be channeled into the sphere through the hollow tubes. As the steam escaped through the nozzles, it created thrust, causing the sphere to spin rapidly. However, this device, despite going down in history as the world's earliest steam engine, was nothing more than a demonstration of physical principles.

The aeolipile was not the only invention that came from the brilliant mind of Hero. The engineer and mathematician also came up with other mechanical devices that were considered centuries ahead of their time. Blending his scientific curiosity with practical application, Hero invented a vending machine. However, instead of dispensing snacks and drinks like the vending machines we see today, Hero's invention was designed to dispense holy water in temples. Similar to modern vending machines, Hero's invention also required a coin. Once inserted, a lever would be activated to release a measured amount of water.

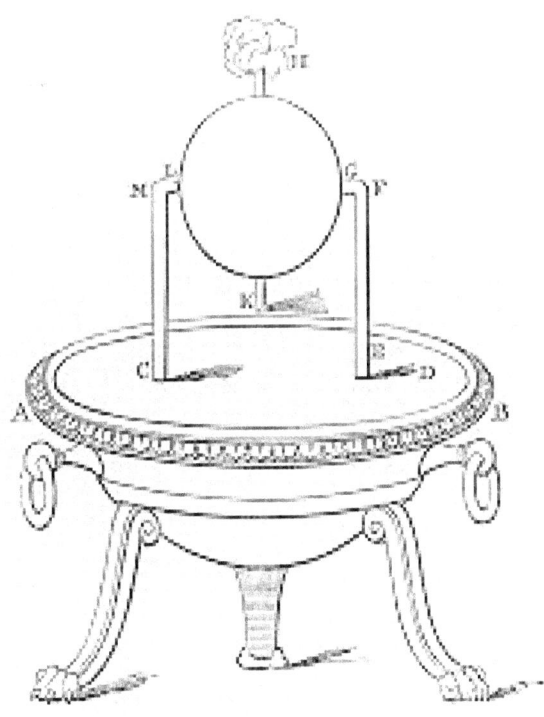

An illustration of Hero's aeolipile.[68]

Hero also devised a type of automatic door that was powered by heat and pressure. They were used at temples to "magically" open and close, giving visitors the impression of divine intervention. He also used air, water, and counterweights to create moving figures called automata. They were often used in theaters to further invoke a sense of magic and spectacle among the audience.

All of his inventions and creations were documented in works such as *Pneumatica* and *Automata*. These writings detail both the construction and principles behind his inventions. They also made sure that his ideas survived the test of time, becoming the precursor to many other modern devices and machines.

The Archimedes Screw

The innovative Archimedes screw was invented sometime in the 3rd century BCE. This device was beyond revolutionary back then, as it was used for lifting water in agricultural settings. This particular mechanism had a helical blade encased within a hollow cylinder tube. To use it, the Greeks would tilt the tube at an angle and rotate the screw manually, often using a handle. As the screw turned, water would be scooped up from a lower level. It was then carried upward along the spiral blade until it emerged at the top.

This invention was very helpful for irrigation and draining marshy areas. It allowed the

A water pump that uses the Archimedes screw mechanism.[69]

ancient Greeks to better supply water to their fields or storage tanks. The Archimedes screw's ability to transport water against gravity made it extremely invaluable in regions with uneven terrain or seasonal flooding.

Although the Archimedes screw—sometimes referred to as the Archimedean screw—had a design that appeared rather simple at a single glance, but the device was agreed by many to be versatile. It required only minimal maintenance and had the ability to handle large volumes of water. Believe it or not, the Archimedes screw is still used today for tasks like wastewater treatment and flood management. Even some amusement park rides, especially those involving water, use this technology.

The Diolkos of Corinth

First constructed in the 6th century BCE, the Diolkos was a stone-paved trackway near the city of Corinth. Used as a route to transport ships overland across the Isthmus of Corinth, the Diolkos was popular back then as a shortcut. By using it, merchants and sailors could save time and avoid the long and treacherous journey around the Peloponnesian Peninsula.

The stone trackway was at least six kilometers long. It featured grooves cut into its surface, which was designed as a guide for wheeled carts that carried the ships. These carts, which were typically made of wood and reinforced with metal, were usually pulled by a group of workers or animals. The grooves along

What remains of the Diolkos today.[70]

the way ensured stability during transport, while levers and rollers were used to assist in lifting and positioning the ships onto the carts.

The Diolkos also served a vital role in military logistics. With this trackway, the Greeks were able to deploy naval forces between the Aegean and Ionian Seas more efficiently. However, as time went by, the Diolkos eventually fell into disuse, largely due to the advent of more efficient transport methods.

The Odometer

Many may be familiar with the odometer, though these days, the device often comes in a digital form or a combination of both digital and mechanical. Thousands of years ago, however, the odometer was purely mechanical. The measuring instrument has transformed over the centuries, yet its function remains the same.

The origin of the odometer remains a mystery; no one can prove who invented it. Some suggest it was invented by Archimedes of Syracuse, who lived in the 3rd century BCE, while others attributed it to Hero of Alexandria, who lived over two centuries after Archimedes. Regardless of the inventor, we can be sure that the odometer was once used to measure the distance traveled by vehicles or carts. The odometer was typically mounted on carts or attached to chariots.

A reconstruction of the ancient odometer.[71]

The odometer was accurate and efficient. Its operation required no additional effort beyond the motion of the vehicle itself. In simple terms, the odometer worked through a series of gears connected to a wheel. As the wheel turned, it activated a mechanism. A pebble would be dropped into a container after a set number of rotations, each corresponding to a fixed distance. This allowed the ancient Greeks to calculate distances for various purposes, from road building to military planning. The odometer was also useful for mapmakers, allowing them to produce more precise maps by measuring distances between key locations.

Chapter 8 – The Cabeiri and Other Lesser-Known Mysteries

Ancient Greece was a land of gods and myths, but beneath the surface of its public religion lay a more enigmatic world—the mystery cults. These secretive groups offered something different from the grand sacrifices and festivals held in honor of the Olympian deities. For those initiated, the mysteries promised personal transformation, hidden knowledge, and often the hope of a better fate after death.

What distinguished these cults was their exclusivity and secrecy. Only initiates could engage in their rites, and they were sworn not to reveal what happened during the ceremonies. This cloak of mystery, along with the rites' promises of divine connection and cosmic comprehension, rendered them both appealing and elusive. Even now, much of our knowledge is based on fragments. We have to rely on archaeological remnants, inscriptions, and secondhand reports from those outside the cults.

Mystery cults touched on universal themes, including life and death, the soul's journey, renewal, and the search for divine favor. Their rituals were intricate and intensive, with purification rites, dramatic reenactments of tales, and symbolic gestures designed to bring participants closer to the divine. Though many of its secrets have been lost to time, what we do know reveals a world where faith was as much about transformation as it was about devotion—a world where the divine was encountered in ways that are as mysterious as they are fascinating.

The Cult of the Cabeiri

Hidden within the complicated web of the ancient Greek religion was the mysterious cult of the Cabeiri. This cult was said to have been dedicated to a group of minor deities whose devotion promised protection, spiritual development, and access to divine mysteries. Though much about the cult has been lost over time, its influence was profound, and its rituals were fundamental to religious life in certain parts of Greece, particularly on the island of Samothrace. The Cabeiri, or Kabeiroi, were frequently associated with chthonic powers linked to the earth and the underworld, as well as maritime protection. Because of this, the cult was particularly held in high regard by sailors and travelers. Their worship, centered on the Sanctuary of the Great Gods, was unique in Greek religion in that it welcomed initiates from all walks of life, from citizens to foreigners, from men to women, and even slaves, which was unusual in a society where most religious practices were closely linked to civic identity and exclusivity.

The cult of the Cabeiri's beginnings are as obscure as the gods themselves. According to some scholars, their devotion stretches back to the Pelasgians, a pre-Hellenic civilization that occupied areas of the Aegean and predated the Greeks. Others indicate Anatolian influences in their mythology and rites, drawing comparisons to religious practices in the eastern Mediterranean. The Cabeiri were assimilated into the larger Greek religious system during the classical and Hellenistic eras and gained more influence as they became protectors of sailors and sponsors of initiates who sought enlightenment or heavenly protection. Their Samothrace sanctuary eventually developed into a significant religious hub that drew followers from all around the Mediterranean.

Only those who had completed the initiation knew the rites of the cult's mysterious rituals. It is safe to assume that the initiation process was multi-staged. Scholars suggest it began with purification rituals aimed at cleansing both the body and soul. Initiates might have bathed in sacred waters, possibly in the nearby streams and springs of Samothrace, before entering the sacred precinct. The fact that ceremonies were often held at night gave the rituals a sense of mystery and solemnity. Animal sacrifices were presumably performed as well to honor the gods and establish a connection with the heavens.

The promise of divine protection, especially for those traveling across the violent seas, was said to have been central to the rites of the cult. To protect them on their travels, initiates were given sacred items—perhaps talismans—that had been imbued with the power of the Cabeiri. Evidence gathered from both literary references and archaeological remains points to the use of fire in the cult's many rituals. This implies a connection to transformation and purification. It is also likely that hymns and dances were performed to invoke the gods and create a communal sense of devotion among the members.

Archaeological finds at the Sanctuary of the Great Gods have revealed invaluable information on the Cabeiri cult. The site featured a certain construction known as the Anaktoron. Historians suggest this structure was once used as a center for initiation ceremonies. Rectangular in shape, the Anaktoron was where the cult's most sacred and hidden ceremonies were held. During such rituals, initiates might have received symbolic revelations or completed consecration rites. Another major structure, known as the Rotunda of Arsinoe, was nearby. This huge circular building was built during the Hellenistic period and was thought to have been used as a gathering place, possibly for communal worship or banquets.

The votive offerings unearthed at the site shed more light on the cult's practices and beliefs. One particularly intriguing discovery is a collection of bronze and terracotta artifacts that could have served as ceremonial tools or personal tokens handed to initiates. While the inscriptions carved into stone tablets provide insights into the rites and prayers performed in the sanctuary, their cryptic language maintains the cult's overall mystery.

The beliefs of the Cabeiri cult revolved around themes of protection, renewal, and the potential for spiritual awakening. Unlike other mystery cults that concentrated on the afterlife, the Cabeiri appear to have prioritized divine intervention and support in the present. Such promises were particularly tempting to sailors, whose jobs and lives were dependent on the whims of the sea. However, the cult's teachings were not restricted to maritime issues; they could have contained esoteric knowledge about the cosmos, human existence, and the interaction between the mortal and divine realms.

The Lesser Eleusinian Mysteries

The Eleusinian Mysteries were among the most prominent religious rites in ancient Greece, providing initiates with deep spiritual experiences based on the tale of Demeter and Persephone. The Greater Eleusinian Mysteries, celebrated every autumn in Eleusis, claimed to inspire a deeper understanding of life and death, spiritual rebirth, and the possibility of a glorious afterlife. Dramatic reenactments of Persephone's abduction by Hades and her subsequent reunion with Demeter were central to these rites, representing themes of death, rebirth, and nature's everlasting cycle.

However, before one could participate in the Greater Mysteries, one had to complete the Lesser Eleusinian Mysteries. The Lesser Mysteries, while smaller in scale and scope, were not a mere formality. These spring rites served as the first stage in a sacred path of purification and spiritual preparation, ensuring that initiates were fully prepared to participate in the autumn festivities.

The Lesser Mysteries took place in Agra, a suburb of Athens near the River Ilissos. These rites were performed every year in the month of Anthesterion (February-March). They served as an entry point for newcomers, introducing them to the Eleusinian tradition while also providing an opportunity to cleanse themselves of bodily and spiritual impurities. At this stage, initiates were led through a series of ceremonies aimed to prepare them for the higher spiritual truths of the Greater Mysteries.

Similar to other mysteries in ancient Greece, the Lesser Mysteries revolved around purifying rites. This particular mystery, however, included swimming in the Ilissos River. This symbolic act of cleansing indicated the removal of sins and the willingness to go on a transforming spiritual journey. As they embarked on their trip, initiates prayed and presented offerings to Demeter and Persephone in hopes of receiving their favor and guidance. The purifications were extremely personal, representing a symbolic rebirth and dedication to the mysteries' sacred path.

A relief depicting a scene of initiation to the Eleusinian Mysteries.[73]

Processions, sacrifices, and symbolic acts associated with the Demeter and Persephone myths were, of course, part of the celebrations. Participants might have carried sacred artifacts, or *hiera*, while they marched in procession. This symbolized Demeter's quest for her daughter. These procedures, albeit less elaborate than those of the Greater Mysteries, immersed initiates in the mythological narrative, giving them a sense of connection with the divine figures at the heart of the tradition.

Membership in the Lesser Mysteries was remarkably inclusive for its time. Unlike most Greek religious rituals, which were usually restricted to male citizens of a particular city-state, the Lesser Mysteries was available to anybody. Men, women, foreigners, and possibly even slaves could participate, provided they were willing to undergo purification and sincerely engage with the rituals. While the Lesser Mysteries were required for the Greater Mysteries, they were not just preliminary. For many, particularly those unable to return to Eleusis in the autumn, the Lesser Mysteries provided a meaningful spiritual experience in and of themselves, bringing purification, rejuvenation, and the hope of divine favor.

The Thesmophoria

The Thesmophoria was one of ancient Greece's most popular and intriguing festivals. It was held entirely by women in honor of Demeter and Persephone. Unlike other mystery cults, which were entrenched in secrecy and exclusivity, the Thesmophoria was a public event, though only married women were permitted to participate. Its rituals, however, were shrouded in mystery due to their extremely symbolic and esoteric character. The festival lasted many days and focused on fertility, agricultural rejuvenation, and the sacred connection between women and the earth.

The festival stemmed from the famous tale of Demeter and her daughter Persephone. According to the story, Hades's abduction of Persephone led Demeter to fall into a great depression. Her sorrow was so immense that the earth withered. This divine narrative served as the foundation for the Thesmophoria, as the festival was held to honor Demeter as the goddess of agriculture and Persephone as a symbol of the cycle of life and death. The name "Thesmophoria" comes from the Greek word *thesmoi*, which means "laws" or "customs." This reflects the ancient Greek belief that Demeter was the one who taught humanity the laws of agriculture and civilized life.

A painting depicting the Thesmophoria procession.[78]

The festival was celebrated in multiple Greek city-states. The exact details differed by region. Typically, the festival lasted for three days, with each having its own set of rites and significance. The first day, referred to as Anodos ("ascent"), commemorated the women's trip to a sacred site, typically a hill or sanctuary, where the festival was held. The journey involved carrying sacred objects and preparing the ground for the ceremonies to follow. The second day, Nesteia ("fasting"), was a day of sadness and introspection. Women fasted from meals and dressed modestly, symbolizing Demeter's sadness while searching for Persephone.

During this phase, most mysterious rites were performed. One particular ritual involved the retrieval of rotting pig carcasses that had been buried months earlier in sacred pits. These carcasses were placed on an altar and mixed with seeds. This was done to ensure a good harvest.

The final day, known as Kalligeneia ("beautiful birth"), was a celebration of fertility and rejuvenation. Here, an obvious mood change could be sensed. Solemnity turned to joy as women performed rituals to invoke Demeter's blessing on the land and their own families. Grains, animal-shaped cakes, and other agricultural products were offered to the goddess. The festival then concluded with feasting and dancing.

The Orphic Mysteries

The Orphic Mysteries was yet another one of ancient Greece's mystifying traditions. This particular Hellenistic mystery cult revolved around the legendary figure named Orpheus. Known in mythology as a poet, musician, and prophet, Orpheus was believed to have possessed the ability to charm every living thing in the world—mighty gods included—with his music. His story, however, was rather tragic. When his beloved wife, Eurydice, died from a snake bite, Orpheus set out on a journey into the underworld to retrieve her. Using his musical talent, Orpheus successfully charmed the underworld beings, including the ferryman Charon and the dog Cerberus. He was able to return to the land of the living with his wife in tow, yet upon failing to abide by Hades's condition, Orpheus lost his wife forever.

Orpheus charming various beasts with his music.[74]

Unlike other Greek mysteries, which focused on specific deities or cults, the Orphic Mysteries were more philosophical and personal. The religion focused more on the soul's journey and its relationship to the divine. Purity was an absolute priority, along with ascetic practices and a thorough comprehension of the universe's divine order. Orphism was founded on a distinct cosmogony that suggested the cosmos had been created by Chronos (Time) and the cosmic egg, a concept that differed from the more anthropomorphic stories of the Olympian gods. The figure of Dionysus Zagreus, Zeus's son who was torn apart by the Titans and then regenerated, was central to this religious system. This tale symbolized the cyclical nature of life, death, and rebirth.

Orphic rituals and practices were designed as a guide for initiates to achieve spiritual purity and the liberation of the soul from the cycle of rebirth. Initiates were expected to follow strict ethical and dietary codes. They had to indulge in vegetarianism since they believed eating meat perpetuated the cycle of violence and impurity. More often than not, rituals included purification ceremonies, chants, and prayers, as well as the study of Orphic hymns and sacred books, which were claimed to hold concealed knowledge about the universe and the afterlife.

Of course, the exact rituals, ceremonies, and practices were only revealed to members, but membership in the Orphic Mysteries was open to anyone, especially those willing to embrace its ascetic lifestyle and philosophical teachings. In contrast to other mystery religions that emphasized communal ceremonies, Orphism typically focused on personal devotion and inner transformation.

Orphic mosaics excavated from late Roman villas.[75]

Those who devoted themselves closely to the mystery were said to have been promised a great reward: freedom from the never-ending cycle of reincarnation and the eventual return to the divine. This belief was immortalized in small inscribed sheets of gold known as the Orphic gold tablets. Uncovered in various burial sites across the Greek world, these tablets were thought to be guides for the deceased, offering instructions on how to navigate the afterlife and achieve eternal bliss.

The Mysteries of the Great Gods

Sometimes referred to as the Samothracian Mysteries, this Hellenistic cult was considered among the most renowned religious rites in Greece, second only to the Eleusinian Mysteries. These rites, which took place on the island of Samothrace in the northern Aegean Sea, centered on a group of obscure deities known as the Great Gods. Unlike other mystery cults associated with individual Greek city-states, the Samothracian Mysteries welcomed all. Men, women, slaves, and foreigners were permitted to take part, making the cult unusually inclusive for their time.

Scholars cannot precisely pinpoint the exact origin of the Samothracian Mysteries. However, many suggest that the cult preceded the Greek colonization of the island. By the classical period, the cult was believed to have been fully integrated into Greek religious life. Its shrine soon became a popular pilgrimage destination, attracting people from beyond the Aegean. Although the Great Gods themselves were never fully recognized in Greek mythology, they were often associated with the underworld and their protective abilities. Even their identities and roles were intentionally concealed, as they were only known by the members of the cult.

First-time participants were known as *mystai*. They would typically begin their journey with purification rites that likely included bathing in the sacred streams or springs around the sanctuary. After preparing themselves for the divine experience, the *mystai* would then participate in processions. Since the processions were often held at night, torches would be lit along the way, further creating a sense of mystery and reverence. Hymns were performed, and prayers were recited to invoke the presence of the Great Gods. These rituals were accompanied by the rhythmic sounds of drums, which were beaten to heighten the participants' emotional and spiritual state.

Similar to the cult of the Cabeiri, sacred ceremonies were usually held in the Anaktoron. Here, initiates were said to have participated in rites that reenacted the stories of the Great Gods. While the specifics of these rites are obscure, ancient records indicate that they included symbolic acts of protection and rejuvenation. Some scholars also suggest that the rites involved the offering of sacred items known as *hiera*, which were given to initiates as part of their spiritual enlightenment.

The foundation of the Rotunda of Arsinoe.[76]

This was not the only holy site for ceremonies and rituals. The sanctuary also featured the Rotunda of Arsinoe. Known to many as the biggest circular building in the ancient Greek world, the site was thought to have been an important gathering spot for initiates. The open-air Theatral Circle was probably utilized for ceremonies that were more public or for meetings.

The Lernaean Mysteries

The Lernaean Mysteries were associated with the ancient site of Lerna in the Argolid region of Greece. Known by some as one of the most cryptic religious traditions of antiquity, Lerna was famous in mythology as the home of the Lernaean Hydra, a serpent-like beast killed by Heracles during one of his famed twelve labors. However, Lerna was also revered as a sacred sanctuary associated with chthonic deities and the underworld.

On the surface, this mystery religion appeared similar to the others. It was most likely centered on themes of death, renewal, and purification. The site of the cult featured a sacred spring known as the Alcyonian Lake, which many thought to be the very entrance to the underworld. Rituals at Lerna might have included symbolic descents into this dark realm to depict the initiates' confrontation with death and their eventual purification and rebirth, though no direct accounts of such rites have survived. Bathing or drawing water from the spring was likely important since the water was thought to have purifying and transformational effects.

Since the cult was closely associated with the underworld, rituals at Lerna appeared to have included sacrifices and offerings to the gods who called the realm their domain. Archaeological evidence indicates the presence of altars and pits, which were most likely used for libations and the burial of sacrificial remains. The rites might have been accompanied by hymns and prayers to the chthonic powers, invoking both their favor and protection.

Archaeologists have also discovered remnants of the House of the Tiles, a Mycenaean-era structure, as well as altars and other ritual sites. These discoveries point to the area's long-standing religious significance, which spanned multiple periods of Greek history.

While the exact details of the Lernaean Mysteries are limited, they appear to be consistent with broader Greek ideas about the cyclical nature of life and death. The emphasis on purification and renewal shows that the mysteries were designed to prepare initiates for both life's hardships and the voyage into the afterlife. The connection to the myth of the Hydra, with Heracles defeating an overwhelming monster, could have represented the soul's triumph over death or other spiritual challenges.

The Mysteries of Andania

The Mysteries of Andania also welcomed everyone, from men to women and even children. Since it was also dedicated to Demeter and Persephone, the cult shared similarities with the Eleusinian Mysteries, though it had its own local characteristics.

Rituals of this particular cult were commonly held in a small town in Messenia known as Andania, hence its name. Since these rituals were often dictated by local circumstances or specific significant events, they often took place at irregular intervals. Processions were an important feature of the rites, with participants wearing specific clothing and carrying religious artifacts. These processions likely recreated elements of the Demeter-Persephone myth, emphasizing the themes of loss, renewal, and divine favor. Sacrifices were likely common during the rituals, along with communal feasting and perhaps theatrical performances that dramatized the myths.

It is safe to say that the Mysteries of Andania were notable for their inclusiveness and detailed organization. The inscriptions uncovered at

Andania provide further insights into the ceremonies' laws. These inscriptions specify the roles, tasks, and directions for all participants, including priests, priestesses, and ordinary initiates. Such painstaking planning indicates the mysteries' importance to the local community, as well as their dedication to maintaining the holiness of the rites.

Chapter 9 – Bizarre Deaths: Empedocles, Aeschylus, and More

The ancient Greeks were known to celebrate drama and tragedy. So, it should not come as a surprise that the deaths of their most influential figures were turned into stories that have an almost theatrical flair. Empedocles, for one, was known to be an extraordinary thinker by the Greeks, but the story of his death intrigued many. By the time he had risen to prominence, the world was still searching for answers to its deepest mysteries. While others pondered their existence, Empedocles was said to have had the ability to understand the world in ways no mere mortal ever had before.

He held strong to the belief that the entire universe was built from four essential elements: earth, air, fire, and water. He also suggested that these elements did not simply exist out of thin air. They were constantly shaped by two opposing forces—love, which brought them together, and strife, which tore them apart. These were forces that he believed to be the architects of everything we see, from the tiniest speck of dust to the countless stars in the galaxy. What made Empedocles even more unique was that he was not just another philosopher. He was also a poet. He often wove his theories into beautiful poetry. Empedocles had a way with words, so his works often feel almost divine, as if they had been whispered by the gods of Olympus themselves.

His story took a dark turn when Empedocles began to feel like something was missing in his life. He was far from content with being an influential thinker or poet. He believed that he was more than just a weak mortal. Some claimed Empedocles thought of himself as a god or a divine being who knew all the truths of the universe. To those skeptical about his capabilities, Empedocles wished to prove them wrong.

Legend has it that Empedocles, eager to prove that he was more than a mortal, made his way to Mount Etna. He stood at the edge of the fiery volcano, ignoring the smell of sulfur and the gurgling sounds of molten lava churning below. Dressed in his flowing robes, he turned to look at his followers who had come to see his actions from a safe distance.

With confidence, he claimed that he was no longer bound by mortal limits. He told his followers that he would not die from the lava below but simply be transported to the divine, the world where he had come from. He even proclaimed that they would not see his body once he leaped into the volcano, believing that he would merge with the divine forces of the universe. Some said this act was intended as a symbolic return to the elements—earth, air, fire, and water—that he believed made up all existence.

Empedocles leaping into Mount Etna.[77]

Empedocles looked into the lava below, glowing as if it were a portal to another world. Without hesitation, the philosopher jumped into the fiery depths. His followers were stunned, silence hanging heavy in the air. Their minds were reeling from what they had just witnessed. However, as if betraying his claims, the volcano erupted one of Empedocles's sandals. The sight of his sandal sitting at the edge of the crater answered his followers' question: Empedocles was, after all, a human bound by mortal limitations.

Aeschylus, the Tragedy Playwright Who Died Tragically

It was just another day for Aeschylus as he strolled under the blazing sun shining over the Sicilian countryside. He gazed at the sky, admiring the beauty of the world. The famed playwright often sought inspiration in nature, but that was not the main reason behind his decision to be outdoors that day. He was also trying to escape his death.

Aeschylus was one of the most celebrated playwrights of ancient Greece. As the "Father of Tragedy," he was no stranger to dramatic twists. His works, such as *The Persians*, *Seven Against Thebes*, and the *Oresteia* trilogy, were some of his most famous contributions that redefined Greek theater. He was credited with producing over eighty plays, but unfortunately, only seven survived the test of time in their complete form. Interestingly, Aeschylus was also the first dramatist to have ever presented his plays in a trilogy.

Like many other Greeks of his time, Aeschylus was a devout believer in the gods. Even his own life was thought to be touched by the divine. Before turning into a playwright, Aeschylus worked at a vineyard. He claimed Dionysus appeared in his sleep one day, urging him to pursue a career in the art of tragedy. He did so, and over time, Aeschylus earned widespread acclaim.

However, that was not the only time the divine had given him a sign. Legend has it that Aeschylus also heard of a certain prophecy that foretold his demise. He would one day be killed by a falling object. He thought that by staying outdoors, where the sky was the only thing above his head, he could trick fate. However, the sky was home to other beings, such as eagles.

One day, an eagle circled the sky with a tortoise clutched tightly in its talons. It was scanning the ground below, searching for a stone large enough to break a tortoise shell upon impact. Once it found its target, the eagle quickly released its grip, sending the tortoise hurtling toward what the bird thought to be a rock gleaming under the sunlight. Unfortunately for Aeschylus, the eagle had mistaken his bald head for a rock. With a sickening thud, the tortoise shell struck Aeschylus's skull.

The last moments of Aeschylus.[78]

The dramatist, who had dedicated decades of his life to producing Greek tragedies, met a tragedy of his own. The absurdity of his death quickly became a subject of legend. Nevertheless, his works continued to inspire many. The Athenians valued his works so much that they allowed his tragedies to be restaged in competitions. His talent and legacy were also inherited by his sons, Euphorion and Euæon, as well as his nephew named Philocles, who all became playwrights themselves.

Draco of Athens

Draco was born in a time when justice was anything but fair. He hailed from Athens, and back in the 7th century BCE, the Athenians had no consistent law system. Because of this, disputes often escalated into bloody feuds. Perhaps growing up witnessing the Athenians constantly fighting each other, Draco wanted to change the way laws worked in the city.

Draco of Athens.[79]

It is unclear at what age Draco first stepped into the realm of law. Scholars have suggested that he was probably in his thirties when he finally obtained a standing in Athenian society. From then on, he was entrusted with the responsibility of codifying Athens' first ever written laws. This was indeed a groundbreaking effort to replace arbitrary decisions with a clear legal structure.

However, Draco's laws were known to be unbelievably harsh. Even those who were caught stealing petty items, such as a cabbage, could be sentenced to death. When asked why his solution to most offenses was the death sentence, Draco simply responded that he could not think of a higher punishment for the greater offenses. In his eyes, petty crimes already warranted the death penalty because of their harmful nature.

There was no more severe consequence he could impose for more serious crimes. His laws were extremely strict and harsh to the point where his name eventually gave us the word "draconian," which is often used to describe overly harsh measures.

Although his laws are controversial, largely due to their severity, the Greeks saw them as revolutionary. Because of him, the Athenians could finally see order and consistency. Draco's laws became the foundation for future reforms that would later lead to democracy. Some might have feared his influence, but many others respected him for his dedication to justice.

Like many other great minds of the Greek world, Draco had to be remembered for his contributions. The Athenians decided to hold a grand gathering to honor him. Silence was immediately replaced with a round of applause when the Athenians saw Draco stepping forward to address them. At a single glance, he appeared modest—he wore only a simple cloak—but his presence commanded attention. However, the Athenians' love for him inadvertently killed him.

Perhaps eager to show their gratitude, the crowd began to throw their hats, cloaks, and other garments on the stage as a gesture of appreciation. As their enthusiasm grew, more and more items rained down until they formed a growing pile around him. Draco stood there, probably trying to calm the audience down. Unfortunately, the deluge of offerings continued, as the Athenians, completely consumed by their enthusiasm, ignored his words. The pile grew so large that Draco eventually collapsed underneath it. By the time the crowd realized what they had done, it was too late. Silence filled the air again. Their celebrated lawgiver had died, having been smothered by their own outpouring gratitude,

Chrysippus, the Stoic Philosopher Who Laughed to Death

Dying of laughter may sound ridiculous, but it is, in fact, a medical possibility, although it is a rare one. In extreme cases, excessive laughter can trigger a range of physiological responses. Asphyxiation might occur if the body fails to take in enough oxygen. Those who already have pre-existing heart conditions might become victims of cardiac arrest. This phenomenon is known today as fatal hilarity and had once befallen a certain Stoic philosopher of the 3rd century BCE named Chrysippus.

Chrysippus of Soli.[80]

According to ancient tradition, Chrysippus once stumbled upon a donkey eating a fig. He found the scene to be so amusing that he shouted, "Now, can someone give the donkey a drink of wine to wash it down!" His laughter escalated uncontrollably. He eventually collapsed to the ground, perhaps due to asphyxiation caused by his non-stop laughter, and died.

This was not the only account of his death. The ancient biographer of philosophers, Diogenes Laërtius, offered an alternative account where he claimed Chrysippus died during the 143rd Olympiad Games. He suggested that instead of excessive laughter, the philosopher met his fate as a result of drinking undiluted wine at a feast. However, without forensic evidence, we will never truly uncover the reason behind his death. Whether it was fatal hilarity or alcohol poisoning, Chrysippus succeeded in immortalizing his name. The philosopher was mostly known for his contributions in logic, the theory of knowledge, ethics, and physics rather than his end.

Heraclitus, the Greek Philosopher Who Spoke in Riddles

Heraclitus of Ephesus had a rather dim view of humanity to the point where he could often be found crying over it. Because of this, the pre-Socratic thinker was known by the Greeks as the "Weeping Philosopher." This was not his only epithet. Heraclitus was also said to have spoken in a cryptic manner, so many referred to him as the "Obscure," "the Riddler," and sometimes "the Dark One." He had some of the best insights and ideas, yet they were all typically expressed in dense aphorisms that challenged even the brightest minds of his time. Heraclitus was also the philosopher whose famous quote was "You cannot step into the same river twice."

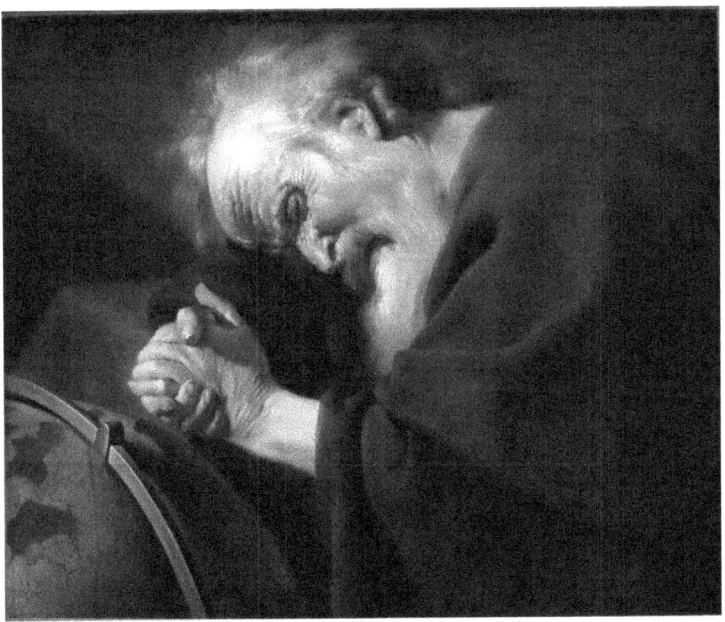

Heraclitus, the Weeping Philosopher."

Heraclitus preferred a reclusive life. Perhaps tied to his view of humanity, he shunned public life and criticized common people and his fellow philosophers, claiming they failed to grasp deeper truths. His ideas influenced later thinkers, including Plato and the Stoics, but the episode where he met his demise is remembered by many.

Heraclitus eventually developed dropsy—today known as edema—as he neared the end of his days. This particular medical condition is characterized by severe swelling due to fluid retention. Possibly caused by either heart or kidney failure, it was undoubtedly a condition that was beyond the medical capabilities of his time. When Heraclitus noticed his condition was getting worse, he made haste to see the doctors. True to his style, the philosopher spoke metaphorically; he asked them whether they could make a drought after a storm. He probably was asking if the doctors could remove the excess fluid from his body. However, none of the doctors could understand him, which left Heraclitus frustrated.

He left the doctors and chose to take matters into his own hands. Believing that warmth was the answer, he devised a rather unconventional remedy. The philosopher covered himself with cow manure. He thought that with the manure's heat and drying properties, he could draw out the moisture that had been causing his medical condition. Unfortunately, this treatment failed, and the philosopher died while still being covered in a mixture of his own invention.

Other ancient records recalled Heraclitus lying still in the manure under the sun. However, the dung dried around him, transforming into a body cast. Unable to move, he could only watch as a pack of dogs came along to eat him.

Philitas of Cos, the Grammarian Who Starved to Death

Many might agree that Philitas of Cos's life revolved around words, but so did his death. Born sometime in the mid-4th century BCE, Philitas built his career as both a poet and a scholar. He was extremely obsessed with language, something that set him apart from other great minds of the Hellenistic world. His appointment as a tutor to the future Egyptian pharaoh, Ptolemy II Philadelphus, further catapulted him into literary stardom to the point where his influence was felt in the works of poets like Callimachus and Propertius.

A bronze statue of Philitas of Cos.[13]

However, some found his expertise in language and obsession with the precise usage of words irritating. He would zealously correct errors in speech, no matter who the speaker was. Once he heard the wrong choice of words being used, Philitas never hesitated to argue and unravel why such a word was wrongly used—a behavior that even his admirers found exhausting. Imagine a man whom you do not know personally leaping into an exhaustive analysis upon overhearing a slip of the tongue and not stopping until the mistake was acknowledged.

His death revolved around his obsession with words and grammar. Ancient sources state that Philitas became so consumed by his scholarly pursuits that it slipped his mind to care for his own needs. He was too deep in his research, investigating a particularly erroneous use of words—Philitas was said to have been preparing an essay to expose the offending mistake—that the scholar forgot to eat. He accidentally starved himself to death, becoming the ultimate victim of his own insatiable pursuit of linguistic perfection.

Milo of Croton, the Wrestler Who Got Trapped in a Tree

When thinking of the strongest men in ancient Greece, many may immediately think of Heracles, the mythical hero whose strength allowed him to perform the famed twelve labors for King Eurystheus of Mycenae. A few may think of Milo of Croton. Like Heracles, Milo was not only popular for his might but also for his larger-than-life feats. He was a wrestler who immortalized his name in history by winning six Olympic titles and seven Pythian championships. He was also a skilled military leader. Milo once led the army of Croton (a Greek colony in southern Italy) to victory against their rivals from Sybaris.

The ancient Greeks claimed Milo possessed an almost superhuman strength. One legend told of his extreme training regimen that bordered on the mythical. He was said to have lifted an ox daily. He began lifting the animal when it was only a mere newborn and continued to do this each day until the ox grew into a full-sized beast. When the ox reached maturity, Milo was said to have been able to carry it with ease, showcasing his otherworldly strength and endurance.

The death of Milo of Croton.[88]

Yet, even Heracles could not escape death, let alone the mortal Milo. While the divine hero died because of a poison, Milo's demise ended because of the brutality of animals. According to traditional sources, Milo was walking alone through a forest. He came across a partially split tree with its trunk held open by wedges. Despite there being no one to watch him, the wrestler saw this as an opportunity to test his strength. With a deep breath, he inserted his rough hands into the gap and, with all his might, tried to tear the trunk apart. At first, it seemed as if he would pass his own test of strength. Unfortunately, the wedges soon fell out. The tree snapped shut, trapping one of his hands.

The mighty wrestler was now a captive of the tree and left vulnerable to Mother Nature. Wolves eventually arrived and devoured him.

Arrichion, an Athlete Announced Champion Despite Being Dead

The *pankratiast* was a type of warrior-athlete in ancient Greece. They typically fought using a blend of wrestling and boxing techniques to topple their opponents. The sport known as pankration was usually brutal; there was little room for mercy. The athletes were permitted to use anything to win the match, save for biting and gouging an opponent's eyes. While strength, skill, and endurance were all must-haves, the athletes also needed strategy and a little bit of trickery. Among the many celebrated *pankratiasts* in ancient Greece was Arrichion of Phigalia.

Ancient Greek pankratiasts fighting.[54]

Arrichion knew he had already cemented his reputation when he won two Olympic titles. So, when the fifty-fourth Olympiad was held in 564 BCE, he was confident that he could take on any opponent thrown at him. Proud of his strength and tenacity, he entered the arena, and as he expected, the crowd erupted with cheers the moment they laid eyes on him. The spectators knew Arrichion was no ordinary competitor. They expected the match to be a swift and easy win for the athlete.

However, much to their surprise, Arrichion soon found himself in a dire situation. He had been a tad too confident. His opponent turned out to be a determined challenger with powerful legs. The opponent wrapped around Arrichion's midsection and arms, trapping the proud athlete in a chokehold. Finding it difficult to breathe, the defending champion appeared as if he were only moments away from defeat. The crowd fell silent as they saw their hero slowly lose consciousness.

But Arrichion was always a step ahead. His unconsciousness was only an act so that his opponent would lower his guard. When his grip loosened, Arrichion made his move. Using every ounce of his remaining strength, the athlete made a sharp motion, twisting and snapping his opponent's ankle. The pain was agonizing, leading his opponent to immediately tap out and signal his defeat. The crowd celebrated with cheers and applause, but little did they know that Arrichion was already dead.

Many were puzzled, but it was later revealed that in his attempt to throw off his opponent immediately after the tap out, the intense pressure from the chokehold had inadvertently snapped Arrichion's neck. Regardless of his death, Olympic tradition held that the opponent's surrender meant victory. So, Arrichion was once again crowned champion, but this time around, only his corpse lay witness to it.

Chapter 10 – The Voyage of Pytheas

The Greeks had a general understanding of the known world, but they were only familiar with regions surrounding the Mediterranean and certain parts of the Near East. While they had heard stories of distant lands, which were typically shared by travelers and merchants, some tended to dismiss the details and descriptions, looking at them as nothing more than just fables and tales. Goods like amber, tin, and silk were commonly traded in Greek markets, but few Greeks were curious about the origins of these items. This was largely due to the Greeks often relying on intermediaries, such as the Phoenicians and the Egyptians, to bring the wonders of faraway places to them.

However, Pytheas had always been curious about the world beyond the Mediterranean. His hunger for knowledge and his desire to explore the world were not solely driven by the chance to expand trade or discover new markets. Pytheas had heard stories of a phenomenon that only occurred in the lands far to the north. In these unknown parts of the world—at least unknown to the ancient Greeks—the sun never set. While today, this phenomenon is considered normal (we now refer to it as the midnight sun), to the ancient Greeks, who lived in a temperate zone with predictable day and night cycles, the thought of not seeing the sun set below the horizon for days was bizarre. Many questions probably lingered in Pytheas's mind. Was it truly possible for such a land to thrive? If so, how were the lives of the people there when nighttime never came?

A statue of Pytheas at Palais de la Bourse in Marseille.[84]

It is safe to assume that Pytheas was not a man who would be content just by listening to secondhand stories and theories. The only way for him to uncover the truth about these lands was to set out on an adventure and experience the wonders of the unknown world himself. Pytheas recorded his extraordinary voyage in his book titled *Ta peri tou Okeanou* (*Things About the Ocean*), but unfortunately for us, the book has been lost to the sands of time. Some said it was once kept in the famous Library of Alexandria, and when the structure was destroyed, so was the book. Only a few fragments of his stories and descriptions of the journey were saved. They were preserved by ancient writers such as Timaeus, Pliny the Elder, Diodorus Siculus, Strabo, and Polybius. Although these secondhand accounts give us a glimpse into Pytheas's voyage, it is important to note that the writings are also full of biases and interpretations of the writers.

According to these secondhand accounts, Pytheas was thought to be a Greek merchant hailing from Massalia (now modern-day Marseille). The city was situated along the southern coast of Gaul, and its strategic location allowed it to thrive as a major hub in the Mediterranean. So, it makes sense for historians to suggest that Pytheas might have grown up surrounded by sailors and traders before becoming a merchant himself.

Even the exact details of his ship remain a mystery. However, since Pytheas could have been a merchant, scholars suggest that he likely sailed in a type of Greek cargo vessel known as the *holkas*. Unlike the oar-driven triremes often used in naval battles, the round-hulled *holkai* were popular for their sturdy build. With the ship's flat bottom, Pytheas was able to navigate shallow waters and haul large quantities of goods. The *holkas* was mainly propelled by sails. Despite not being particularly fast, this type of ship was reliable and a fitting choice for explorers like Pytheas who prioritized endurance and capacity rather than speed.

Pytheas likely began his voyage in Massilia. He would have then set sail westward, passing through the Pillars of Hercules (the modern-day Strait of Gibraltar) and into the Atlantic Ocean. This was where his voyage must have faced its first challenges. The Atlantic was an uncharted and treacherous frontier even for the most experienced Greek navigators. Nevertheless, Pytheas succeeded in overcoming all of the tests that the ocean had in store for him. He sailed northward along the coasts of Spain and France, observing the lands, and eventually made landfall in Brittany. Records claimed that Pytheas crossed the English Channel, reaching a place he referred to as "Belerion," which historians suspect to be Cornwall.

Ancient writers like Pliny the Elder and Timaeus also preserved Pytheas's record of an island he stumbled upon. Referred to as "Mictis," the island was said to be accessible by sailing inland from Britain for six days. This was where Pytheas observed the inhabitants mining tin. He also recorded his observation of the Britons traveling to the island using only lightweight wicker boats covered with animal hides. Tin was a crucial material for producing bronze, and the tin mined by the inhabitants was usually traded to Gaul. From there, it was transported to the

Mediterranean markets. This was undoubtedly an important discovery for Pytheas, as it provided insights into the supply chain of one of antiquity's most valuable resources. While the exact location of Mictis remains unknown, some scholars speculate it could have been St. Michael's Mount in Cornwall, the Mount Batten peninsula in Devon, or even the Isle of Wight.

As a curious explorer, Pytheas's observations were not only limited to geography and trade. He was also said to have taken a keen interest in the people he encountered. He observed their way of life, culture, and customs. In one of his writings preserved by Diodorus Siculus, Pytheas noted that Britain was densely populated, which he thought was surprising given the region's cold climate. Its inhabitants lived in humble houses made of reed and timber, and the people were organized into tribal societies. Pytheas also wrote that they were governed by kings and aristocrats, which was pretty similar to other ancient societies. Agriculture was the Britons' main source of sustenance. Pytheas even described their unique method of harvesting grain. According to his observations, the people did not cut entire stalks; instead, they harvested only the heads of the grain. These heads were stored in roofed buildings until they ripened. Every day, the people would grind the ripened heads and use them as part of their diet.

Perhaps satisfied with his observations of Cornwall and southwestern Britain, Pytheas finally made the decision to continue his adventure. He sailed northward along the coast of Wales, where he explored rugged landscapes and possibly witnessed the lives of the remote tribes of the region. This was not his last stop; scholars suggest that he sailed farther north. Pytheas landed on the Isle of Man before continuing his exploration along the rugged western coast of Scotland. From here, he made his way between the Outer and Inner Hebrides. It is possible that the explorer made several landfalls in this area, where he studied the unfamiliar terrain and the people who inhabited it. The geographer Strabo noted that Pytheas explored as much of Britain as was accessible by foot, though Strabo also claimed that Pytheas might have exaggerated his adventures.

Pytheas did not venture into these unknown regions empty-handed. One of the tools he brought along on his journey was a gnomon, a vertical rod or stick used to measure the shadow cast by the sun. This ingenious device served as a precursor to modern navigational tools like sextants (used to measure the angular distance between two visible objects) and

GPS. Many may agree that the gnomon was a relatively simple navigational tool, but it was highly effective at the time. Typically, a sailor would place the rod upright on a flat surface and record the shadow it cast when the sun finally reached its highest point in the sky. By calculating the length and angle of the shadow at noon, one could determine one's current latitude. Although the tool is considered crude by today's standards, back then, it was a groundbreaking innovation that allowed many explorers to venture farther into unknown regions.

A sundial with a gnomon (the triangular blade) on it.[96]

According to Pliny the Elder, Pytheas also explored another group of islands north of Britain that he referred to as the "Orcades." Scholars have suggested that the Orcades might be the Orkney Islands, yet this is nothing more than speculation. Pliny's count of the Orcades does not align with the actual number of islands in the Orkney archipelago. What we can be sure of, though, is that Pytheas moved on from Britain after exploring the Orcades. This time around, he sailed into the frigid waters of the North Sea.

This daunting journey took him six days before he finally reached a landmass he called Thule. This was where Pytheas finally got to answer his own question: was there really a part of the world where the sun refused to sink beyond the horizon? According to the ancient writers, Pytheas described the phenomenon in great detail. Although we will never uncover his exact words and description, it is safe to assume that Pytheas might have been in awe when he experienced continuous daylight during the summer months. After all, this concept where night ceased to exist—at least for several days or weeks—was almost mythical to the Greeks, who were well accustomed to the predictable cycles of day and night in the Mediterranean.

Pytheas documented what lay north of Thule. After sailing another day, the explorer was said to have come across what he called the "Congealed Sea." Scholars thought this was a term he used to refer to the icy waters of the Arctic Ocean. Pytheas wrote about the region being full of thick fog and floating ice floes, which were probably the main obstacles that stopped him from sailing further. Regardless, the extremely cold temperature, heavy mist, and dozens of ice floes were likely an alien sight for Pytheas and his crew, who all came from the temperate Mediterranean.

Perhaps one of the most intriguing parts of Pytheas's lost writings about his northern travels was something he referred to as "sea-lung." This term has long puzzled scholars and historians. Some believe that Pytheas was simply trying to describe something he had never seen before, and there was no existing word for it in Greek. What he saw was probably pancake ice, which is a type of sea ice that forms in circular patterns and floats on the water's surface.

Pancake ice.[87]

But why did he call it "sea-lung?" While we can never be entirely sure, some historians provided an explanation. Pytheas might have borrowed the term from jellyfish. According to Aristotle in his work *Parts of Animals*, jellyfish were known in Greek as *pleumōn thalattios*, or "sea lung." So, Pytheas, who had no word to refer to the pancake ice, might have thought of a jellyfish. These sea creatures are round and float near the surface of the water, just like pancake ice. Whether or not this is true, Pytheas's description of his northern travels really captured the bizarre and dynamic nature of the Arctic waters. It was indeed a place where the boundary between sea and land seemed to blur.

Of course, just like the Orcades, the exact location of Thule has been a topic of debate for many years. While some suggested Pytheas landed in Iceland, there are others who argued it was Norway or the Faroe Islands. The Canadian explorer Vilhjalmur Stefansson—best known for his Arctic expeditions—sided with the idea that Pytheas went to Iceland. Stefansson, in his book *Ultima Thule*, wrote that Pytheas's descriptions of Thule aligned with both Icelandic geography and astronomical details, especially the phenomenon of the midnight sun near the Arctic Circle. However, without definitive evidence, this is nothing more than just a theory. The exact identity of Thule and whether it was true that Pytheas succeeded in sailing as far as Iceland remains a debate.

Nevertheless, according to what remains of his records, the Congealed Sea and its "sea-lung" marked the northernmost point of Pytheas's journey. Since the environment was completely inhospitable, Pytheas began his return voyage home. Scholars suggest that he likely sailed down the eastern coast of Britain. He then rounded the Kentish peninsula, which he wrote down as "Kantion." This referred to the region of Kent, located at the southeastern tip of England, facing toward continental Europe (modern-day France).

This meant Pytheas had effectively achieved a circumnavigation of the island of Britain. Without modern navigational tools and the unpredictability of the fierce Atlantic water, this was a giant feat for his time. However, instead of turning westward and heading toward the Mediterranean, Pytheas made the decision to go on one last detour into uncharted territories.

He turned eastward and sailed along the northern coastline of Europe. Pliny the Elder recounted Pytheas's journey in his writing, narrating that the Greek explorer encountered various groups of people along the way. The Germanic tribe Gutones was one of them. They lived near the shores of an estuary (the tidal mouth of a large river) of the ocean he called "Mentonomon." This was possibly the mouth of the Elbe or another major river whose stream meets the North Sea. Always a keen observer, Pytheas likely recorded the people's customs, descriptions of their dwellings, and trade practices, all of which would have been invaluable to the Greeks who were unfamiliar with the northern Germanic tribes.

Pytheas also reached an island known for its amber. Some historians have proposed that the island he landed on was none other than Heligoland, a small yet historically significant archipelago off the coast of modern-day Germany. The Greeks considered amber to be extremely precious. Apart from its beauty, amber was revered for its mystical properties. The Greeks often associated it with sunlight and divine power. Referring to it as "electron," it was best known for its ability to attract lightweight objects when rubbed—a scientific phenomenon we now know as static electricity. Therefore, Pytheas's discovery of a land abundant with amber might have been a revelation.

Pytheas continued his journey, venturing into the Baltic Sea. Scholars suggested that he might have gone as far east as the Vistula River in present-day Poland. This theory is further supported by ancient accounts that recalled Pytheas's own descriptions of the amber trade and peoples living in the Baltic region. Moreover, given its proximity to rich amber deposits, it would have been a logical destination for someone keen on understanding the trade networks that brought this precious material to Mediterranean markets.

This region offered Pytheas a change of scenery. If he had indeed reached the Baltic, Pytheas might have encountered an environment that was vastly different from the rugged coasts of Britain or the biting cold of the north. The Baltic Sea was calmer compared to the harsh waters of the Atlantic and Arctic. The Baltic was also hugged by dense forests along its shores, providing Pytheas with rather green scenery.

It was only after he was done with exploring the Baltic that Pytheas continued the long journey back to the Mediterranean. It is unclear whether he decided to retrace his route along the northern European coast or took a different route southward. However, we can be sure that his return voyage was challenging.

Pytheas safely arrived at Massalia. With his memories fresh in his mind, the explorer dedicated himself to documenting the extraordinary voyage. Since his book *Things About the Ocean* was cited by Dicaearchus, a student of Aristotle, who lived between 350 BCE and 285 BCE, historians believe that Pytheas wrote his accounts sometime around 320 BCE, only a few years after he finished his expedition. This early acknowledgement of his work suggests that Pytheas's accounts were not only remarkable for their content but were also a significant contribution to the geographic and scientific understanding of the ancient world.

Things About the Ocean quickly gained traction and was widely circulated throughout Greece. It served as one of the primary sources of knowledge, especially about Britain and the mysterious lands far north, for over two centuries. His detailed descriptions of Britain, its inhabitants and trade, and stories of Thule and the Arctic were studied and dissected by a range of scholars and historians. It was not until the emergence of accounts by Tacitus and Julius Caesar that Pytheas's writings began to be overshadowed.

Unsurprisingly, despite his detailed writings, not everyone took his work in a favorable way. Strabo and Polybius, for example, were critical of Pytheas's work. As two of the most prominent ancient geographers, they often dismissed Pytheas's descriptions, claiming them to be exaggerated or fabricated. Strabo himself claimed Pytheas to be unreliable. He particularly mocked the explorer's claims about the midnight sun and the frozen sea, dismissing the descriptions as improbable and fantastical. Polybius also viewed Pytheas's accounts of the distant north with skepticism. Their criticisms, however, were less about Pytheas's methods and more about the incredible nature of his claims; to them, Pytheas's descriptions seemed to challenge the established understanding of the world at the time. The idea of a vast ocean filled with frozen sheets of ice and a land where the sun never set was so bizarre to the Greeks that many contemporaries found it easier to doubt his writings.

However, today, Pytheas's voyage has been acknowledged as one of the most incredible feats of the ancient world. His journey is often underappreciated in the history of exploration, often overshadowed by famous voyages of later explorers like Marco Polo and Christopher Columbus, but Pytheas's journey was no less daring. His curiosity led him to venture into uncharted territories with only his knowledge and the help of a primitive gnomon. Not only did he return to his homeland in one piece, but Pytheas also worked to compile his accounts, which ultimately expanded the geographic boundaries of his time.

Conclusion

Ancient Greece is a place that feels both familiar and endlessly fascinating. It was a world full of epic battles, intricate marble temples, and powerful gods who mirrored the mortals they ruled over with their flaws and passions. But beyond the famed story of the Trojan War or even the wisdom of the Olympian gods, one will discover a range of stories that reveal the Greeks as more than just legendary figures. They were also humans who were curious, contradictory, and delightfully peculiar.

Throughout this journey, we have encountered the unexpected. We have met Neaira, a woman whose trial provided us with a glimpse into the lives of those navigating a world where freedom was tenuous and societal expectations rigid. We followed Pytheas on his voyage to the frozen edges of the known world. There were narratives of ancient Greece's greatest minds and warriors who left us with ideas that shaped the world. We also learned about their odd deaths. Who would have thought that history could include a cryptic philosopher experimenting with manure to ease his sickness or a celebrated war general falling to his demise upon being hit by a roof tile?

Everyone knew the Greeks had a love for drama, but not everyone was aware that it was not confined only to their theaters. The Greeks wove drama through every aspect of their lives, from politics to war. Even their greatest city-states were not an exception. Athens, for one, had its history written with a dramatic flair. It reached incredible heights with its democracy, art, and naval power, yet the city was not invincible. The city-state was eventually brought to its knees by an invisible enemy. The plague that wreaked havoc throughout Athens reshaped its destiny, giving the world a clear reminder of the fragility of human ambition.

What makes ancient Greece so captivating is not only its awe-inspiring achievements but also its many contradictions. True, this was the very civilization that built and championed democratic systems, yet it also marginalized much of its population. Ancient Greece was a melting pot of rational thought and groundbreaking philosophy, but the people were also deeply superstitious at the same time, often turning to the gods for even the smallest omens. For every gleaming temple or visionary thinker, there was also a tale of human error, rivalry, or unexpected tragedy.

It is clear that ancient Greece left us far more than myths and ruins. It provided us with stories and episodes that ask questions about life, ambition, and what it means to be human. These tales remind us that history is not just about polished monuments but also the rough edges that make it real, surprising, and relatable.

Part 3: Ancient Rome

Discovering Lost Stories from Roman History

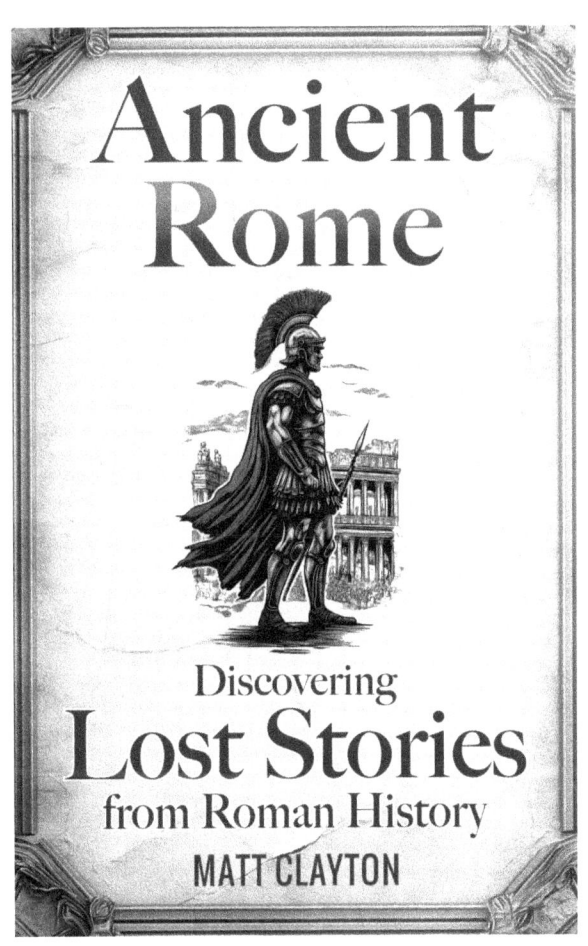

Introduction

The ancient Romans were a proud people. They were proud of their military might, their engineering inventions, and, of course, their empire, which stretched across continents. However, their pride was not only limited to their achievements; it also extended to how they viewed their legacy. Romans took their reputation seriously and believed in the power of memory. In their eyes, to be remembered was to live on. Emperors, generals, and heroes were deified after their death to preserve their legacy. Statues were built, and grand monuments were commissioned to honor them.

To be forgotten, however, was to truly die. It is safe to say that the Romans' obsession with their legacy had a darker side. Indeed, they celebrated those they viewed as successful, but the Romans also had a way of ensuring those they despised or even feared remained forgotten. Known as *damnatio memoriae* (translated to "condemnation of memory"), this was a form of punishment for figures who had greatly harmed the empire and fell out of favor. Once an individual was subjected to this punishment (often after their death), the Romans would do everything in their power to remove evidence of their existence. The individual's statues and portraits would be destroyed, their name would be scratched from public records, and buildings once dedicated to them would be demolished, only to be replaced with another dedicated to someone better. But no matter how meticulous they were in erasing the legacies of these people, some stories were never meant to be buried forever.

Of course, not all of the forgotten history of ancient Rome was the result of *damnatio memoriae*. Many people simply struggled to survive the test of time or were overshadowed by bigger figures, such as Julius Caesar, Augustus, or Justinian of the Byzantine Empire. Few are aware of powerful women like Agrippina the Younger and Livia, who quietly controlled the Eternal City and influenced the decisions of the mighty emperors. Julia Domna, for one, was a woman of philosophy who followed her husband on military campaigns across the empire, yet her name is unfamiliar to many.

Although emperors were on the highest tier of the Roman hierarchy, they were often exposed to assassination plots, which were sometimes arranged by their most trusted allies. These tales of betrayal and political intrigue are rarely highlighted, as writers often expanded only on the triumphs and successes of the emperors. In our version of untold stories, we shed light on emperors who met their end not on the bloody battlefield but through a weapon many thought to be used only by the weak: poison.

While the ancient Romans typically took pride in their success on land, few today are aware of the secrets that the Mediterranean Sea held. The empire emerged victorious in countless battles, but there were times when the threat of pirates pushed Rome to the brink. Pompey the Great, for instance, led an impressive campaign to suppress the marauders, but his story and reputation were often reduced to being Caesar's greatest opponent. The same could also be said about Sextus, whose maritime prowess was forgotten due to ancient historians who sought to forever name him as the Roman Republic's enemy.

When speaking of entertainment in ancient Rome, one cannot help but imagine a duel between two muscular gladiators who must fight to the death. Few are aware of the *bestiarii*, fighters who fought against wild beasts in the Colosseum. These brutal fights were not the only entertainment that the Romans enjoyed; chariot races also existed, although gladiatorial games often take the spotlight in modern-day books and films.

We will explore only a small fraction of the untold history of Rome, from the women of Rome to poisoned emperors to forgotten slave rebellions. The Eternal City might have been built on pride and had a long story of successful conquests and victories, but the stories that Rome attempted to bury truly show us the complexity of one of the greatest empires in history.

Chapter 1 – The Life of Julius Caesar

The Aegean Sea appeared serene and peaceful to the untrained eye. Yet, the threat of danger was always present beneath its surface. The pirates of Cilicia were some of the biggest challenges that one had to face whenever they were on a voyage across the sea. For years, these marauders had built a fearsome reputation. Their ships were as swift as an eagle. Those with little experience in the ocean could only dream of returning to their homeland unscathed once they were spotted and chased by these vicious pirates.

The Cilician pirates were not typical bandits. They were a well-organized force with years of experience. Their wealth typically came from various illegal activities. Not only did they seize merchant vessels and take the cargo that they deemed valuable, but these pirates also occasionally kidnapped those on board. However, the people they chose to kidnap were not random; the Cilician pirates were particular about their victims, as they wanted to demand the highest ransom possible.

There was a day when the pirates of Cilicia found the perfect victim to kidnap. He was aboard a small Roman vessel. The Romans were quick to recognize the sight of the pirate ships on the horizon. Knowing they could not go on a direct assault against the pirates, the crew attempted to flee. However, their efforts were in vain, as the pirate ships proved to be much faster and more agile. It only took a moment until the pirates surrounded them completely. Without wasting any time, the pirates boarded the

Roman ship, each drawing their swords to add a sense of intimidation. Fighting was absolutely out of the question, and the Romans were forced to watch as the pirates took some of them captive.

The pirates were eager to make a quick profit out of their hostages. They scanned a particular victim who appeared to be of noble lineage. He had fine clothes, and every movement showed that he was not a commoner. They began discussing the young man's ransom. They eventually settled on a ransom of twenty talents (a sum that was almost equivalent to a soldier's annual salary at the time). However, much to their surprise, the nobleman interrupted their discussion.

"What audacity!" he exclaimed. "You clearly do not know who you've captured if twenty talents is the amount you came up with!"

The pirates were stunned. They had never captured anyone so bold; typically, once the hostages were brought aboard their ship, they would be either trembling or begging the pirates to spare their lives. It was at this moment that the young man finally revealed his identity–he was none other than the young Julius Caesar.

Before Caesar's ship was surrounded by pirates, he was on his way to Rhodes. He was supposed to sharpen his oratory skills under the tutelage of Apollonius Molon, an esteemed Greek rhetorician. In ancient Rome, it was a must for a noble to strive for excellence and conquer knowledge. Thus, Caesar made it his top priority to master the art of oratory, knowing well that it would be essential for his future in the harsh Roman political world.

"I am worth fifty talents at least," Caesar announced, his voice a mix of pride and irritation.

The pirates were initially amused by his outlandish demand. After all, Caesar was but a young man at the time, and his name was not widely known yet. Nevertheless, they eventually agreed to a higher ransom. However, despite his age, Caesar was ready to assert his authority. He planned on turning the tables on those who had captured him.

He remained in captivity—or rather, custody—for eighty-three days, but he was not a typical prisoner. He never begged for the pirates to return him to Rome. Instead, he behaved as if he was their superior. The pirates, somehow amused and in awe of his behavior, allowed him to participate in their activities. Caesar exercised with the pirates and never held back when it came to criticizing their lack of sophistication. Once, he practiced his poetry and speech in front of them, but the pirates mocked him. Never one to be embarrassed, Caesar pointed at them, claiming they were nothing more than vagrants who had no idea of knowledge. The young nobleman also told the pirates that he would one day return to capture them and crucify them—a statement that the pirates thought to be a joke.

CÉSAR

est fait prisonnier par des pirates.

An illustration of Julius Caesar being taken captive by pirates. [88]

Julius Caesar was known to be a very determined person. His words were far more than just a mere boast. Everything he said came true after the ransom was paid. In the name of eradicating the Roman Republic of violent pirates, Caesar raised a fleet months later and searched for his former captors relentlessly.

It did not take long until he caught up with them. The sight of Caesar with his troops probably widened the eyes of the pirates who once laughed in his face. They now faced the full wrath of the man they had underestimated. Caesar stayed true to his words and crucified them. However, their throats were first slit before being tied to the wooden cross. While some suggest it was an act of disdain, others claim Caesar was showing his final act of mercy on the pirates. They were spared from the prolonged agony of crucifixion. Although one could never be sure about his intention at that moment, many can safely agree that Julius Caesar was not a man to be trifled with.

Caesar's Early Life and Image

Whenever Caesar's name is mentioned, the image that often comes to mind is that of a powerful general whose ambitions and strategies brought his legions dozens of victories across the Roman provinces. Some might even imagine the famous scene of the general crossing the Rubicon, his first step to reshaping the Roman Republic. Julius Caesar was often seen as the embodiment of strength, a man who was showered with greatness the moment he was born. To those unfamiliar with his story, they might even think that his path to glory was a series of successes. Given his privileged upbringing, it is not a surprise that many think he had it all from the beginning.

However, Caesar's early life was full of struggles, setbacks, and even insecurities. While he was a noble, Caesar was born in 100 BCE when the gens Julia (one of the most prominent patrician families in ancient Rome) was politically weakened. The Julians were believed to be descendants of Venus, but this did not spare them from the turbulent politics of the Eternal City. Caesar's father died when he was sixteen. The responsibilities of the head of the family fell onto him.

When Caesar reached young adulthood, Rome had already tasted chaos, as figures like Sulla and Marius vied for control. Caesar was made familiar with danger. Since he had familial connections to Marius (Sulla's bitter rival), he became one of Sulla's prime targets. Caesar had also married Cornelia, the daughter of Lucius Cornelius Cinna, who was a prominent Marian supporter. This undoubtedly complicated his position. Sulla demanded Caesar divorce his wife, but he refused. He was stripped of his inheritance and left with no choice but to go into hiding. It was only through the intervention of influential family friends that Sulla eventually allowed Caesar to return home, though Sulla did not entirely trust him, declaring that he saw "many a Marius" in Caesar.

Instead of remaining in the shadows, the dangers that plagued Caesar's early life and career only fueled his ambition. He grew more resilient as the years went by, and he knew that his survival and success depended heavily on alliances and boldness. Nevertheless, Caesar could not help but compare his successes to those of Alexander the Great.

The Macedonian king was Caesar's greatest idol. Caesar was captivated by the stories and legends of Alexander's brilliance. He knew everything about the conqueror's battles, strategies, and even his ways of inspiring loyalty in his subjects. He held Alexander in such high regard that he often felt insecure about his own accomplishments. According to certain historical accounts, Caesar once encountered a statue of Alexander in Spain. After staring and admiring the statue for a moment, he was said to have broken down in tears. When asked why, he responded that he was envious of the conqueror. He lamented that Alexander had conquered much of the world when he reached thirty, but he had achieved so little.

Of course, Caesar's lament was not an empty complaint; it was a vow for success. From this point on, Caesar's life was filled with the pursuit of power and glory.

Caesar's Path to Greater Power

Strong alliances were key to dominating the Roman political sphere. So, one of the things that Caesar did to strengthen his position was to get into strategic marriages. His marriage to Cornelia was undoubtedly significant. But when she died, Caesar knew he had to secure another bond since that could be a stepping stone to his ascent to power. After all, marriage in Roman society (especially among the elites) was not merely a personal matter. It was more than often a political tool. Therefore, he married Pompeia, Sulla's granddaughter.

Unfortunately, the union ended after a scandal that took place in 62 BCE. Caesar, who was the pontifex maximus at the time, hosted a religious ceremony at his home. Since it was dedicated to Bona Dea, a deity whose rites were strictly reserved for women, men were forbidden from attending, including Caesar himself.

The scandal happened when a Roman politician named Publius Clodius Pulcher sneaked into the ceremony fully disguised as a woman. He was said to have done so with the intention of seducing Pompeia. However, his presence was soon discovered. It was never confirmed whether Pompeia knew of Publius's plan, but the scandal damaged her reputation. Despite refraining from publicly accusing Pompeia of any wrongdoing, Caesar divorced her. He claimed that his decision was a must since, as pontifex maximus, his wife must be above suspicion.

In 59 BCE, Caesar was elected consul. That same year, he married Calpurnia, the daughter of Lucius Calpurnius Piso Caesoninus, a powerful senator. Calpurnia remained loyal to Caesar until his death. However, the same could not be said about him. Julius Caesar was known for his charm and wit. Thus, it should not be surprising that he had numerous other lovers, likely both male and female. Apart from his notorious affair with Cleopatra, Caesar was rumored to have a relationship with Servilia, the mother of Brutus, one of Caesar's assassins.

Interestingly, despite the influence and successes that he had achieved throughout his life, sources claim that Caesar had insecurities about his physical appearance. He was particularly concerned about his thinning hair. In an effort to hide this, he often combed his hair forward—a detail that a few of his critics and ancient writers noted with a hint of amusement.

Caesar's influence shone even more thanks to the political machinations of the First Triumvirate. After being made a consul in 59 BCE, he achieved another milestone in his career when he was appointed the governor of Gaul. Here, Caesar was given an opportunity to demonstrate his military brilliance as a general. He worked day and night to conduct campaigns that not only expanded Rome's borders but also solidified his reputation as one of the greatest leaders of Rome. It is safe to say that his conquests in Gaul were not just a display of Roman might; they were also a means of securing the loyalty of the Roman soldiers. Caesar knew that he would need the trust of his troops to navigate the rough waters in the future.

The Roman Republic in 40 BCE after Caesar's conquests. [89]

Of course, like many other leaders in the world—both ancient and modern—their ascent to power was not only due to their military prowess and strategic governance. Some were believed to have been involved in many covert operations. Caesar himself was thought to have been involved in the Catiline conspiracy, which portrayed the dangerous scene of Roman politics in the late republic.

This conspiracy unfolded years before Caesar became a general (it happened sometime between 63 and 62 BCE). The conspiracy was a plot arranged by Lucius Sergius Catilina (famously known as Catiline), an ambitious aristocrat who grew dissatisfied with the Roman government. After failing to become consul several times, the frustrated Catiline began to believe that the government was corrupt. Apart from being disillusioned with the Senate, Catiline was also deeply in debt, which further drove him into voicing his opinions. He began rallying support from other dissatisfied nobles and even veterans who never got the lands they were promised. He even turned to the urban poor, who were suffering from economic hardships. His next step, according to Cicero, was to lead an armed uprising. He allegedly planned on assassinating key senators, including Cicero himself, before taking control of the republic.

Nevertheless, the plot was eventually suppressed. Cicero, who was consul at the time, discovered the plan. He presented evidence to the Senate, which led to the execution of the conspirators without trial. Catiline managed to flee Rome and found refuge in Etruria, where he attempted to raise an army. This failed; he was defeated and killed in battle.

Cicero exposed the Catiline conspiracy in the Roman Senate. [90]

As for Caesar, some claimed that he was among the many who stood behind Catiline or at least showed sympathy to the conspirators. Rumors claimed that Caesar debated in the Senate over how to deal with the conspirators; he was said to have argued against the death penalty and instead voted for life imprisonment. Perhaps it was this action that led to suspicions he was involved in the conspiracy. However, the exact details of his involvement are rather murky. Nevertheless, from here on out, Cicero always had his eyes on Caesar, judging every decision that he made.

Debt was a common issue in the Eternal City; even the elites lost sleep at night thinking about it. Caesar was no exception. Historical accounts claimed that the general was deeply in debt himself, but he was able to use this to his advantage. Instead of using the borrowed wealth to make his life comfortable and live in luxury, Caesar used it to secure loyalty from various allies, even those he owed money to. He used the fortune to bribe those who initially did not see his way and produced propaganda to broaden his network of supporters.

Caesar understood that controlling the narrative was key to winning a republic that was constantly engulfed in wars and scandals. His *Commentaries on the Gallic War* is a great example of how he shaped public perception. His public image was indeed important when it came to cementing his power in the republic. Known for his charisma and ability to speak to the commoners as easily as to the aristocracy, Caesar succeeded in swaying negative public opinions. Through the *Commentaries on the Gallic War*, he was able to bypass the Roman Senate and communicate with the Roman public directly. This way, he succeeded in presenting himself as the hero of Rome, thus diluting the more controversial comments of his campaigns.

His meticulous care for his image did not end with the *Commentaries*. He understood that calculated charm was a necessity in order to maintain both power and the support of the masses. Caesar held games, banquets, and feasts to win over the people of Rome. By doing this, he was seen as their champion. Like modern politicians who create their public personas through social media, Caesar also ensured he used every tool available to shape his image.

Another one of Caesar's aspects that many could not dismiss, even those who wrote about him with full bias, was his exceptional memory. The general was said to have remembered the names of all his men, which undeniably earned him the respect of his soldiers. To the military, this simple gesture of remembering their names was seen as a personal connection. His men would not hesitate to follow him into battle, no matter the odds.

Some might agree that Caesar was something of a fashion icon in his time. He was a trendsetter. When he started wearing his toga slightly differently—he often draped the loose end over his shoulder and arm—the public began to follow suit. Caesar always had a clean-shaven look, although during the republic period, the Romans preferred to keep their beards, as they were considered signs of maturity and wisdom. It was only when Rome transformed into an empire that its people began to adopt the practice of shaving.

In his later years, Caesar again gained the public's favor when he refused kingship. He famously displayed this refusal during Lupercalia, a festival, in 44 BCE. His closest ally and general, Mark Antony, offered him a diadem, which Caesar turned down without hesitation. He knew that the Roman Republic's greatest enemy was the monarchy; therefore, an act of humility was the only way to capture the public's heart.

Caesar refused the diadem during Lupercalia. [91]

Internal struggles within the Roman government were common. However, this did not stop Caesar from expressing his care for the Roman citizens. While displays of kindness and care by leaders were, at times, nothing more than an act, Caesar's displays were likely genuine. This can be seen in his will. He left instructions that his villa, gardens, and art gallery be made accessible to the public. He even left his riches to be divided among the citizens. Along with his other deeds, this act of generosity made it possible for his name to be remembered forever.

The Dictator and the Queen of Egypt

Caesar's relationship with Cleopatra is a topic often explored by scholars and history buffs. Their first meeting was as dramatic as it was strategic. Our story begins in 48 BCE after the Battle of Pharsalus. Pompey, having been defeated by Caesar in the battle, made his way to Egypt, where he hoped to earn refuge from the reigning pharaoh, Ptolemy XIII. Unfortunately for the Roman, the pharaoh ordered his assassination instead of providing him shelter. This affected Caesar, who was said to be either saddened by the unjust murder of Pompey or enraged since he had planned on killing Pompey himself. Nevertheless, this opened a door for Cleopatra, who had been exiled by her brother, the pharaoh.

Cleopatra wasted no time in planning her entrance into Egypt and meeting the Roman general herself. Legend has it that Cleopatra had her most trusted advisor, Apollodorus, carry her to Caesar's chamber in the city. Since she was rolled up in a carpet, none of the guards suspected anything when Apollodorus passed through. Once they were in Caesar's chamber, Apollodorus unrolled the carpet to reveal Cleopatra in all her splendor. Although dressed in a simple tunic and perhaps a diadem encircling her head, her charisma immediately captured Caesar's attention. From there on, the two quickly became allies and lovers.

Cleopatra unveiling herself before Caesar. [93]

Their union was more than just a romantic affair. It was one of the most powerful political alliances in ancient history. Caesar recognized the value of supporting the Egyptian queen. He assisted her in defeating Ptolemy XIII, allowing her to reclaim the Egyptian throne. Once the civil war in Egypt ended, Caesar remained in the kingdom for a time, enjoying lavish treatment. In another romantic episode, the two went on an extravagant voyage along the Nile.

Egypt was a wealthy kingdom, and by cementing a relationship with its queen, Caesar could direct some of the wealth back to the Eternal City. Cleopatra never shied away from showering the general with gifts. Apart from natural resources and large sums of money, Cleopatra also gifted Caesar with a giraffe, which he brought along the streets of Rome during his procession later on. That was the first time the Romans ever saw such a unique animal.

While his affair with Cleopatra expanded his influence beyond Rome, the relationship also caused a stir back in the city. The majority of Romans viewed Cleopatra with suspicion. After all, in the Roman tradition, it was bizarre for a woman to rule a kingdom. The Romans were also worried that Caesar might become too accustomed to foreign traditions and customs. Their fear worsened with the birth of Ptolemy Caesar, also known as Caesarion, whom Cleopatra claimed to be Caesar's heir.

In 44 BCE, Julius Caesar was declared dictator for life, a title that did not sit well with the Romans, who deeply valued the republic traditions. Caesar's reforms were aimed at centralizing power in his own hands. The Senate had always been a thorn in his side, so he restructured it. He filled the Senate with his supporters and passed laws that curtailed the power of the provincial governors to ensure ultimate loyalty.

Caesar also introduced the Julian calendar, which corrected the inaccuracies of the previous system; this is the basis of the calendar that we use today. Some praised his reforms, but there were also many who criticized his decisions. Although the reforms gave Rome stability after years of chaos, they also alienated many of the old guard who saw signs of tyranny in Caesar's eyes.

This act of power consolidation sowed the seeds of his downfall. The Senate grew restless as they witnessed Caesar's influence grow each day. Even those who once claimed to be his most loyal allies began to doubt him. They worried that Caesar would one day abolish the republic entirely and establish a monarchy, with himself sitting on the throne. And so, they began plotting.

Chapter 2 – The Women Who Ruled Rome

The ancient civilization took omens seriously. They believed that certain events that occurred were signs sent by the divine as either a warning or a clue that could lead humans to the right path. The sibyls' words, for instance, were extremely revered by the Romans and Greeks. As priestesses of Apollo, sibyls were believed to have been given the gift of prophecy by the god. They were thought to have access to divine knowledge beyond human comprehension. Their words, however, were usually cryptic. Nevertheless, the priestesses often received visits from various kings and generals who strongly believed that the fate of their empires could be foretold through their visions.

One of the prophecies told by a sibyl was about the rise of a ruler born from a noblewoman whose lineage was both ancient and pure. When the prophecy spread across the Eternal City, many began to imagine it could be their family's destiny. Among those was Livia Drusilla, a noble who belonged to the Claudian family. Born in 58 BCE, Livia was the wife of Tiberius Claudius Nero, a staunch supporter of the Roman Republic and a strong opponent of Julius Caesar and Octavian (later known as Augustus Caesar).

Livia lived in a period of turmoil. Her early marriage was far from peaceful. When the civil war erupted, she and her husband were forced to flee Rome and live as exiles. During this period of hardship, Livia gave birth to a son, also named Tiberius, in 42 BCE. Little did she know, this was the very child that the sibyl had mentioned.

Things began to change for Livia three years later when she met Octavian. Some said that their connection was immediate. It was believed that Octavian wished to marry her at that very moment, either because of personal attraction or because he had heard of the prophecy and thought Livia was the woman the sibyl foretold. However, Livia was still married to Tiberius Claudius Nero at the time, and she was pregnant with their second child. However, this did not stop Octavian even though he, too, was married to Scribonia.

The future emperor soon arranged his plans. He divorced Scribonia in 39 BCE. On the day of their separation, Scribonia gave birth to Julia the Elder, Octavian's only biological daughter. Then, he persuaded Tiberius to divorce his wife for the sake of a political advantage. Seeing that it could be useful to get on Octavian's good side, Tiberius complied. Octavian and Livia married just three days after she gave birth to her second child, Drusus. This union set in motion the foundation of the Julio-Claudian dynasty, which would rule Rome for nearly a century.

From there on, Livia remained loyal to Augustus. She stood by his side for over four decades and witnessed her husband transform the republic into a vast empire. Unfortunately, when Augustus died in 14 CE, Livia's life also changed. While the great emperor was deified, Livia's reputation was not viewed positively. The historian Tacitus described her as a manipulative figure who played the strings from the shadows. Livia was thought to have had only one goal when she saw Augustus take the reins: to clear the path for her son Tiberius to succeed Augustus and control the empire behind the scenes. Whether these accusations were true or simply political slander, writers of that period never held back in criticizing Livia, painting her more like a villain in Roman history.

Livia was not just a wife to Augustus. Her influence over the late emperor was immense. She was considered his most trusted advisor, and she helped him shape the empire's policies and other decisions. Unlike other powerful women of her time who showed their power openly, Livia thought it was enough for her influence and power to be hidden behind the curtains.

Augustus also entrusted his wife with other administrative responsibilities. He was aware of her capabilities, so he gave her the power to manage the mines in Gaul, which was one of the major sources of revenue for the Roman Empire. Although records are scarce, they are enough to confirm that she succeeded in her role. Her competent administration was efficient and brought immense profit to the empire's coffers.

Much like an emperor would, Livia was given her own court with advisors and patrons. Through this, she was able to gain allies and ensure those who were loyal were rewarded with a good position within the government. Of course, Livia was aware of the importance of public perception. She always had eyes watching her every move, so it was necessary for her to work on garnering respect and admiration from the public. She took the ideal of a Roman matron close to heart and cultivated an image of virtue and piety.

Of course, being a woman of power, especially during ancient times when gender bias was prominent, Livia was not free from obstacles. The biggest of all was managing the succession of the imperial throne. As age was catching up with Augustus, many began to question his successor. It was up to Livia to ensure that her son would be the one to inherit the throne.

Manipulations, plots, and persuasion were common scenes in the court of power. Augustus initially favored his grandsons, Gaius and Lucius Caesar, to succeed him. However, Livia managed to persuade her husband to consider Tiberius. She even persuaded the emperor to adopt Tiberius as his own son. Of course, there would always be rivals to challenge Tiberius's rights, but Livia used everything in her power to ensure that her son was positioned as the natural and inevitable successor to her husband. Although debated by many modern-day scholars, Tacitus claimed that Livia was the one responsible for the early deaths of Gaius and Lucius Caesar. Whether or not this was true remains unknown, but in the end, Livia was successful in placing Tiberius on the throne.

Statues of Livia and her son, Tiberius. [98]

While her son sat on the imperial throne, Livia continued to expand her influence. Although she lived long enough to witness her son's rule, her relationship with Tiberius was often strained. The new emperor sought to assert his power independently without the supervision of his mother. Livia Drusilla eventually died of natural causes in 29 CE. Unlike her husband, her deification was not immediate. Tiberius perhaps resented her influence and delayed any posthumous honors. When her grandson, Claudius, came to the throne years later, Livia was finally deified.

Agrippina the Younger

Agrippina the Younger had a rather rough start. Although she was the great-granddaughter of Augustus (her mother was Agrippina the Elder), the tragic end of her parents changed her life in almost an instant. Her father was none other than Germanicus, the biological grandson of Mark Antony. He was adopted by Emperor Tiberius. Together, Germanicus and Agrippina the Elder were considered the golden couple of Rome. Their dedication to the empire, combined with their nobility and charisma, earned them the respect of the Roman citizens. Many saw their marriage as the perfect union of power and grace. Germanicus had an immense influence over the military. He was a popular general whose deep loyalty to Rome was unquestioned.

242

In 19 CE, everything changed. Germanicus suddenly died while on a campaign in the East. The cause was a mystery, but almost everyone believed that the culprit was the reigning emperor. Tiberius was allegedly threatened by Germanicus's rising popularity. He might have had concerns that Germanicus could one day steal the throne from him.

Among those who were suspicious of Tiberius was Agrippina the Elder. In a bold move, she openly accused the emperor of murdering her husband. This, of course, did not end well. Her defiance eventually led to her persecution. Agrippina the Elder was sent into exile, and on the emperor's merciless order, she was starved to death. Other sources, however, claimed she starved herself out of despair. Her two eldest sons also faced the same fate.

After losing both of their parents and two brothers, Agrippina the Younger and her sisters were left unprotected, fully exposed to the treacherous world of Roman politics. Despite having been born into a noble family, they were treated with suspicion by the paranoid emperor. Once Agrippina the Younger reached the ripe age of thirteen, she was married off to her cousin, Gnaeus Domitius Ahenobarbus, who was known for his cruelty. Tiberius ordered this union; he thought that the marriage would remove any threat she might pose to the emperor.

Tiberius finally met his end in 37 CE. The throne then passed to Gaius Caesar Augustus Germanicus, who was better known by his childhood nickname, Caligula. With her brother as emperor, Agrippina saw the first ray of light after years of hardship.

For a long time, Tiberius had stained Caligula's family name. In order to undo the damage, Caligula gathered his sisters and bestowed upon them all the honors the empire could give. Agrippina the Younger and her two sisters were elevated to positions of great influence and power. They were given the titles of "Augusta," and their images were minted on coins alongside Caligula—a rare honor, even for royal families.

Coins during Caligula's reign featuring his three sisters. [94]

Unfortunately, Agrippina and her sisters were not allowed to enjoy this period of favor for too long. When one of her sisters, Drusilla, died in 38 CE, Caligula began to transform into a whole different person. Drusilla's death affected Caligula deeply. The emperor had grown attached to her sister to the point where rumors began to circulate that their relationship was unnaturally close. Caligula, perhaps unable to process his grief, turned paranoid, which led to erratic behavior. Rome saw the first signs of political unrest. The court grew tense, and Agrippina was forced to go through another episode of misfortune.

However, it was in this chaotic environment that Agrippina's ambition and survival instincts began to form. She was eventually involved in a plot to remove Caligula, which she did to safeguard her future and spare Rome from experiencing another disaster. Unfortunately, the plot was discovered before it could be carried out. Its failure resulted in severe consequences. Despite being a member of the royal family, Agrippina was publicly humiliated, stripped of her honors, and exiled from the Eternal City. Her life was once again thrown into uncertainty. Nevertheless, this was not the end of her journey. Caligula was assassinated by the Praetorian Guard (the royal bodyguards) in 41 CE. Much to the surprise of many, the throne passed to Claudius, Agrippina and Caligula's paternal uncle.

In an effort to mend the royal family fracture, Claudius allowed Agrippina to return to Rome and reunite with her son, Lucius Domitius Ahenobarbus (named after his father of the same name). Since Claudius did not see Agrippina as a threat, she was allowed to live a life as a minor royal, away from the dangers in court. For a time, Agrippina remained behind the scenes and away from the public eye. Her focus was mainly directed on raising her son.

However, Agrippina and her son could not escape the prying eyes of the Romans forever. Her son soon became a figure of great interest in Rome. He was, after all, the youngest descendant of Augustus. By this point in time, Agrippina was the lone surviving member of her family. Her youngest sister, Livilla, had previously been executed by Caligula for treason. Because of this, Lucius was the only male left who had the right to take his great-great-grandfather's throne. Agrippina was well aware of this. But her experiences in life made her extra cautious. She knew that one small mistake could be disastrous. So, she remained low, at least until the death of Messalina.

Messalina was not only Augustus's great-grandniece but also Claudius's wife. Since Claudius's rise to the throne was a surprise—he was not listed at the top of the list due to his physical disabilities and perceived lack of political ambition—it is safe to assume that Messalina never thought of becoming an empress. She was known for her beauty and intelligence among the Roman citizens, but her reputation changed shortly after she found herself in a position of immense power. Suetonius, Tacitus, and Cassius Dio were among the many ancient historians who wrote Messalina as a figure with insatiable greed.

Other than her desire for more power, Messalina was also said to have had a high sexual appetite. According to traditional sources, she was allegedly involved in a number of extramarital affairs. Tacitus once noted that Messalina once competed with a prostitute in a contest of endurance and won it after twenty-four hours. Although the claim was most likely exaggerated, the story highlights how Roman historians often portrayed her as a symbol of excess and immorality, even by the standards of imperial Rome.

Messalina was entangled in a few plots in the court. She was believed to have orchestrated the downfall of several politicians, mostly wealthy senators and equestrians. She did so by simply pointing fingers, accusing them of treason, adultery, or any other major crime. Because of her influence and power, these accusations were easily proved. Those unfortunate enough to have had their names mentioned by Messalina faced either execution or forced suicide. Messalina was able to seize their wealth and property, adding them to her already full coffers. Her political enemies lived in constant fear, and they could not turn to the emperor, as she would always be around, whispering in her husband's ear to eliminate those who bore even the slightest sign of disobedience.

It could be safe to assume that the bond between Messalina and Claudius was not forged out of love. Messalina was described as a lustful woman—whether this held any truth or was simply a smear campaign by her enemies remains unknown—and the constant absence of her husband made her restless. When Claudius was in Ostia in 48 CE to perform a sacrificial ceremony, Messalina made a move that shocked many. In a public ceremony, she married Gaius Silius, her lover. Gaius was not unfamiliar to the court officials; he was an ambitious man who had always had his eyes locked on the imperial throne. The two conspired to secure their power. Word went around the imperial court claiming that Messalina and Gaius were plotting the emperor's death.

News of the marriage soon reached Claudius, who refused to believe it. However, a certain official managed to persuade the emperor to believe the news; this man was Narcissus, the emperor's advisor, who had long despised Messalina for instigating the execution of many senators. Claudius rushed back to the Eternal City and immediately ordered the arrest of his wife and Gaius Silius. It was said that Claudius was extremely saddened by his wife's actions and drank the entire night. He could not find the will to sign her death warrant.

However, Narcissus was not planning on letting Messalina get away. Messalina requested an audience with the emperor, but Narcissus was worried that Claudius might change his heart and spare her. The vengeful advisor ordered centurions and tribunes to head to where Messalina was being held and execute her. Messalina begged for her life at first, but seeing that there was no hope, she calmly held the tip of a tribune's sword to her breast. The blade was then pushed through her flesh until her soul left her body.

The death of Messalina. [95]

Messalina's death opened a door of opportunity for Agrippina the Younger. In an unexpected move, she married Claudius. This marriage stirred the public, as it was seen as an illegal union. Why Claudius agreed to marry his niece remains debated, but he did change the law, allowing incest marriages. Agrippina successfully solidified her position and saw her path to controlling the empire clear up.

Unlike Livia, who was content with having power over the empire behind the scenes, Agrippina sought to exercise real authority. It was not enough for her to merely influence those around her. Early on, she successfully persuaded her husband to elevate the status of her birthplace in Germany. Known as Colonia Claudia Ara Agrippinensium (modern-day Cologne), the settlement was turned into a Roman colony.

Agrippina also began changing her fashion. After securing ties with the emperor, she was often seen donning the imperial colors of gold and purple, which were typically reserved only for the ruling emperor. She also sat beside Claudius in court. Of course, the sight of Agrippina everywhere in the imperial court disturbed many. In a world where men dominated the government, it was hard for Roman officials to acknowledge a woman's power. Agrippina was also believed to have authored her own autobiography later on, though it did not survive the test of time.

Agrippina remained on the highest level of the hierarchy, along with her husband, for five years. Throughout this period, Rome barely saw any major political intrigues happen. No major coup attempts were made, and no significant violence erupted in the Eternal City. Claudius and Agrippina were busy grooming Nero to be the next emperor. Everything seemed to be going well until October 12th, 54 CE. In her final effort to clear the way for her son's rise to power, Agrippina poisoned Claudius.

Agrippina crowns her son, Nero. [96]

With sixteen-year-old Nero officially the successor of Claudius, Agrippina became the most powerful woman in the empire. She had her portrait minted on coins and carved on friezes. Although her face often appeared alongside Nero, their heads were depicted as equal in size, meaning they possessed equal power and influence. Agrippina was also sometimes portrayed as the personification of a fertile Rome crowning her young son. Agrippina had achieved her goal, but obstacles came in the form of her own son's jealousy.

For years, Agrippina had been sharpening her wits and strategies. Everyone in the imperial court knew her power, and many chose to bow to her command instead of go against her. Nero noticed this and grew resentful of his mother's immense influence. He sought ways to distance himself from Agrippina. He barred her from participating in political events and would occasionally humiliate her in front of both Roman officials and foreign delegations. Nero even went as far as to remove his mother from the palace, leaving Agrippina with no choice but to live in the imperial residence. However, it was not that easy to break her will. Agrippina continued to be a formidable figure in the empire for at least three more years.

Knowing that the only way to curb his mother's power was to remove her entirely, Nero eventually came up with a plot to kill Agrippina. However, assassinating a person of such influence required careful planning. Since she was well connected, a direct attack could be risky and politically dangerous for Nero. So, the emperor staged an elaborate accident. According to his plan, Agrippina was supposed to drown at sea, yet by some miracle, she survived. Desperation soon consumed Nero, and he quickly sent three men to finish the job.

Agrippina was killed at the age of forty-three. Nero denied her a state funeral, which was perhaps due to his resentment of his mother, whom he saw as beyond controlling. The emperor succeeded in eliminating Agrippina, but he failed to erase her memory in Rome. This was the beginning of his downfall as well. Nero's popularity soon waned, and his reign spiraled into chaos.

Julia Domna

Julia Domna was the wife of Emperor Septimius Severus. He was originally born in Leptis Magna in modern-day Libya, part of the Roman province of Africa. Despite being the emperor's second wife, Julia Domna went down in history as one of the most influential women in

Rome. Having been born in 170 CE in Emesa (modern-day Homs, Syria), Julia was the daughter of Julius Bassianus, the high priest of the Syrian sun god Elagabal. It was not a surprise that she had deep religious connections.

Julia married Septimius Severus in 187 CE when Septimius was not yet an emperor. However, his name was not unfamiliar in the empire. As a rising star in both the Roman military and political arena, Severus knew the importance of strategic marriages. After all, he had just lost his wife, Paccia, in 186 CE. He knew it was important to align himself with another influential family. This was when Julia came into the picture. Their marriage brought mutual benefits. While Septimius gained the support of the Eastern provinces, Julia successfully elevated her position in the heart of the empire. She saw Severus as a man of ambition and capability, but Julia also had her own set of abilities.

Julia's influence shone brighter when Severus's career progressed. He eventually claimed the throne in 193 CE after a series of civil wars. Julia was made the emperor's most trusted advisor. She was the one he would turn to for counsel on critical decisions. Her role and involvement in the state's administration was significant. Julia even obtained the trust of the emperor to oversee justice and the empire's financial matters. She was well versed in state affairs, a skill that not every empress could master.

Julia was not tied to the imperial palace. Perhaps not content with remaining in the safe walls of the Eternal City, Julia often accompanied her husband on his military campaigns. Her presence on these campaigns cemented her reputation as a capable empress who cared; she was thought to have a genuine interest in the welfare of the empire. The Roman troops appreciated her decision to stand alongside them. Her presence more or less solidified their loyalty to the Severan dynasty. Julia was given the title Mater Castrorum, which means "Mother of the Camp."

Aside from official state matters and administrative tasks, Julia was also a woman of arts and philosophy. Once she transformed the imperial court into a center of learning and philosophical discourse, Rome began to experience many visits from philosophers, scholars, and artists who hailed from different parts of the known world. The empress was particularly interested in Stoicism, a philosophical school that emphasized self-control, rationality, and virtue. She also appreciated the works produced by Greek philosophers.

The empress even supported the famed Greek writer Philostratus in writing the semi-biographical piece called *Life of Apollonius of Tyana*. Seen as a wise and almost divine figure, Apollonius's life story was composed to deliver messages to readers about the ideals of classical paganism. This work was, of course, meant to counterbalance the rising influence of Christianity. Because of her deep interest in philosophy, Julia often encouraged discussions and debates around these topics in her court, which eventually shaped the intellectual climate of the era.

In an effort to further unify the diverse peoples of the empire under her husband's reign, Julia engaged in the many religious traditions of the Roman Empire. Although she descended from an Arab family whose devotion was to the sun god Elagabal, Julia never failed to show her respect to the traditional Roman gods.

Portraits of Julia Domna, Septimius Severus, and their sons Geta (face erased) and Caracalla. [97]

Julia's life began to take a darker turn when Septimius died in 211 CE. The empress found herself in a difficult position when her two sons, Caracalla and Geta, were made co-emperors. The brothers were constantly at each other's throats, each planning to rise to the throne free from the other. Julia was the mediator between the co-emperors, but maintaining peace between them seemed to be impossible. Their rivalry reached a tragic climax in 212 when Geta was murdered by Caracalla's soldiers right in front of Julia.

Caracalla managed to realize his dreams and claimed the throne for himself. Yet, he hated the fact that his brother's name still lingered in the Eternal City. The new emperor sought every way to erase Geta's memory from history. As for Julia, who was around forty-one years old at the time, she remained a powerful figure in court. Her role was pretty much similar to decades before; she was to advise her son and steer the empire through the chaos.

Despite her counsel, Caracalla was never a favorite among the Romans. His rule was characterized by cruelty and heavy taxation. The growing anger among the Romans soon turned violent in 217. Caracalla met his demise while he was on campaign in the East. He did not die in battle; he was assassinated by his own troops, which were possibly supported by the praetorian prefect, Macrinus, who rose as the next emperor, albeit for a short period.

Although Rome was grateful for the departure of Caracalla, Julia felt otherwise. In addition to facing the sudden loss of another one of her sons, Julia also had to live in a court controlled by her enemies. She eventually took her own life in the same year Caracalla died, marking the decline of the Severan dynasty.

Chapter 3 – Rome's Forgotten Rebellions

A man could be seen staring into blank space. For days, he had been transported from one town to another. His hands were bound tightly in shackles, and he wore only a dirty tunic. The man could not remember the last time he had eaten and drank. The scorching weather weakened him, yet he was unable to leave the world.

The man hailed from Gaul, and his people had just lost to the Romans in a vicious battle. His family was gone, and the man himself was taken prisoner. He was to be taken to the markets, where he would be sold as a slave. From a man who had everything, he was reduced to becoming the spoils of war. He had no value, and the Romans were now free to trade him as if he were livestock.

This was the reality for those who lost in wars back then. The Roman Republic was a force to be reckoned with. It was constantly hungry for more power and land. Wars became common, especially in the unfamiliar lands beyond their borders. Prisoners of war were first marched back to Rome. Those who had been on the higher level of the hierarchy would be paraded during triumphs. They were displayed in chains, and their last stop would be the Temple of Jupiter. Here, the fate of the prisoners would be determined. Former leaders, generals, and kings would either face execution or imprisonment for ransom. Ordinary soldiers and commoners were spared, only to be made into slaves.

Slaves were a necessity in the Roman Republic, especially when large estates (called *latifundia*) began to grow in the countryside like mushrooms. They eventually became the backbone of the Roman agricultural economy, as these estates were the ones producing grain, olives, and wine—resources that fed the population of the Eternal City. But, of course, the booming of the estates came at a terrible human cost. The wealthy patricians needed dozens of slaves to work the fields. Slaves were also a status symbol for the Romans; the more slaves they owned, the higher their reputation. Luckily for them, with each successful conquest Rome achieved came more captives for these landowners to buy. The most notorious slave market was located on Delos.

Just like slavery in modern history, the life of a slave in ancient times was one of relentless toil. Those who were placed on *latifundia* or mines had to work until their body gave up entirely. They were exposed to the scorching sun and the chill of the early morning every day. The slaves had eyes watching them from every corner. The overseers were always ready to inflict pain on those they caught lagging behind. Their status in the Roman hierarchy was the lowest; even freed criminals had more rights than them. And so, it is not surprising that they were housed in the worst way possible. Those who worked in the fields were usually placed in barrack buildings where the interior was nothing more than a prison. They had a roof over their heads, but the food was barely enough to sustain them. Chronic arthritis and the distortion of limbs were common issues they faced.

However, the fields and mines were not the only places these slaves were sent to. There were also those who served in the homes of the wealthy. Referred to as household slaves, their conditions were slightly better than those forced to work outdoors. Their tasks usually included cooking, cleaning, and educating the children of their masters. Nevertheless, they were still at the mercy of their owners; every word that came out of their master's mouth was law, and a simple or even accidental mistake could lead to severe punishment. The only time slaves could breathe freely was during the Saturnalia festival, where they were at least given some freedom.

There was a possibility for the enslaved to win their freedom. Those lucky enough to have a decent master could earn their freedom after years of good service. This, however, was a rare occurrence, as the slaves usually had to buy their freedom with their own money. Nevertheless, even if they were finally free from the chains, life as freedmen was not a breeze. They were still viewed as socially inferior, and more often than not, they were still tied to their former masters through ongoing obligations.

Eunus, the Prophet and King of the Slaves

On the rocky hill of Sicily was the town of Enna, where one of Rome's greatest slave revolts took place in 135 BCE. The slaves had been forced to face inhumane treatment by their owners. A wealthy merchant named Damophilus and his wife, Megallis, were two of the cruelest slave owners in town. Beatings, starvation, and labor without rest were the norm for those who served under Damophilus. Branding of slaves was also practiced, adding more horror to their lives. Megallis was as brutal as her husband. She displayed her viciousness toward her female slaves without hesitance.

Yet, every living being has its limits. The slaves, tired and enraged from their continuous suffering, began to plot for the downfall of their masters and pursue freedom. But, first, they needed a capable leader. This was where a man named Eunus came into the picture.

Eunus was not merely a slave. He was believed by his fellow slaves to have been gifted by the gods themselves. Although records of his early life have been lost to the passage of time, the story of how he came to be the king of the slaves has been preserved. Despite being a slave, Eunus was not tasked with typical work in his master's house. Instead, he was used as an entertainer or "wonderworker" for guests. Eunus had various abilities that could enchant his master's honorable guests, such as breathing fire, telling jokes, and other theatrical performances. Eunus also claimed to have a divine power to see what others could not; in other words, he could tell prophecies. Once, he told the guests that he was approached by a Syrian goddess who told him that he would one day become king. Instead of worrying about his claim, his master and the guests enjoyed his story, thinking it was nothing more than a joke.

It is unsure what Eunus might have felt when his master and the guests thought of his words as tales and fables. However, we can be sure that other slaves viewed him as more than just an entertainer. They saw a potential leader in him, someone who could finally lead them to freedom.

The slaves of Enna, likely just Damophilus's slaves, began gathering in secret to discuss a plot. It did not take long until they decided to seek Eunus's counsel and listen to his prophecies. When they finally met the entertainer, they asked a simple question: what were their chances of success if they rose against their masters? Eunus, claiming that he heard whispers from the gods, told them that the heavens were on their side. He firmly insisted that with the gods favoring rebellion, the time for them to throw off their chains and take up arms against their master had finally arrived.

Perhaps Eunus's words had some truth, and the gods really did favor their decision because the Roman Republic had its attention fully booked at the time. Rome was preoccupied with a conflict in Spain. The Romans had been busy preparing for the Numantine War. This cleared the way for the enslaved in Sicily to make their first move.

With Eunus's blessing and reassurance of divine favor, the slaves who once faced oppression by Damophilus united. There were about four hundred of them ready to strike those who had wronged them for years. They made their way to Enna, and under cover of darkness, they launched an assault. Perhaps fueled by years of pent-up rage and desperation, the town was razed. Damophilus was among their primary targets. He was captured and dragged through the streets of Enna by the very people he had once gladly punished. He pleaded for mercy, yet his cries fell on deaf ears. He was beheaded in a theater by his own slave named Zeuxis.

Megallis was not spared from the wrath. She was killed without hesitation. The only person the slaves spared from that family was their daughter, who had shown kindness and mercy to the slaves in the past.

Their rebellion did not stop at Enna. With their success, the enslaved chose to continue their cause. But, of course, they needed strength and numbers. They turned to Eunus again, although it was not for counsel this time around. Eunus was crowned their king at the very location where Damophilus had been executed. From here on, the slave king went on by the name Antiochus, which he chose after the Hellenistic monarchs of the East.

As king or *cyrios* ("supreme commander"), Eunus did not waste a second planning their next movement. Ironically, his first decree was based on brutality and violence; he ordered the execution of the citizens of Enna. Only blacksmiths were spared from tasting their blades since they were needed to forge weapons. With Enna cleansed from its oppressors—even Eunus's master, Antigenes, was killed—Eunus assumed the regalia of a Hellenistic monarch. This was a move to legitimize his new position and inspire more slaves to take a stand against their masters.

The decision to elect Eunus as king proved to be fruitful, as in just three days, the rebels had transformed into a formidable force. News of the successful uprising spread across the land, reaching hundreds of slaves who yearned for freedom. By this point in time, Eunus had successfully armed six thousand men, all prepared to display their defiance in other parts of Sicily.

Meanwhile, in the coastal town of Agrigentum (modern-day Agrigento, southwest of Enna), another figure rose. Known as Cleon, his first move came after he heard about Eunus's victory. Leading a revolt of his own, Cleon rallied the oppressed and formed a massive force. However, Cleon had no intention of rivaling Eunus as king. He acknowledged his sovereignty and submitted himself to Eunus's command. Since Cleon also brought his forces along, the number of the rebel army grew tremendously.

When the ranks of the rebels swelled, Rome finally decided to take matters seriously. Worried that the insurrection would one day reach the gates of the Eternal City, the Senate dispatched a praetor named Lucius Hypsaeus to Sicily. His task was simple: to quell the rebellion and restore order on the chaotic island. Hypsaeus had every reason to be confident in defeating the slaves. The Roman legions were known to be far superior to many other forces across the globe. However, things quickly turned south when the Romans laid eyes on the rebels.

While Hypsaeus had eight thousand men at his disposal, Eunus and Cleon had successfully gathered over twenty thousand men. Nevertheless, the Roman legions were not planning to back down and return to the Eternal City in shame. Therefore, battles ensued until the Romans were forced to retreat.

With Hypsaeus's legions dealt with, the rebels grew more confident. News of their triumphs spread like wildfire. Distant lands like Attica and Delos were beginning to see revolts breaking out. Those in Rome were beginning to be plagued by fear; not only were they in the midst of war, but they were also endangered by dozens of slave rebellions.

Eunus was fierce in achieving his vision. He led the rebel forces in several key locations on the island. The town of Morgantina (southeast of Enna) was captured along with Tauromenium (modern-day Taormina) on the northeastern coast. They successfully conquered any obstacles thrown at them. They grew so confident that they often performed acts of mockery outside towns garrisoned by Roman troops. Theatrical mimes were among their favorite performances; they were used to mock the soldiers who trembled behind the walls. Each time they achieved a victory, celebrations were held publicly.

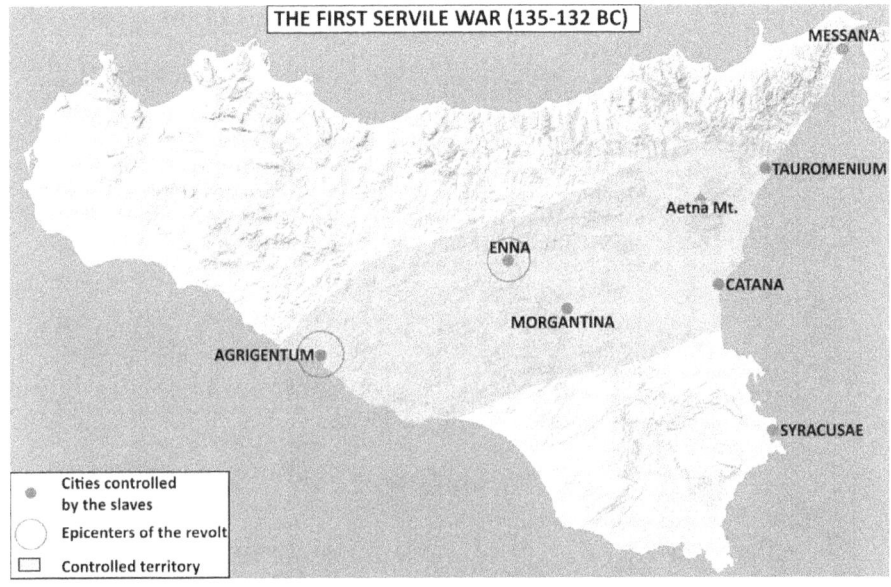

Territories controlled by the slaves under the command of Eunus. [98]

Unfortunately for the rebels, their success would eventually turn into disaster by 132 BCE. The Roman Republic finally chose to display its full might in Sicily. The Roman legions, under the command of the consul Publius Rupilius, successfully laid siege to the many strongholds of the rebels. Eunus could only watch as his forces gradually dwindled. The slave king himself was eventually captured and brought to Rome, where he breathed his last in captivity. While some suggested that he was executed for his defiance, others claimed he resorted to suicide. Whichever it was, his journey ended in the Eternal City, and his death crushed the hope of the thousands who had followed him.

Another Rebellion

Sicily was not meant to enjoy peace forever; it was plunged into chaos by rebellious slaves yet again in 104 BCE, some thirty years following Eunus's and Cleon's uprisings. This time around, a certain decree ignited the first spark of rebellion. By 104 BCE, Rome found itself in another conflict. They were up against the Cimbri and Teutons, two tribes that had proved their might against the Roman legions. With their numbers gradually dwindling, General Gaius Marius decided to seek help from Rome's client kings. One of them was Nicomedes III of Bithynia.

Perhaps desperate for reinforcements, Marius did not hesitate to request soldiers from Nicomedes, though the king's reply was rather shocking. Nicomedes claimed he could not help the Romans even if he'd like to. This was because the Romans had already taken most of his capable men and turned them into slaves.

General Gaius Marius appeared victorious among the Cimbri. "

Because of this, the Roman Senate was spurred into action. A decree was soon issued that ordered the Romans to free those slaves who had been unlawfully taken; this was especially common in regions like Sicily. The decree was made so that these freedmen could be conscripted into the Roman army. However, this was only the start of another chaotic episode in the Roman Republic.

The decree did not sit well, especially with the wealthy Sicilian landowners. They had profited greatly from slave labor. Freeing them would mean a decrease in revenue. They resisted the decree, refusing to tarnish their reputation and diminish their wealth. Governor Publius Licinius Nerva was stuck in between; the landowners were expressing their dissatisfaction day and night while the Senate was pressing him to enact the decree. He attempted to satisfy both sides. Nerva assured the landowners not to worry about their status, caving into the pressure and freeing only a small number of slaves to appease the Senate. This undoubtedly inflamed tensions and enraged the slaves who had been waiting to be released from their daily torment.

The first revolt of this period began outside of Syracuse. Eighty slaves had united, and together, they launched an assault and killed their masters before building a fortification on a nearby hill. News immediately reached Nerva, but he did not have enough men at his disposal to lay a siege on the fortification. However, Nerva was a cunning man, and he had an idea to bring down the rebels. He picked his most loyal slaves and ordered them to get into the fortification while pretending to betray the Romans. Once they were in the fortified hilltop, these loyal slaves opened the gates for Nerva's forces to storm in. The rebels were not ready to go against proper Roman troops and were immediately overwhelmed. Most were slaughtered, while others who survived chose to commit suicide rather than be recaptured.

Nonetheless, the flames of rebellion had already been ignited. Not long after Nerva's success, another revolt broke out, this time near Heraclia. In this rebellion, the slaves successfully claimed the life of Publius Clonius, an eques whose wealth was only a step lower than the senators. With their victory, many others became inspired to break free from their chains. They murdered the overseers and their masters and raced to join the others on Mount Caprianus. At this point in time, their numbers had swelled to over eight hundred strong. Nerva only learned of this uprising when the rebel forces had grown to over two thousand men.

Nerva turned to the commander of Enna, Marcus Titinius, to deal with the rebels. The attempt, however, ended in failure, which led to the rebels increasing in number and experience. The slave army numbered over six thousand following the defeat of Marcus Titinius. It was high time for the rebels to elect a new leader. They chose a man known as Salvius, who took the name Tryphon, a Seleucid king. Just like Eunus, Tryphon claimed to have the ability to tell prophecies and divinations.

The newly elected slave king knew he had to build a larger force if he were to challenge the other Roman cities of Sicily. He had his men rampage the countryside. They pillaged homes, seizing their resources and welcoming new slaves into their ranks. Tryphon ordered his men to do so until he was able to amass an army of twenty thousand men. Now a full-fledged force, Tryphon did not waste a minute going against the Romans, eventually defeating Nerva himself. With the city of Morgantina falling in his grasp, Tryphon easily gained the upper hand and dominated the eastern part of Sicily.

Another slave leader was busy building his reputation in the west. Known as Athenion, the Romans saw another slave army that numbered at least ten thousand men. Athenion and his forces tried to besiege the city of Lilybaeum, but the effort ended in vain. Not planning to give up,

Athenion, perhaps drawing an example from Cleon during the First Servile War, pledged his loyalty to Tryphon, hoping that together they could achieve greater success. Given his fierce determination, Athenion was made Tryphon's general and closest advisor. With their leadership, the slave army was able to capture Triocala, a city that Tryphon turned into his capital.

At Triocala, Tryphon fully embraced his destiny as king. He established a formal court where he surrounded himself with advisors and war generals. He even donned symbols reserved for the Roman royalty, such as the purple toga. While the slaves enjoyed the sight of this new king, for the Romans, this was their ultimate nightmare.

However, history was about to repeat itself again. Like Eunus, Tryphon's reign was never meant to last for too long. He soon died due to unknown reasons, and Athenion wore the mantle next. Athenion worked tirelessly to maintain the momentum of the rebellion. Unfortunately, Athenion lacked in a few areas. Although he was a skilled leader, he did not possess the political acumen of Tryphon and had no gift for telling prophecies. The rebellion began to lose its flame.

In 101 BCE, Rome's greatest general, Gaius Marius, was once again made consul alongside another respected veteran named Manius Aquillius. The two had both fought in the Cimbrian War. Although the rebels had lost Tryphon and gradually lost their grip, they still posed a massive threat to the republic. After all, Sicily was the breadbasket of Rome, and without its usual grain supply, the Eternal City would eventually falter. It did not make it any better that the Cimbrian War was still ongoing; resources were desperately needed for the Romans to win against the invading tribes.

Since Marius had his hands full in the Cimbrian War, the Senate dispatched Aquillius with a full consular army (about 20,000 men, including 2,500 cavalry) to crush the slave revolt once and for all. Athenion was confident in emerging victorious. He outnumbered the Romans by about ten thousand, and most of the rebels already had experience going against the Roman legions. Nonetheless, he clearly underestimated the brilliance of Manius Aquillius. War was not something new to him; Aquillius was a seasoned commander who was further hardened by years of direct combat against the Cimbri. Therefore, when the two forces clashed on the battlefield, it quickly became apparent to Athenion that their chances of winning were not as high as he had thought.

Of course, Athenion never planned to take a step back. He came face to face with Aquillius himself. He managed to wound the seasoned commander in battle, yet that was not enough to turn the tide. Despite bleeding all over, Aquillius fought the rebel leader and ultimately killed him. With another one of their kings dead, the rebels saw no hope of winning. Their resolve was diminished, and the majority of the forces were demoralized. Those who survived quickly retreated to their strongholds, yet Aquillius refused to let them recuperate. He and his men pursued them without mercy. One by one, these strongholds became targets of a siege. The slaves who were trapped inside did not have enough strength or resources to fight. They had only two choices: death by starvation or submission. Many chose the latter.

With the submission of over a thousand rebels, Aquillius succeeded in his goal. These slaves did not return to their work in the fields or mines. Instead, they were thrown into the gladiatorial arena to fight against wild animals as a form of entertainment for the Romans. This was an execution. However, the slaves were not done with their act of defiance; instead of fighting the animals, they killed each other quietly, with the last one pushing a blade into his own chest.

The Most Famous Slave Rebellion of All

The Third Servile War, which was the most famous slave rebellion of ancient times, erupted less than two decades later. It was led by none other than Spartacus. Beginning in 73 BCE, initial whispers of a revolt could be heard in the gladiatorial training school of Capua.

Spartacus hailed from Thrace and was believed to be a part of the Roman auxiliary forces. His life took a turn when he deserted the Roman army. After getting captured, he was made into a gladiator, living his days fighting men in the arena for the Romans to cheer on. When Spartacus and about seventy other fighters had their limits reached after having to go through harsh training and orders, they decided to make a daring escape. They armed themselves with whatever items they could find, including kitchen utensils. Even though the gladiators lacked proper equipment and weapons, they succeeded in fighting their way out of the school. They struck down anyone who tried to stop their escape and made their way to Mount Vesuvius.

Spartacus was made their leader, and before he knew it, many others joined their ranks. Unlike Eunus, Cleon, Tryphon, and Athenion, who were believed to have had ambitions to overthrow the republic itself,

Spartacus only wished to lead his fellow fighters and other slaves who joined his cause out of Italy and away from the Romans' clutches. Once he accomplished his mission, Spartacus planned on disbanding his army so that they could return to their homelands.

However, what began as a small-scale escape later grew into a full-scale war. Perhaps utilizing the experience he gained from being a part of the Roman army and the training he went through in the gladiator school, Spartacus and his men were able to defeat one Roman force after another. His forces were remarkably disciplined and mobile, allowing them to outmaneuver the Roman legions. At one point, it seemed as if the Romans had no chance of defeating the rebels.

The Senate grew ever wary, afraid that Spartacus would come knocking on their door with his vicious fighters. Their fear grew even worse by 72 BCE when they witnessed the immense growth of Spartacus's army. In their eyes, this was not a minor slave uprising; it was a direct threat aimed at toppling the Roman order. It was only after the Senate called upon Marcus Licinius Crassus that the senators were able to finally sleep at night. With at least eight legions under his command, Crassus began his campaign, pursuing the rebels day and night. Crassus aimed to push the rebels to the south, which he eventually succeeded in doing.

The death of Spartacus. [100]

The final battle took place near the River Silarius in 71 BCE. The only way to demoralize the Romans was to slay their commander. Spartacus fought against those who stood before him, charging straight into the heart of the Roman lines. He aimed to find Crassus and strike a blow to the commander himself. Unfortunately, the gods were not on the rebels' side. Spartacus was eventually killed in battle. Six thousand rebels survived the day, but they only lived for a short while. According to historical accounts, they were crucified along the Appian Way.

Chapter 4 – The Mystery of the Ninth Hispana

Gallic King Vercingetorix knew he had to change his strategy after suffering a series of defeats at the hands of the Romans. Continuing to face Julius Caesar and his highly disciplined forces in the open would mean a certain death. So, Vercingetorix retreated to Alesia in 52 BCE, hoping he could use the natural defenses—a hilltop surrounded by rivers—as a shield against the fierce Romans. His forces had been worn down by Caesar's men, yet the Gallic king remained confident. The retreat was not a sign of his defeat but a part of a larger strategy; he planned on luring Caesar into a siege, and when the time came, he would conduct a pincer attack on the Romans. Then, the Gallic king would summon reinforcements and crush Caesar and his remaining men.

A bronze statue of Vercingetorix in France. [101]

However, the Gallic Wars were not Caesar's first military campaign. The general had extensive experience from years of being on the battlefield. He was able to anticipate Vercingetorix's moves. Caesar's siege preparation was impressive. Not only did he order the construction of a double wall—one facing the fortress and another to shield the Romans from the incoming reinforcements—but he also had the Ninth Legion by his side.

The Ninth Legion was unlike any other Roman force. Their ultimate discipline and battle-hardened resolve separated them from the others. Marching under the eagle standard (a symbol of Roman supremacy), the Ninth Legion was a force to be reckoned with. There was no terrain that could stop the legion from advancing, and their battle tactics were highly effective. Whether they were facing cavalry charges or infantry assaults, the Ninth Legion always showed their might.

Each legionnaire was equipped with the finest weapons. The gladius was used for quick and lethal strikes in close combat, while the rectangular scutum shields gave them great defense against enemy blows. They were also equipped with a heavy javelin that featured a sharp tip capable of penetrating enemy shields. These javelins would also bend upon impact so that they could not be reused by enemies. In addition to the scutum shields, the legionnaires also wore durable *lorica hamata*, a type of chainmail armor.

A modern depiction of Roman legionnaires. [109]

A statue of a soldier wearing the Roman lorica hamata. [108]

When the Gallic relief army arrived, Vercingetorix launched the assault. Waves of Gallic warriors threw themselves at the outer Roman fortification, while Vercingetorix's forces attacked the inner walls. Unfortunately for the Gauls, this simultaneous assault failed. Another series of attacks was launched by the Gallic forces, yet the Romans held their ground. The Gallic warriors found it especially difficult to break through the shields of the Ninth Legion. They stood firm, and whenever there was an opportunity, their gladii never failed to cut down the enemy.

Eventually, victory belonged to the Romans. Vercingetorix had no choice but to surrender. This was the last major engagement between the Gauls and Romans.

As for the Ninth Legion, their legendary status grew as they followed Caesar in his many campaigns. We can never be sure of the legion's origin, but some believe that it existed decades before Caesar achieved adulthood. Many believe that the Ninth Legion was active on the battlefield as early as 90 BCE when Rome was struggling in the Social War.

We can be sure that when Caesar was appointed governor of Cisalpine Gaul in 58 BCE, the Ninth Legion's loyalty to him was unmatched. They never left the general's side, not even when Caesar crossed the Rubicon, which ignited the civil war in 49 BCE. Throughout this period of turmoil, the legion was at the forefront of the battlefield. The Ninth Legion witnessed Pompey's wrath, as his cavalry pierced through Caesar's forces at the Battle of Pharsalus. However, due to their harsh training and experience, the legion successfully held their ground. Their discipline was out of the world, and combined with Caesar's strategies and tactics, they were able to overwhelm Pompey's forces. It is sufficient to say that the legion played a prominent role in Caesar's success in cementing his control over the republic.

Of course, the Ninth Legion was not without its flaws. In 47 BCE, they were put to yet another test. After years of continuous campaigns, the Ninth Legion, along with three other legions (the Seventh, Ninth, and Twelfth), were beginning to experience extreme fatigue. Not only were they exhausted, but they were also frustrated by the false promises of rewards. They demanded to be discharged since they had been campaigning for over a decade. To display their dissatisfaction, the soldiers of these four legions mutinied.

At the time, these legions were under the command of Mark Antony, who failed to regain control over the mutineers. Diplomacy was out of the question, at least it was until the arrival of Caesar himself. The general knew he had to regain control of his golden quartet in order to win the fight in his upcoming campaign against the Optimates (Pompey's supporters) in Africa. Yet, Caesar had little in his coffers; the general could not offer money so that the men would reenlist. So, he resorted to a speech.

It was said that the legions went silent the moment they saw Caesar standing before them. He began his speech by addressing the men not as soldiers but as citizens, which signaled to them that they had been discharged. He questioned their loyalty to the republic and acknowledged the fact that he owed them their pay. He told them that he would hold on to his promise and pay them what was due after he returned from the African campaign. He spoke as if he no longer had plans on bringing his four favorite legions—the ones that had stood by his side for so long—with him to Africa. Caesar also threatened to decimate the entire Ninth Legion (a rare punishment in the military where every tenth man was executed).

The soldiers were disheartened by his speech. How could they let their commander charge onto the battlefield without them? They began surrounding Caesar and asked for forgiveness. They begged for the commander to spare the Ninth Legion. The legionnaires even expressed their desperate wish to be reinstated. While Caesar first feigned indifference, he changed his mind when the legionnaires agreed to hand him the names of those who instigated the mutiny. They were then executed.

Having been narrowly spared by Caesar, the Ninth Legion continued to be on his side throughout the rest of his upcoming campaigns. When Caesar was assassinated in 44 BCE, the Ninth Legion continued its service under Octavian in his quest to rise as the first Roman emperor. Perhaps one of the legion's biggest contributions under the emperor was their involvement in the Cantabrian Wars (27-19 BCE).

These wars were some of the most challenging ones under Augustus's reign. The Cantabri and Astures tribes resisted Augustus's rule. They resorted to guerilla tactics, which, more often than not, managed to overcome the Romans. Despite the Ninth Legion being seasoned by many decades of warfare, the difficult terrain and unconventional warfare of the Cantabrian forces posed a great challenge to them. Nevertheless, the legionnaires were known for their ability to hold their formation and respond quickly to an enemy ambush. Combined with their discipline, the Romans eventually won the day. The legion's act of valor in Hispania was recognized by Augustus, who bestowed upon them the honorary title Legio IX Hispana. From here on, the Ninth Hispana was stationed in Spain to assist the Romans in asserting their control over the newly conquered territories.

The legion continued to contribute to the empire for years to come. In 20 CE, the Ninth Hispana was dispatched to North Africa, where they were put under the command of Gaius Fulvius. Their mission was to join the Third Augustan Legion and assist in suppressing a rebellion. Led by Tacfarinas (a former Roman soldier-turned-leader of the Berber Musulamii tribe), the rebellion had been a thorn in the side of the empire. Their guerrilla tactics had been disrupting the settlements and supply lanes of the Romans. The arrival of the Ninth Hispana was supposed to contribute to the Romans' success.

However, things didn't go as planned. A centurion of the Ninth Hispana, Decrius, took a cohort of 480 men and launched a direct assault against Tacfarinas's forces. The Numidian warriors proved to be faster than the Roman soldiers; they managed to evade their attacks and swiftly counter their slashes. Although Decrius fought bravely, he was eventually killed in battle. The defeat was humiliating for the Romans to the point where the Ninth Hispana again faced the threat of decimation. Nevertheless, the legion regrouped and launched a successful counterattack. Tacfarinas was forced to retreat into the desert and never succeeded in reclaiming victory against the Romans.

The Ninth Hispana also survived to witness the unexpected rise of Emperor Claudius and joined his campaign of invading Britain in 43 CE. Little is recorded about their exact activities during this time in Britain until 60 CE when the Boudican revolt surfaced.

Led by Boudica, the queen of the Iceni tribe, it all began with the betrayal of Suetonius Paulinus, the Roman governor of Britain at the time. Not only did he annex the Iceni territory outright (the late Iceni king had left his kingdom jointly to his two daughters and the Roman emperor), but the Romans also seized the Iceni tribe's resources and wealth. The final straw came when Boudica was publicly flogged while her daughters were viciously raped by Roman soldiers. From here on, Boudica worked to unite several tribes under her banner and launched several attacks on Roman settlements.

A statue of Boudica and her daughters in London. [104]

The Ninth Hispana was then dispatched to Camulodunum (modern-day Colchester, Essex) under the command of Petillius Cerialis. During their march, four cohorts were suddenly ambushed by Boudica's forces. Driven by rage, the Britons quickly overwhelmed the Romans. Since they were outnumbered, slaughter was inevitable; nearly all of the infantry fell. Only Cerialis and a few cavalry narrowly escaped. The loss was so massive that the Ninth Hispana had to be reinforced with two thousand men from Legio XXI Rapax.

This was not the end of the famous legion. They remained in action, serving in Britain for several more decades. Their worst challenge came in the late 1ˢᵗ century when the Caledonians (tribes from the north of what is now Scotland) began to show their teeth. The Romans, ever hungry for more territories, were encroaching on their lands. To retaliate, the Caledonians raided multiple Roman outposts and settlements. The Romans were left with no choice but to launch another campaign aimed at crushing the tribes. Led by governor Gnaeus Julius Agricola, several legions, including the Ninth Hispana, marched north in 77 CE.

On one particular night, the Caledonians launched a surprise raid on the Ninth Hispana's camp. This wreaked havoc across the camp, and the Roman soldiers scrambled to get their weapons and hold their ground. For a moment, it seemed as if it was the last time the legion would see action. However, perhaps thanks to Agricola's quick maneuvering, he was able to get reinforcements from the other legions nearby. The Romans managed to repel the Caledonians and secure the camp.

Victory was again awarded to the Romans at the Battle of Mons Graupius in 83 CE, allowing Rome to solidify its control over much of Britain, though the full conquest of the Caledonians was not yet complete. Agricola intended to launch a second invasion to get his hands on the northern territories. However, he was recalled to the Eternal City by Emperor Domitian in 85 CE, as he feared that Agricola's rising popularity would pose a threat to his rule. Because of this, the Roman campaign in northern Britain never got its ending.

The situation in the region became ever precarious under Emperor Hadrian, who rose to power in 117 CE. Hadrian was well known for desiring peace over war. Instead of launching invasion campaigns like his predecessors, the emperor focused on fortifying Rome's frontiers. Hoping to keep the Caledonians at bay, he issued the construction of Hadrian's Wall in 122 CE, which stretched across the width of northern Britain. Many suggest the construction was the result of a certain dark event that took place in the Roman military: the end of the Ninth Hispana.

One theory claimed that the Ninth Hispana met its doom when the men were lured into a trap by the Caledonians. Knowing that Hadrian would always choose the path of peace, the Caledonians were thought to have invited the Romans into a peaceful meeting to discuss terms. The commander of the Ninth Legion, believing that it was an opportunity to finally end the hostilities at the northern frontier and also a chance to earn favor from the peace-loving emperor, agreed to the meeting. Being based at Eburacum (modern-day York) at the time, the legion marched north into Caledonia, where the tribe had set up a meeting point in a rather remote location.

Unsurprisingly, peace was never an option in the eyes of the Caledonians. The Ninth Legion was welcomed with an ambush. Being far from their reinforcements, the legion faced merciless slaughter. Their sacred eagle, which they had sworn to protect with all their might, fell to the ground, and none of the legionnaires were left to pick it up. While some said the Caledonians killed every last one of them, others suggested there were survivors, though their honor was shredded into so many pieces that they were engulfed by shame to recall the event.

By 120 CE, mentions of the Ninth Hispana had vanished completely from the Roman military records. Two years later, another legion was created. Known as the Sixth Victrix, this legion replaced the Ninth Legion. For centuries, the theory that the Ninth Hispana had been removed by the Caledonians stood. The Roman legions were the primary builders of Hadrian's Wall, but interestingly, the Ninth was the only legion that did not participate in its construction. It is hard to dismiss that it was a mere coincidence that the legion mysteriously disappeared right before Hadrian's visit to Britain and his commission to construct his famous wall. This particular theory is also further supported by the discovery of inscriptions bearing the legion's name in York, where they were stationed before meeting the Caledonians. In 1886, the world was shocked by another discovery. A bronze Roman eagle, believed to be the imperial standard of the lost legion, was found in Silchester.

IM P CAESA R
DIVI·N ERVAE·FIL NERVA
TRAIA NVS·AVG·GE M·DAC
ICVS·PO NTIFEXNIAXIMVS·TRIBV
NICIAE·PO TESTAT·IS·XII·IMP VI·COS·V·P·P
PORTAM·P ER·LEG·VIIII·HIS SP FECIT

The inscription bearing the legion's name discovered in York. [106]

Of course, there is another theory that suggests otherwise. Some claim the Ninth did not meet their fate in Britain after all. This was due to another archaeological discovery that uncovered inscriptions with the words "Ninth Legion" and "Vex Brit" (which stands for Vexillation Britannica, a detachment of the British Ninth) in Nijmegen, the Netherlands. These findings led scholars to argue that the legion might have been relocated to the Rhine to defend the northern frontier of the empire from the Germanic tribes. Whether or not this is true remains unclear.

Another possibility is that the Ninth might have sealed their fate in 132 CE during the Second Jewish Revolt (also known as the Bar Kokhba Revolt). Since the revolt in Judea was named the most destructive catastrophe to ever happen in the Roman Empire at that time, several legions were deployed to defeat the rebels. The Ninth could have been reassigned to the East and been defeated in battle. However, there is no concrete evidence to support this theory.

If the men of the Ninth Legion were not annihilated during the revolt in Judea, it could be plausible that they fell at the hands of the Parthians. Roman-controlled territories in the East, including Armenia and Syria, were invaded by the Parthian Empire in 161 CE. This undoubtedly sparked a major conflict between the two colossal powers. When several Roman legions were dispatched to defend the empire from the Parthians, the Ninth could have been one of them, though they were among the unlucky ones. The Parthians were exceptionally skilled in mounted warfare and archery, so it was not impossible for the Ninth to have been destroyed by them. However, like the theory where they fell in Judea, this particular theory is nothing more than speculation.

What we can be sure of is that the Ninth Legion completely disappeared from the official Roman record starting from 120 CE. The reason behind this remains a mystery. Apart from being a topic of study by scholars, the disappearance of the Ninth has also given ideas to those in the entertainment industry. They fill the gaps with speculative narratives and different scenes of battles toward the end of their story. The 2010 film *Centurion*, for example, depicted the Ninth Hispana taking its final stand against the Caledonians.

Rosemary Sutcliff wrote and published a fictional book inspired by the mystery of the Ninth Hispana. It follows a Roman officer named Marcus Flavius Aquila, whose task was to recover the lost eagle of the Ninth Hispana. This piece of fiction drew inspiration from the theory that the legion was wiped out by the northern tribes. This novel was also adapted into a film in 2011, bringing the history of the Ninth Hispana to a new generation of viewers. Despite the lack of records, the legacy of the Ninth Hispana has been successfully immortalized.

Chapter 5 – Conspiracies in the Senate

Caesar woke up slightly earlier than usual. His dreams last night gave him an uneasy feeling, but he chose to brush it off. As he got ready for another day, his wife, Calpurnia, approached. She appeared to be far more disturbed than Caesar, as she herself had been troubled by nightmares of her husband's demise.

"Stay," she said, her voice almost like a whisper. "Don't go to the Senate meeting today. Your blood, Caesar. I see it streaming down the steps of the Senate."

Caesar was moved by her distress, but he was not highly superstitious like a typical Roman usually was. He assured his wife that nothing would happen to him. He had, after all, survived decades of war.

"The Senate will not wait for me, my dear," he responded before leaving.

Caesar made his way through the streets and passed by the Temple of Jupiter. He suddenly remembered the words of a certain soothsayer who approached him during a triumph. "Beware the Ides of March" was what he said. But Caesar had so many things on his plate that he chose not to think about it further.

Meanwhile, in the Senate House, Cassius could be seen pacing back and forth. He was looking forward to this day, yet he had to be more vigilant than usual. He tightened his grasp around the small dagger hidden beneath his toga and looked around at his fellow conspirators, namely,

Casca, Brutus, and Decimus. Once they met, they exchanged looks. They knew there was no turning back. Today was the day to save the republic from continuing to bow down to a dictator.

The Roman Senate had always been a center of plots and assassinations. The Senate was an advisory body and was once regarded as the cradle of the Roman Republic. It possessed a significant influence over every aspect of the Eternal City, from legislative decisions to foreign policy to military affairs. But, of course, as the republic expanded its influence and territories, its political landscape grew more complex. Many senators, driven by greed, sought to outmaneuver one another just so they could have more control. Alliances frequently shifted, and loyalty meant almost nothing. Debates were, at times, skipped, as the senators preferred tools like assassinations, purges, proscriptions, or exiles to eliminate their rivals.

Cassius claimed to be a staunch defender of Roman liberty. Therefore, it was not a surprise that he had always viewed Caesar with disdain. His rise as dictator for life meant the erosion of republic values. In his eyes, Rome would certainly crumble under Caesar, whose thirst for power would only keep growing. If Caesar came out of the meeting alive, he could only sit and watch as the dictator used his absolute authority to render the Senate powerless and, with it, the concept of Roman democracy.

The same could be said about Cassius, who would do anything to see Caesar's downfall. In fact, he was the one who planted the seeds of discontent, especially in Brutus. Although it was said that Brutus loved Caesar—the dictator was not only his mentor but a father figure—his love for the republic ran deeper. He grew up listening to stories of Roman virtue, and he idolized men who never hesitated to risk their lives for the sake of freedom. True, Caesar declined the crown thrice, but he continued to display his ultimate power over Rome. The idea that Caesar's rule might put that legacy to an end made him restless. Cassius saw this wariness in Brutus's eyes and saw an opportunity to plant the seeds of doubt in his mind.

"You are the descendant of Lucius Junius Brutus, the one who bravely expelled the last king of Rome!" Cassius might have said. "How could you stand idly by as Caesar crowns himself the ruler of our beloved republic?"

Brutus eventually understood Cassius's intentions, and he agreed with him; the Eternal City must rid itself of Caesar if it were to survive.

The great dictator finally arrived with his customary grandeur. He made his way through the Porticus of Pompey and entered the Senate, where he was met with murmurs of the senators who were beginning to quiet down as he entered. They watched him stride forward, his regal purple toga brushing the stone floor. The silence in the air was heavy. Suddenly, as if they had an urgent matter to discuss, several of the conspirators rose and encircled Caesar. They greeted the dictator warmly, though their expressions were cold. Caesar attended to them, exchanging pleasantries as they guided him toward his golden seat.

Then, Tillius Cimber rose and approached the dictator. Claiming he had urgent matters to discuss, Caesar immediately shifted his entire focus onto him. The senator quickly begged him to recall his exiled brother, and Caesar firmly dismissed his request. Cimber, who had perhaps already rehearsed this motion the night before, held his hand out, reaching the dictator as if to plead further. In a sudden move, he pulled Caesar's toga down from his shoulders. Little did the dictator know that this was a signal.

The assassination of Julius Caesar. [106]

Casca was the first to unveil his dagger. His blade sliced into the mighty dictator's flesh. Stunned by both pain and treachery, Caesar glanced at his first assailant and attempted to fend off the upcoming blow. However, his effort was in vain, as Casca was not the only one to have stepped forward. One by one, the other conspirators lunged forward, their daggers slicing his torso brutally. Blood quickly spilled on the marble floor, pooling around his feet. Caesar, a man who had survived dozens of battlefields, tried to get on his feet, but his strength was clearly fading away.

Shakespeare described the incident vividly in his play. The dictator staggered, hoping he could at least take a final look at the faces who betrayed him, the same men he had trusted and whom he called his friends. One face made his eyes widen.

"Et tu, Brute?" he whispered.

The man he had loved and mentored as a son slowly approached the already dying dictator with his dagger drawn. Brutus gifted the dictator with the final blow. Caesar collapsed, his lifeless body slumping to the ground. The only thing that could be heard was the ragged breathing of the conspirators.

The soothsayer was right all along. The Ides of March had come and gone, as had Julius Caesar. The conspirators thought they could finally breathe easy now that the tyrannical ruler had died. They thought they had spared the Senate from its doom. Yet, Caesar's death did not restore the Roman Republic like the conspirators had hoped for. Instead, it plunged the Eternal City into chaos. Some praised Brutus and Cassius, seeing them as liberators, but the public viewed them as nothing more than traitors.

The streets mourned Caesar. Caesar's most loyal ally, Mark Antony, displayed his grief. Not only did he dress in mourning attire for a period of time, but the war general also refused to shave. Antony further expressed his grief during his famous funeral oration, where he showed to the public Caesar's blood-stained toga. This was also the time when he read Caesar's will and emphasized the Senate's betrayal. The general was attempting to ignite the public's fury and direct their rage toward the conspirators, which eventually worked, as Rome witnessed another civil war.

Mark Antony, Octavian, and Lepidus formed the Second Triumvirate with a goal to hunt down each of the conspirators. Brutus and Cassius paid the ultimate price at the Battle of Philippi, but peace for Rome was still far from reach. When Octavian and Antony's fragile alliance finally came to an end, the two fought each other, plunging the already shattered republic into further conflict. It was only when Octavian rose as Emperor Augustus that Rome began to see the first light of the Pax Romana.

The Ultimate Danger of Those Who Wore the Purple Toga

Although the emperor held supreme authority now that the republic was a thing of the past, senators, generals, and especially the imperial bodyguards (known as the Praetorian Guard) were still considered key players in the treacherous game of Roman politics. Aside from keeping a close eye on the borders and neighboring tribes in case there were revolts or invasions, Roman emperors had to watch out for those closest to them. Emperor Caligula was among the many Roman emperors who failed to do so; he was assassinated in 41 CE by those who were tasked with keeping him safe.

At the very beginning, Caligula's rise to the throne was warmly celebrated by nearly everyone. He came from a distinguished family. His father was Germanicus, one of the greatest Roman generals. He was admired by both the legionnaires and the common people, so many held high hopes for the new emperor. After all, the Romans had suffered under his predecessor, Emperor Tiberius, who was popularly known for his paranoia, absence, and assassinations. Corruption was common under Tiberius, and the Senate was nothing more than just puppets.

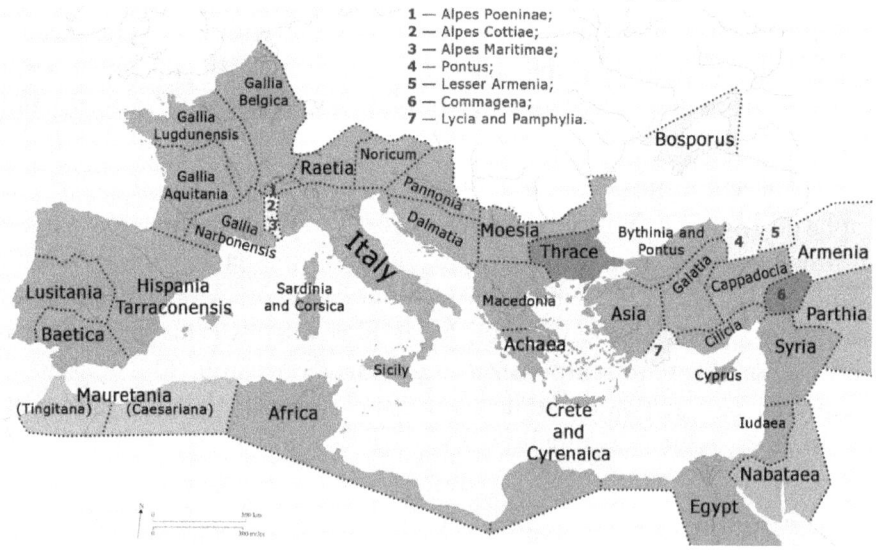

Map showing the extent of the empire. (Red - Italy and Roman provinces. Blue - Independent countries. Yellow - Client states. Magenta - Seized by Caligula. Purple - Former Roman provinces made client states by Caligula). [107]

So, when Caligula sat on the throne, he was expected to cleanse the Eternal City of its misfortunes and terror, which he successfully did in the first few months of his reign. Not only did he set everyone free who had been wrongfully imprisoned by Tiberius, but Caligula also wasted no time in pleasing the public. He abolished the harsh taxes that had long dragged his citizens down and used his newly acquired wealth on games and public spectacles. In just a few weeks, Caligula had earned the admiration of the masses. However, things took a sharp turn when the emperor suddenly fell ill.

Although he recovered from the mysterious illness, he seemed to become a different person. What began as signs of eccentricity soon spiraled into full-blown madness. He turned from an honorable and benevolent leader into a tyrant. Policies changed based on his mood swings, and his behavior turned increasingly erratic and cruel as the days passed. He once declared himself a god. It was common for Roman leaders to be deified, but this only happened after their death. Caligula went as far as to demand his subjects worship him. Caligula squandered the empire's coffers by commissioning personal projects, be it his own statues and palaces or the construction of ships for his own entertainment. There were also accounts that told how the emperor, disappointed and enraged with the senators, threatened to make his horse (known as Incitatus) a member of the Senate. He even took pleasure in mocking and humiliating the senators. It was almost like Tiberius's paranoia was contagious. Caligula often purged his government, with the senators and other aristocrats either facing execution or forced suicide.

This combination of paranoia, cruelty, and madness sealed his fate. The Senate seethed under his erratic reign, but the senators were not the ones who hit the final nail in his coffin. It was the Praetorian Guard.

The Praetorian Guard was an elite unit established by Rome's first emperor. Initially, their task was to protect the emperor, but as time went by, this prestigious unit became a significant force in its own right. Some might even describe them as a double-edged sword; they could either make or break emperors. Their loyalty could be bought, but it was far easier to displease them, which could make them extremely deadly.

Caligula had repeatedly abused them. The respected Praetorian commander, Cassius Chaerea, was among the men who had experienced the emperor's erratic behavior firsthand. Chaerea was publicly mocked and belittled more than once. Caligula would often insult his masculinity and refer to him with derogatory names such as *effeminatus*, which implied effeminacy. Since the commander had a rather soft or high-pitched voice, the emperor never held back from making crude jokes about how he sounded. In the ancient Roman culture, personal honor, especially for soldiers, was of immense importance. Caligula's abuse of power and mistreatment contributed to Chaerea's desire for revenge.

The conspiracy took place during the Palatine Games (also known as the Secular Games) on January 24th, 41 CE. The unsuspecting Caligula was first lured into a corridor beneath Palatine Hill, away from the eyes of the public. Once the emperor arrived, the members of the Praetorian Guard ambushed him. Caught off guard, Caligula attempted to flee, but Chaerea was quick enough to stab Caligula in the neck. As if mirroring the assassination of Julius Caesar centuries before, the other conspirators wasted no time in joining in, each leaving a wound on the emperor. The emperor was not the only victim of the conspiracy; his wife, Caesonia, and their infant daughter were also murdered to prevent any possible claim to the throne.

Caligula's assassination. [108]

With the throne left vacant, the Senate hoped to reassert its power. However, the senators knew they could not be that ambitious without the support of the military. At the same time, the Praetorian Guard had another plan. Although the blood of Caligula was on their hands, they had no intention of erasing the imperial system. They turned to one particular candidate to replace the mad emperor: Claudius, Caligula's paternal uncle. This move surprised many, as none expected Claudius to ever wear the wreath. He was kept on the fringes of politics largely due to his perceived physical disabilities (a limp and a speech impediment). Many saw flaws in him, including his lack of ambition. The Praetorian Guard saw these weaknesses too, but these flaws were the reasons why they put him on the throne. They wanted a malleable figure who would secure their interests.

The Senate had long lost its claws, and it had no choice but to accept Claudius as the empire's legitimate ruler. Claudius had lived through the reigns of three emperors (he was four years old by the time his grand-uncle Augustus died), so he had seen the harsh reality of what happened when one donned the purple toga. Knowing both his reign and survival depended on the very people who had put him on the throne, Claudius rewarded the Praetorian Guard with substantial bribes, which earned him their loyalty. Gone were the days when emperors rose solely by their lineage or political support. The Praetorian Guard now had the power.

Decades after the assassination of Caligula, the Eternal City witnessed yet another deadly plot to remove its emperor. This time around, it was Nero, whose reign is infamously known for both extravagance and cruelty. Much like Caligula, Nero had a good start. He ruled the empire with promise, yet by 65 CE, his increasing paranoia, coupled with his wasteful spending on personal projects and persecution of political rivals, stirred deep resentment among the Romans, especially among the aristocrats. The art-obsessed emperor further eroded his support after the Great Fire of Rome in 64 CE. Rumor says that the fire was started by the emperor himself when he ordered a land clearance for the construction of his lavish palace known as the Domus Aurea ("Golden House"). Despite fires being common in Rome, this particular one ravaged the city for several days, destroying over half of it. Interestingly, Nero was not even in Rome when the fire broke out.

When the public began to point their fingers at the emperor, his reaction was to blame the Christians. Leveraging on the public's negative view of Christians, Nero accused them of being the culprits. He arrested, tortured, and brutally executed them. Tacitus recalled that the emperor ordered horrific punishments. While some Christians were torn by dogs, others were crucified in the Circus of Nero. They were burned alive and served as torches in the emperor's garden.

Eventually, the Romans had enough of the emperor's violent charades. Gaius Calpurnius Piso was a well-connected aristocrat who was respected by both the elites and commoners. Piso was known for his oratory skills. His home was a gathering spot for those who quietly wished for the return of the republican system. They often met to criticize Nero's brutal rule, but by 65 CE, their complaints had turned into a discussion of a plot. Joined by a group of senators, equestrians, and even the Praetorian Guard, the group planned on overthrowing Nero and putting Piso on top, as they believed he had the capabilities to restore order and respect to the empire.

Known as the Pisonian conspiracy, it involved some forty men, including Seneca, Nero's former tutor. Their strategy was rather straightforward. They were to assassinate the emperor during a public performance in the Circus Maximus and declare Piso the new ruler. Since they had the support of the Praetorian Guard, the plan was supposed to go smoothly. However, the conspiracy was foiled before it could even begin. One of the conspirators, Milichus, chose to betray the group. The freedman went to Nero's trusted advisor, Tigellinus, and revealed the details of the coup. As expected, Nero, who was already struggling with paranoia like his predecessors, acted hastily and brutally. A relentless purge was initiated across the Eternal City, targeting not only the conspirators but also anyone who was suspected of disloyalty. Piso and Seneca were forced to commit suicide.

The Great Fire of Rome. [109]

The conspiracy had failed terribly. Nero only grew more paranoid and was on guard day and night. As for the Senate, it was humiliated further since Nero's reign of terror resumed. Eventually, a series of political and military upheavals took place. Revolts plagued the empire, and Nero's royal bodyguards turned against him. Nero was eventually declared a public enemy by the very Senate he had constantly humiliated. When he finally had no other way out—even after fleeing Rome and hiding in one of his freedmen's villas—Nero stabbed himself in the throat.

Cicero, Whose Speeches and Words Cost Him His Own Life

Of course, emperors and dictators were not the only ones who became targets of assassination. Even senators had the possibility of meeting their demise in a brutal fashion. One such tragic figure was Marcus Tullius Cicero, who lived before Rome was made into an empire. Aside from being a member of the Senate, Cicero was also a skilled orator whose life was dedicated to defending the foundations of the Roman Republic.

Born in 106 CE, Cicero had it all. He was born into a wealthy equestrian family. He was neither a soldier nor a war general; the senator was described by many to be a man of words, law, and politics. He was made a consul in 63 BCE and polished his reputation when he successfully thwarted the Catiline conspiracy. Cicero had a hand in saving the republic from internal revolts multiple times. So, it was not a surprise when Cicero pledged his support to Pompey the Great during Caesar's civil war.

Ever a man of politics, the senator sought reconciliation after Caesar gained victory, perhaps somehow believing that Rome could still be saved and its republican roots fully restored. However, everything changed when Caesar was assassinated. Power was quickly divided between a new set of leaders: Mark Antony, Octavian, and Lepidus. Mark Antony, in particular, was considered a threat to the Roman Republic, at least in the eyes of Cicero. He saw Antony as a corrupt and tyrannical figure. Antony's relationship with Cleopatra fueled Cicero to throw even more negative criticism at the general. With Caesar gone (Cicero knew he could not act when the dictator was alive since Antony was his closest friend and ally), Cicero was free to strike. He launched a series of speeches known as the *Philippics*, which were modeled after the orations of Demosthenes against Philip of Macedon. These speeches were thought of as a way to bring down Mark Antony. They labeled the general as a grave danger to Roman liberty and acted as a plea for the Senate to take a stand against him.

Some senators wasted no time in joining Cicero's cause. However, this success also signed his death warrant, as Antony began to plot his revenge. Cicero's life was threatened when the Second Triumvirate was formed. Mark Antony, Augustus (then Octavian), and Lepidus joined hands and drew up a proscription list, which contained the names of their enemies. These names were then marked for death, and their properties were seized. Antony insisted Cicero's name be included on the list. Octavian hesitated at first since Cicero had shown him support during the early years of his career. However, for the sake of maintaining the alliance with Mark Antony, he relented.

Soldiers under the order of Mark Antony dragged Cicero out of his litter. [110]

With the triumvirs aiming for his head, Cicero planned on fleeing Rome. He first sought refuge at his villa in Formia before leaving by sea. Unfortunately for the senator, Antony's soldiers tracked him down. Knowing that his time had come, legend has it that Cicero accepted his fate with calmness. He extended his neck and famously uttered, "There is nothing proper about what you are doing, but at least do it properly."

The severed head of Cicero, inspected by Fulvia, the wife of Mark Antony. [111]

Although Cicero's final act was one of dignity, his enemies were not planning to act the same. The soldiers severed his head and hands. These parts of Cicero were then taken back to the Eternal City, where they were nailed to the Rostra, a large platform, in the Roman Forum. Ironically, this was the very platform where Cicero had once delivered his speeches defending the Roman Republic and condemning tyranny. The sight of his severed body parts served as a vicious warning to others who dared to even think of opposing the Triumvirate.

Chapter 6 – The Cult of Mithras

Secret societies are not only limited to the modern world. They have existed for centuries. Their meetings and discussions were often cloaked in mystery and, most of the time, controversial intrigues. Secret rituals were common among the members of these kinds of societies, with each of them sworn to oaths and codes of conduct known only by their members. The purposes of these societies varied; some sought to protect a certain knowledge, others aimed to wield power, and some were spiritual in nature. The one thing they had in common was their need for secrecy, as they aimed to hide their true motives and actions from the larger world.

Today, many may be familiar with the Illuminati and the Knights Templar. Founded in Bavaria in 1776, the Illuminati was an intellectual movement aimed at promoting Enlightenment ideals and opposing religious and state control. However, as time went by, different views of society arose, many of which were based on conspiracy theories. Today, many claim that the members of the Illuminati are the ones who secretly control global political and economic systems.

The Knights Templar, on the other hand, was founded back in the 12th century. Created by a medieval order of warrior monks, its mission was to protect Christian pilgrims traveling to the Holy Land. The knights were also famous for their role in the Crusades.

These knights were known for their white mantles with a red cross and their strict vows of poverty, chastity, and obedience. They were involved in early banking activities (which made them one of the first organizations to provide financial services like loans and safekeeping), and they generated a fortune from donations made by kings and nobles. Their wealth and influence brought about their downfall.

In the 14th century, King Philip IV of France, who was said to be deeply in debt to the Templars, accused them of heresy. They were arrested, and their assets were seized. By 1312, the order had been disbanded, with some members subjected to execution. The order's sudden downfall soon led to various conspiracy theories. While some believe they had grown too powerful for the ruling class to tolerate, others thought they held secret knowledge or treasures like the Holy Grail or the Ark of the Covenant.

If we were to journey further back into time, when Zeus and Poseidon were still actively worshiped and the pyramids were still being constructed, we could find other secret societies. Both the Cult of Isis and the Cult of Dionysus played a big role in the religious and social life of the ancient world.

While the Cult of Isis originated in ancient Egypt and was established to worship the goddess of fertility and magic, Isis, the Cult of Dionysus was formed in ancient Greece. Popularly known as the god of wine, fertility, and ecstasy, Dionysus was worshiped differently compared to Isis. The cult's rites involved drinking, dancing, and revelry. Its rituals were designed to break down societal norms and constraints, allowing worshipers to experience a sense of freedom from the rigid structures of Greek society. Of course, these rites did not sit well with the authorities; they were seen as a potential source of social unrest. To avoid any mishap, the Cult of Dionysus operated in secret, with its members sworn to protect the mysteries of their worship.

In ancient times, it was normal for a secret society or cult to emerge from the worshiping of a certain god. The Cult of Mithras captured the imaginations of many in the 1st century CE. The cult was popular among the Roman military. The Cult of Mithras held the deity Mithras in high regard, though he was not openly worshiped in Roman temples like the gods of Olympus. In fact, Mithras was a figure of worship hidden from the public eye. Rituals involving the deity were practiced only by a select few.

Mithras originally belonged to the Persian pantheon, where he was acknowledged as a powerful divine being associated with light, truth, and the cosmic order. Being one of the central figures in the Zoroastrian religion, Mithras was also thought to be the mediator between the supreme god known as Ahura Mazda and humanity. As a guardian of cosmic balance, Mithras's task was to maintain justice and truth in the world. He was to oversee contracts and oaths while ensuring the forces of chaos and darkness were kept at bay.

Because of this, his worship among Persians centered around his role as the protector of the faithful and the god who upheld justice. His usual depiction was a solar deity riding a chariot across the sky, ensuring the sun would shine upon the earth. Of course, as time went by, the worship of Mithras transformed, especially when Persia's influence came into contact with other cultures beyond its borders.

The same could be said about the Roman Empire as it expanded its borders eastward. Although the Romans conquered many territories, bringing them under the empire's banner, they did not shy away from adapting new traditions and religious beliefs originating from these regions; the Cult of Mithras was definitely one of them. The worship of Mithras began with the Roman soldiers stationed in the eastern provinces (particularly those in modern-day Turkey and Syria). Perhaps impressed by the Persian god's warrior-like qualities and his associations with loyalty, truth, and victory over darkness, the Roman military found a sense of purpose in looking up to the divine being. After all, the soldiers were a long way from home and had been constantly facing the violent threat of war. Mithras offered them a sense of protection and strength.

When these Roman legions returned to the Eternal City after years of campaigning in the east, they brought along new religious ideas. Mithras became fully integrated into the Roman religion. Although most of the god's attributes remained, Mithras was not exactly the same as in Persian mythology. In Rome, Mithras was brought in as the god of soldiers. He was a symbol of discipline, loyalty, and victory. His role as a mediator was retained, though it took on a new significance in the Roman world; members of the Cult of Mithras saw themselves as part of a cosmic struggle between the forces of order and chaos.

Archaeological discoveries have revealed to us how far the Cult of Mithras flourished across the Roman Empire. One of the most significant discoveries was the Mithraeum, or temple dedicated to Mithras, found at Carrawburgh, a site along Hadrian's Wall in Britain. Hadrian's Wall was a Roman defensive fortification, and Carrawburgh was a military outpost. This underground temple, complete with an altar and reliefs of Mithras slaying a bull, shows that even soldiers stationed in far-off places, like the edges of the Roman Empire in Britain, practiced Mithraism. This was, of course, not just an ordinary bull. According to myth, the bull represents a primal cosmic creature whose death gave birth to life. When Mithras performed the sacrifice known as tauroctony, the bull's body and blood were believed to have generated new life—a ritual that symbolized the cycle of life, death, and rebirth.

The Mithraeum could also be found in the heart of the empire itself. Located in Rome under the Basilica of San Clemente, the Mithraeum was first rediscovered in the 19th century. Its intricate frescoes and carvings depicting the Persian god were still intact. This discovery confirmed the deep connection between the cult and elite Roman society. At the Roman port city Ostia, archaeologists discovered several temples dedicated to Mithras. Only one was well preserved, but it shed light on the activities held by the cult members. The temple featured stone benches arranged along the walls, which scholars believe were used for ritual feasts, a common activity held by those in cults.

The ruins of the Mithraeum in Ostia Antica, Italy. [113]

The Mithraea were unique. Unlike the grand temples of Jupiter, Mars, or Apollo that dotted the cities of the empire, Mithraea were typically smaller in size. Usually built within underground caves, it was common for the temples to be only dimly lit. This subterranean setting was not just for the sake of design. It was symbolic of the hidden nature of the cult and represented the journey from darkness to light. The cave-like atmosphere was also thought to be a reflection of the mythological setting where Mithras slayed the sacred bull. Although the Mithraea were not as spacious as the grand temples of Rome—they could hold only a few dozen members at the same time—the spaces were more intimate, allowing a tight-knit brotherhood to be formed among the initiates.

Each Mithraeum featured a centerpiece, an image of Mithras slaying the bull. The deity could be seen posing heroically as he thrust a dagger into the neck of a mighty bull. This scene was accompanied by various other animals, including a dog, a snake, and a scorpion. Scholars believe that this iconography also represented the cosmic struggle between life and death and light and darkness. The bull's blood, in Mithraic belief, was thought to bring fertility and renewal, while the act of sacrifice symbolized the victory of order over chaos. For members of the cult, the image was a reminder of their role in this cosmic battle and that they had aligned themselves with the forces of light, represented by Mithras.

The cult bore several similarities to other secret societies in our modern world; its appeal lay in its exclusivity and secrecy. Those who chose to be a part of its mysteries were bound together in brotherhood, with Mithras acknowledged as their divine leader. Perhaps it was this very sense of camaraderie that attracted many soldiers of the empire to take a vow and become initiated into the cult.

Not every soul could gain entry into the Cult of Mithras. Its teachings, rites, and rituals were held in secret, known only to initiates who had undergone a series of complex and symbolic initiation rites. These rites were not just a requirement for entry; they were designed to test both the physical and spiritual strength of the initiate so that they could further prepare themselves on a deeper journey to understanding the cosmic mysteries associated with Mithras.

To enter the cult, initiates had to pass through seven levels of initiation. Each of these levels represented a higher state of spiritual understanding and connection to Mithras. Apart from being symbolic, these stages were also practical, as they each carried specific duties and responsibilities. The first level of initiation was known as Corax (Raven). The lowest rank among all seven, Corax was associated with the element of air. Initiates at this stage were symbolically connected to the raven, a bird that served Mithras and carried messages. This was also when an initiate would take oaths of loyalty to the cult and to Mithras himself; it was the very beginning of their spiritual journey.

The second level was Nymphus (Bridegroom), which was associated with water, which symbolized purity and transformation. At this level, initiates would take on the role of a bridegroom and be metaphorically wedded to Mithras. This represented a bond or commitment to the faith. The third initiation level was Miles. Those at this level were considered soldiers of Mithras, emphasizing the militaristic nature of the cult. Initiates had to portray courage and dedication in battle in Mithras's service.

The fourth level was named Leo. Associated with fire and the image of a lion, this level marked a significant advancement in the cult. Initiates who reached this level were considered guardians of the Mithraeum, and their main responsibility was to maintain the sacred space. Once they passed this level, the initiates would go to the fifth level, Perses. Named after the Persian origin of Mithras, this level symbolized spiritual wisdom. Initiates were seen as intermediaries between the earthly and divine realms. They were almost like Mithras himself.

The sixth level of initiation was named Heliodromus or the "Sun-Runner." Just as its name suggested, this level was associated with the sun, the symbol of ultimate light and truth. Those who had come all this way and reached this rank were considered to have attained a close connection to Mithras. Last but not least, the highest rank of all was Pater ("Father"), which was reserved only for the elders and leaders of the secret cult. As the "Father," those in this rank were the spiritual guides or teachers responsible for leading rituals and the initiation of new members. They were also seen as fully integrated into the cosmic mysteries of Mithras.

Much like the depiction of the tauroctony (where Mithras slayed the bull), initiation ceremonies often mimicked the struggle between life and death. The most essential part of the Mithraic practice was the communal meals, which mirrored the brotherhood of the Roman army. Bread and wine were consumed by members of the cult, and they could have been symbols of the sacred bull's flesh and blood. Apart from being a ritualistic practice, this act was also a way to strengthen bonds between initiates, creating a sense of loyalty that greatly defined the Mithraic brotherhood.

A relief showing a depiction of the tauroctony found near Heidelberg. [118]

The Mithraic mysteries also had a strong astrological connection. The depiction of the tauroctony alone was believed to have been more than just a sacrificial image. Many agreed that it might have had astrological connotations. The bull, for instance, was thought to represent the zodiac sign Taurus. Meanwhile, the scorpion could be identified with the zodiac sign Scorpio. Its depiction of stinging the bull's genitals could symbolize Scorpio's position opposite Taurus in the zodiac. Its act of attacking the bull might also be a symbol of cosmic struggle. While the image of the dog leaping up at the bull's wound might not be directly linked to a specific zodiac sign, scholars agree that it might represent the constellation Canis Major or Canis Minor.

As for the snake, which could be seen near the bull and, at times, depicted drinking its blood, its image could be linked to the constellation Hydra, though its specific astrological role remains debated. The raven, which at times appeared perched near Mithras, represents the constellation Corvus, the messenger between gods and humans.

Of course, like many other mystery cults of the ancient world, the influence of the Cult of Mithras began to wane as time passed by. When

Christianity rose under Emperor Constantine and officially turned into a state religion by Emperor Theodosius I in 380 CE, Mithraism and many other pagan beliefs were suppressed. The cult's exclusivity and secretive nature contributed greatly to its decline. While Christianity sought to convert the masses and offered salvation to all, Mithraism was only open to a select group of men, particularly soldiers and the elites. When Christianity spread across the edges of the empire, carrying a universal message of salvation and eternal life, the mysterious cult struggled to maintain its foothold.

With Christianity becoming the official religion of the empire, the Romans saw an increasing number of decrees outlawing pagan practices. Churches and basilicas began to be constructed to replace temples. While some were repurposed and converted into churches, the Mithraea were left abandoned or destroyed. The cult's decline was indeed rapid. Mithraism disappeared from public life just as the curtains were about to close on the 4th century CE.

What is left for us today is only questions. Unlike Christianity, which left behind scriptures, letters, and early theological works for us to dissect, Mithraism left little to no written doctrine. The teachings and rituals of the cult were likely passed down orally from initiator to initiates. They were never recorded in a way that could survive the test of time, or if they were any, it could be plausible that they were purposely destroyed. The remains of the Mithraea, the relics and images of the tauroctony, and a few surviving inscriptions are the only ways we can get a glimpse into the religious practices of the cult. Much of its inner workings are forever lost, making them a true untold story.

Chapter 7 – The Roman Entertainment: Gladiatorial Games and Chariot Races

Excitement filled the air as the citizens of Rome made their way into the Colosseum. They were eager to see a certain figure: Carpophorus, the legendary *bestiarius* who had already cemented his name in the history of Rome for his mastery of the deadly art of combat against beasts.

Carpophorus was far from an ordinary *bestiarius*. Typically, *bestiarii* were either criminals or prisoners of war thrown into the arena to fight wild animals as punishment. It is safe to assume that most *bestiarii* were condemned to death. Many often resorted to suicide rather than face their demise in the jaws and claws of a lion or bear. Carpophorus took his fate as a challenge. He rose above the expectations and slew some of the most ferocious beasts ever brought to Rome. He turned these battles into spectacles of strength and cunning, leading to the cheers of the blood-loving Romans.

Some even believed Carpophorus possessed a supernatural ability to read the minds of these beasts. They claimed that he was able to predict every move of the creatures with ultimate precision. Others suggested that he was favored by the gods, who generously gifted him with otherworldly strength.

The time had finally come. The heavy iron gate creaked open, and loud cheering soon burst out when the audience saw Carpophorus stepping into the arena. He was a sight to behold. Like the seasoned gladiators, Carpophorus was muscular yet lean, and his body showed marks created by years of combat. His armor was minimal. It was designed not for protection but for speed and agility. He only had a spear in his hands, its tip sharp enough to pierce through even the toughest of hides.

A 5th-century mosaic in the Great Palace of Constantinople picturing a fight against a tiger. [114]

The first beast was unleashed. It was a lion, his golden mane suggesting that it was mature enough to lead a pride. The crowds hushed and leaned forward, wondering if this was the last time they would ever see Carpophorus in action, though it was unlikely since the *bestiarius* had slain many lions before. After a few moments of scanning the arena, the lion let out a roar and charged forward. This did not shatter Carpophorus's resolve; he held his ground and waited for the right opportunity. When the lion was inches away from him, the *bestiarius* quickly sidestepped the beast, avoiding its giant claw of death. Then, with a single, powerful thrust, Carpophorus drove his spear deep into the lion's side. The creature's roar turned into a weak growl before the lion collapsed to the ground.

The crowd stood and cheered for the talented *bestiarius*, yet Carpophorus remained calm. This was just the beginning of the day. Legend has it that there was a time when the *bestiarius* fought relentlessly against twenty wild beasts in a single day.

A bear was released into the arena. It rose onto its hind legs and towered over the muscular Carpophorus. The *bestiarius* circled the beast and read the animal's movements. When the bear swiped its massive paw, Carpophorus ducked. Noticing an opening, he drove his spear into the bear's exposed chest.

At this point in time, the crowds were chanting his name. More beasts were unleashed. Next was a tiger, its stripes striking and jaws deadly. Then came a hulking rhinoceros, its every footstep making the ground tremble. Afterward, a group of hyenas came running out, their snapping jaws attempting to end the Carpophorus's life. Last but not least, a wild boar charged forward with unrelenting fury. Carpophorus successfully put an end to each one, and when the last beast fell, he raised his spear in triumph.

But, of course, beneath the glory of the arena lay the harsh reality of a gladiator's life. Fighters like Carpophorus were not always born into fame and opportunity. The majority of them had rather difficult beginnings. They were prisoners of war, criminals, or even slaves whose careers in the arena were actually a form of punishment. This was not always the case, though. There were those who joined the arena willingly so they could get their hands on wealth to escape a life of poverty. Regardless of the reasons, all of the gladiators were subjected to relentless training before their names were called to enter the violent contests.

Gladiators were divided into multiple classes, and each of them was defined by its equipment and fighting styles. The *retiarius* fought with a trident and a net, which he used to ensnare his opponents, and the *secutores* were best known for their helmets with small eye slits, heavy shields, and short swords used for close combat. The heavily armored *murmillo* usually wore fish-shaped helmets, while the *Thraex* were armed in the Thracian style. They carried curved swords and a *parmula* (a small shield) and were lightly armored. Each class had its own strengths and weaknesses, allowing game hosts to orchestrate a balanced match to enthrall spectators.

A 2ⁿᵈ-century CE mosaic depicting gladiators. [115]

The *bestiarii*, like Carpophorus, were unique among the gladiators. Instead of going against other men, they fought wild beasts brought into the Eternal City from lands far away; this included lions, bears, bulls, and other exotic animals to the Romans, such as leopards and rhinoceroses. The *bestiarii* were, more often than not, supplied with minimal armor compared to the typical gladiators. This was so that they could fully utilize their speed and precision rather than their brute strength. Carpophorus usually favored fighting primarily with a spear and, at times, a dagger.

Interestingly, historical records suggest the *bestiarii* were often of African origin. This conclusion was made due to the fact that Rome had brought in a large number of slaves from North Africa. The Africans were also thought to have possessed a unique understanding of wild animals, especially those native to their homelands. However, this remains a topic of debate; even Carpophorus's origin is a mystery to us.

Although the arenas were mostly dominated by male gladiators, historical accounts suggest that female gladiators existed, though they were not as common. Known as gladiatrices, they were considered a novelty, and their participation in fights was meant to add excitement for the spectators. These women who chose a life in the arena were thought to have made the decision willingly; they were either motivated by a desire for independence or financial rewards. Although it seems a woman gave up any claim to respectability as soon as she entered the arena, there is some evidence to suggest that female gladiators were honored as highly as their male counterparts.

Perhaps one of the misconceptions about gladiatorial combat was the idea that every fight ended with a single gladiator standing. This misconception was made popular by modern films. While some matches—especially the ones where the fighters were condemned criminals or hated individuals—were to the death, the majority of them were not. Owning gladiators was expensive. They had to be fed, trained, and housed. Losing a gladiator in every game meant losing an investment. Unless a fight was specifically designed to be a punishment, many fights ended with more than one gladiator surviving. A match did not have to end when blood was shed. Some ended when one gladiator was too injured to continue. Once this happened, the editor, the sponsor of the games, or even the roaring crowds could decide the loser's fate. Nevertheless, death in the arena was far less common than Hollywood has led many to believe.

A depiction of a gladiatorial fight (with audiences giving their thumbs down), painted in 1872. [116]

Gladiators who managed to earn a reputation were rewarded immensely. They were showered with prizes and wealth, but the most precious of all was an offer for freedom. Some gladiators were allowed to hang their weapons and never worry again about their fates in the arena.

A gladiator named Flamma was one of the fighters offered this chance. Originating from Syria, Flamma was a prisoner of war who successfully earned renown through victories in the arena. He was believed to have participated in thirty-four fights; he won twenty-one, drew nine, and lost only four matches—a feat very few could claim. Flamma was a crowd favorite. As he built his reputation, he was granted a golden chance to break free from the chains of servitude.

He was offered the wooden *rudis* more than once. The *rudis* was a public acknowledgment that the gladiator had earned his place among the free citizens of Rome. However, to the shock of many, he refused his freedom, turning down the *rudis* time and again. Many were puzzled by his decision, but perhaps Flamma had become fond of the Colosseum and the roar of the crowd. Perhaps the honor of combat outweighed the peace and freedom offered to him. The arena had become both his life and identity; stepping away from it meant he was abandoning the very thing that made him legendary.

The Colosseum was not the only place where Romans—regardless of their status in the hierarchy—flocked in search of entertainment. The elites, the plebeians (commoners), and even slaves sought blood-pumping spectacles at the Circus Maximus, where chariot races were held. The roots of chariot racing trace back to the Etruscans and Greeks, and it became a favorite pastime for the ancient Romans. Similar to the gladiators, charioteers were also made up of either prisoners of war, slaves, or those from humble or unfortunate backgrounds.

The Circus Maximus could house up to 150,000 people. Known to be the largest and most famous venue, the Circus Maximus featured an oval-shaped track on which charioteers would race each other at breakneck speeds. There were different teams in the race, which were often sponsored by wealthy elites. Divided into four factions (Red, Blue, Green, and White), each of them had their own loyal fans who would, at times, get involved in violent outbursts in the stands.

A model of the Circus Maximus (left) in the 4ᵗʰ century CE, along with the Colosseum in the far right. [117]

Since speed was key, the chariots were lightweight and not designed for protection. They were pulled by two, four, or even six horses. The charioteers had to steer their horses at high speeds while maintaining their balance during the sharp turns. This was not the only danger the racers had to face, as they were allowed to use violence in their bid for victory. Some would use their whips not only to lash their horses but also to strike a blow to their opponents. This attack would knock their opponents off balance and send them crashing, especially at the sharp turns of the track, where things could quickly turn deadly.

The charioteers had to complete all seven laps around the two-thousand-foot sand track. Reaching a top speed of nearly forty miles per hour, the charioteers had to stay vigilant at all times; even the smallest mistake could lead to a disastrous crash that could possibly claim their lives. The final stretch was where the brutal struggle between the racers reached its peak, as they would do everything in their power to ensure victory was theirs.

One of the most renowned charioteers was Gaius Appuleius Diocles. Born in the province of Lusitania (modern-day Portugal), Gaius began his career at the age of eighteen, racing for the White faction. By the time he reached 25, Gaius was said to have participated in over 4,200 races. Despite the dangerous nature of the sport, Gaius won 1,462 races, forever immortalizing his name as one of the greatest charioteers in Roman history. His victories undoubtedly rewarded him with immense wealth, with some sources claiming that he reportedly owned a fortune equivalent to millions in today's currency. He was named one of the richest athletes in the ancient world.

A modern depiction of a chariot race held in the Circus Maximus. [118]

A typical race involving Gaius Appuleius Diocles would have been a show of speed, violence, and danger. Before every race, the chariots lined up at the starting gates. Tension was probably high during this moment for both the racers and the audience. With a blast of the starting horn, the gates would fly open, giving way for the horses to gallop, leading the chariots forward. Dust would fill the air as the chariots skid around the curved track. As for Gaius, who had substantial experience, the sharp turns were no longer a challenge.

However, the race was not only about speed; survival was also of the utmost importance. Gaius aimed to tangle his closest opponent's reins, hoping it would send the chariot into a vicious crash at the sharp turn known as the *metae*. Collisions were common, and they were almost always followed by the cheers of spectators.

Betting was also a common sight among the spectators, with fortunes won and lost based on the outcome. Those who were desperate to tip the scales in their favor even went to the extent of relying on supernatural means. Archaeological findings of curse tablets found near Roman race tracks suggest that the spectators believed in divine intervention; these curses were usually written to harm racers from rival factions.

Gaius knew exactly when to pull the reins and to balance the aggression with caution. When he arrived first on the finishing line, his victory would be announced with a blast of a trumpet. Gaius would then be escorted to the judges' box, where he was presented with a wreath, a palm branch, and a prize in the form of money. Afterward, he would return to his chariot and take a quick lap around the track before the next race began.

Gaius Appuleius Diocles survived the race track for twenty-four years, yet not everyone could share his luck. Another famous figure on the track who went by the name Scorpus gained public recognition, yet his demise happened too soon.

Similar to Gaius, Scorpus achieved substantial success in the Circus Maximus, granting him both fame and wealth. Born as a slave, Scorpus raced for the Green faction and quickly became a fan favorite after the crowd witnessed his incredible speed and tactical skill on the track. He was highly talented, especially when it came to daring maneuvers. His quick reflexes also spared him from crashes—at least for a while—while his fearless approach around the *metae* made him a formidable opponent. Throughout his career as a charioteer, Scorpus won over two thousand races.

Unfortunately, his career was cut short when a tragedy struck him on the very track he had built his reputation on. Despite being known for his reflexes and skills at maneuvering the horses, Scorpus was killed in a collision at the *metae*. Many agreed that he died before his time. Scorpus was likely in his twenties when the crash took his life, a stark contrast to Gaius, who lived well into his forties. Although both men successfully achieved legendary status, Scorpus's early death proved the dangers of racing, as it only took a minor misstep before the gods could snatch away their lives. The young charioteer's passing affected his fans tremendously. They mourned the loss of a man who had once seemed invincible on the dusty track.

The Romans enjoyed these brutal forms of entertainment, yet when Christianity rose later on, the Roman Empire began to change its views on both gladiatorial games and chariot races. Seen as nothing more than barbaric, both games were banned by the end of the 4th century CE.

Chapter 8 – The Poisoned Emperors of Rome

Caligula's paranoia had turned into reality. He could only widen his eyes to express his disbelief. He wished to speak once more, yet not a word left his lips. It was all too late—the daggers had pierced his flesh, giving way for his thick blood to flow, staining the ground. The emperor had finally collapsed; Rome's most despised tyrant had been killed in cold blood.

News of Caligula's sudden death soon spread across the palace, resulting in more chaos in the Eternal City. The Senate had mixed feelings about the tyrant's death. The senators saw this as an opportunity to restore the republic, but the Praetorian Guard stood before them; they had other plans in mind. In one of the palace's chambers, the royal guards stumbled upon Claudius, the awkward and stuttering uncle of the dead emperor. He had seen it all, but fearing the same fate, Claudius hid himself behind a curtain. Much to his terror, the Praetorian Guard dragged him out. But instead of putting a sword to his throat, the royal guards hailed him as the new emperor—a decision that shocked many.

The Praetorian Guard proclaiming Claudius as the new emperor of Rome. [119]

Claudius was never on the list to run for emperor. Despite being the paternal uncle of Caligula, their relationship was complex and tense. He was a member of the imperial family, yet his reputation was nearly nonexistent, largely due to his perceived frailty and awkward demeanor. Claudius was initially treated fairly by his nephew when he first rose to the throne. He even held minor positions under Caligula, although they were mostly ceremonial, but as the young emperor's reign progressed, his deteriorating mental state began to corrupt him.

The very moment Caligula descended into madness, he became tremendously suspicious of those around him. He saw them as his enemies or even conspirators planning his murder. The early days of promise soon gave way to multiple episodes of cruelty and paranoia. Even Claudius was not free from Caligula's suspicions. Although Claudius never posed a threat to the throne, he was still a member of the imperial family. In Caligula's paranoid mind, Claudius could easily shift his support and turn into a potential rival.

According to the historian Suetonius, the emperor took pleasure in embarrassing him, often ridiculing his physical condition. Claudius was essentially turned into a jester before the Senate and the public, further reinforcing the idea that he was unfit to lead. At times, Claudius was even forced to participate in public spectacles where he was made to play the fool at banquets and feasts. Caligula also once jokingly auctioned off Claudius's wealth to embarrass his uncle.

Nonetheless, Claudius managed to survive his nephew's reign. Wanting to maintain a low profile, Claudius often relented to the emperor's orders, no matter how ridiculous they were. He endured the humiliation in silence and avoided displaying any political ambition. However, Caligula's paranoia knew no boundaries; although Claudius remained submissive, the emperor never stopped making threats, even toward his closest family members.

By the time Caligula breathed his last, Claudius had long since become disillusioned with his nephew. There is no direct evidence that shows Claudius's involvement in the assassination of Caligula. Although it could be plausible that he was at least aware of the growing discontent, especially among the Praetorian Guard and the Senate, Claudius likely kept his distance. He avoided getting involved in conspiracies, knowing that it might cost him his own life.

Whether or not he was actually informed about the plot, we can be sure that Claudius's life took a different turn the moment Caligula's lifeless body hit the marble ground. The Praetorian Guard saw him as a figure they could easily manipulate, which was why a wreath was handed to Claudius.

Rome was already unstable when Claudius sat on the throne. However, despite being known for his disabilities, Claudius showed a willingness to rebuild the empire. He knew the importance of the very people who had placed him on the throne. Thus, one of his first moves to secure his power was to reward both the Praetorian Guard and the military. He spoiled the Praetorians with a large *donativum* (a gift of money) to ensure he had their loyalty and allegiance. He also made generous grants to the Roman legions, pleasing them as a result. Although not exactly groomed to rule, Claudius was aware of the most important lesson as a ruler: in a time of turmoil, the person who controls the army controls the entire empire.

Claudius also paid attention to Rome's public infrastructure, which had long needed improvement. He continued the construction of two major aqueducts—named Aqua Claudia and Aqua Anio Novus—which had been started by his nephew. Completed in 52 CE, these structures drastically improved the water supply for Rome. Along with two other aqueducts (Aqua Anio Vetus and Aqua Marcia, which were commissioned in 272 BCE and 144 BCE, respectively), they became known as the four great aqueducts of Rome.

Aqua Claudia. [120]

Claudius undoubtedly surprised many with his capabilities to bring Rome back to its glory, albeit for a while. Understanding the importance of trade and grain supply, the emperor made the decision to expand the harbor at Ostia. This way, Rome was able to have a reliable supply of food at all times. Claudius also paid attention to improving the roads that connected the city with distant provinces. Because of this grand construction project, the military could respond to threats more efficiently. Claudius also took a personal interest in handling matters on the administrative front. He was involved in the judicial process, often presiding over cases himself.

The Roman bureaucracy improved when Claudius took the mantle. Through his legal reforms, the emperor was able to streamline governance and reduce corruption. Another major decision he made was to open bureaucratic positions to freedmen (former slaves who had been granted freedom). These men, perhaps appreciating his move not to favor only the aristocrats, were loyal to him.

The emperor was also said to have increased women's privileges and often displayed humility whenever he was with his subjects. Once, the emperor apologized to visiting pensioners after finding out there were not enough chairs prepared for them. This was the kind of behavior that, according to Suetonius, made the public love their emperor.

The most defining act of Claudius's reign came in the form of military conquests. The emperor launched the invasion of Britain in 43 CE, which resulted in the expansion of the empire's borders. New wealth was obtained from these campaigns, and the emperor solidified his rule. Claudius wished to stay away from the same mistakes his predecessors had made.

Unfortunately, no matter his efforts, the gods had already decided his fate; Claudius could not escape the brutality of politics. However, unlike Caligula or even Julius Caesar, Claudius would be a victim, not of the blade but of poison.

Roman conquest of Britain. [191]

Poisoning was—and still is—considered a popular method of eliminating people of power. Its subtlety made it a preferred tool for those seeking power without the risk of public spectacle. Compared to daggers, which left obvious evidence of murder, poison allowed the assassin to remove their targets in a quieter and more calculated way. During a time when forensics was not yet advanced, the cause of death could often be wrongly concluded. The dead could be thought to have died from natural causes while the real culprit was actually poison. Suspicions would, of course, linger, especially if it was a sudden death, yet without concrete proof, nothing could be done.

As for Claudius, his greatest weakness was, ironically, his trust in others. Despite being a capable ruler, Claudius tended to misplace his trust. His greatest enemy turned out to be none other than his wives, first Messalina and later Agrippina the Younger (who was also his niece).

Agrippina had one ambition: to secure the throne for her son, Nero. When Claudius's health worsened and his performance in governing the empire began to see the first few signs of deterioration, Agrippina made a move. Instead of using sharp weapons to eliminate the emperor, she chose poison, hoping it could mimic natural causes. Of course, Agrippina did not plan on removing Claudius all by herself. She had the help of those closest to the emperor, particularly the servants, advisors, and the freedmen-turned-officials whom Claudius had appointed years ago. The plan was to serve the emperor a dish of mushrooms—said to be his favorite food—with poison injected in them. It was also widely believed that the poison was created by Locusta of Gaul, a notorious poisoner and possibly the first serial killer in history.

Unsuspecting of the plot, Claudius devoured the mushrooms, only to fall ill afterward. However, the emperor did not die. Agrippina was quick to administer a second dose of poison, possibly through a feather that was used on the emperor to induce vomiting. The emperor finally met his demise. It was ruled that Claudius had died of illness. Because of this, Agrippina successfully avoided suspicion, though whispers of the emperor being murdered followed her.

Despite Claudius's tragic ending, the emperor's name was not listed in the same category as his nephew. He was able to maintain a reputation as a competent ruler, even though he was once the black sheep of his family.

Yet, years after Claudius, Rome would again be thrown into a period of chaos when a new emperor rose to the throne. Named Commodus, the emperor would be forever known as the worst tyrant to ever hold the throne.

Commodus came to power in a very different Rome from the one Claudius knew. By the time he rose as emperor, the Roman Empire had endured different episodes of crisis, including a brief experiment with co-emperors. This system was initially established as an attempt to share the burdens of leadership. After all, Rome had transformed into a sprawling empire that stretched from Britain to the Near East. However, this system of co-rulership did not curb the issues that the empire was struggling with. Competition for power only intensified, leading the Eternal City to enter another state of political unrest. It was not until the rise of the philosopher-emperor Marcus Aurelius in 161 CE that the empire finally got its taste of stability once again.

Marcus Aurelius's reign, in many ways, represented the height of Roman virtue. Apart from his Stoic philosophy, the emperor was also a man of ultimate discipline. He was best known for his strategic governance. Although Rome faced constant wars on its borders and battled a plague that shook the city, Marcus Aurelius never faltered. Being one of the Five Good Emperors, Marcus Aurelius ruled over the empire and watched it flourish for nearly two decades. His only decision that would haunt the empire for years to come was when he appointed his son, the fifteen-year-old Commodus, as co-emperor in 177 CE (three years prior to his death).

It did not take long for the Romans to notice that Commodus was the complete opposite of his father. While Marcus Aurelius was often praised for being thoughtful and disciplined, Commodus was impulsive, cruel, and indulgent. The historian Aelius Lampridius later described the young emperor with words such as dishonorable and lewd—he even claimed Commodus to be defiled of mouth and debauched. Other historians agree that although Rome had suffered under the reign of emperors like Caligula and Nero, at least they began their reigns with promise. With Commodus, however, terror could be seen the very moment he first sat on the throne.

Commodus officially took over the reins in 180 CE when Marcus Aurelius died. He inherited an empire that was relatively stable, largely thanks to his father. Yet, the young emperor had little, if any, interest in governance. He only had his eyes on the luxury and privileges of wearing the purple toga rather than the burden of leadership. Instead of handling state matters in person, Commodus delegated the day-to-day tasks to several of his most trusted lieutenants. However, just like his predecessors, Commodus developed trust issues. Whenever he smelled even the slightest scent of disobedience, he would turn against his lieutenants. Even without securing concrete evidence, the emperor would have them murdered and find another person to fill the position.

Commodus did not pay much attention to governing the vast empire, yet it was clear that he enjoyed its spoils. As an emperor, the immense wealth of Rome was at his disposal, and he never hesitated to use it to pursue his own desires. Commodus was especially passionate about the gladiatorial games. However, unlike most emperors who enjoyed the games from the imperial box, Commodus took a more active role in the arena. While his father was well known on the battlefield (Marcus Aurelius spent much of his reign leading Roman armies in the Marcomannic Wars), Commodus only showed his teeth fighting against gladiators and beasts, though most of the combat was staged. The historian Cassius Dio once noted that Commodus boasted that he personally slayed a hundred lions in a single day.

Commodus's participation in the gladiatorial games. [189]

The arena was also where he displayed his cruelty. In one particular spectacle, the young emperor brought out a group of men, all of whom had lost their feet, and dressed them as serpents. Armed with sponges instead of rocks, these people had to pretend they were giants attacking the emperor. Perhaps playing the hero, Commodus clubbed them to death. Nevertheless, despite enjoying these violent performances, Commodus toned down his excitement whenever he was going against actual gladiators. Although there were records suggesting that the emperor did kill men in the arena, historians debate whether or not his victims were real fighters. Since the spectacles were usually manipulated to save the emperor from embarrassment, many suspected his opponents were not skilled gladiators but people forced into combat.

As his reign continued, his delusions grew more pronounced. Commodus was infamously obsessed with Hercules, the god of strength. He even went as far as to claim that he was the reincarnation of the god. In an attempt to convince his subjects of his claim, the young emperor could often be seen dressed in a lion-skin cloak and, at times, wielding a club. He spent an enormous amount of money building statues of him as the demi-god and hosting festivals. The statues of Nero were demolished to be replaced with ones of Commodus dressed as Hercules.

It is not surprising that Commodus was described as a narcissist. He once attempted to rename the months of the calendar so they would all be his name. This was a tradition that had been briefly adopted by earlier Roman leaders. July, for example, was named after Julius Caesar, and August was named after Augustus. However, most Romans refused to acknowledge the changes that Commodus made. He further displayed his narcissistic side when a massive fire engulfed parts of the Eternal City in 191. Instead of leading the recovery efforts, the emperor's contribution was to rename the city Colonia Lucia Annia Commodiana, which translates to Commodus's Colony. He then announced his decree that required

A statue of Commodus as Hercules. [188]

his subjects to be referred to as Commodiani, and the Roman Senate was rebranded the Commodian Fortunate Senate.

The young emperor's erratic behavior undoubtedly alienated much of the Roman aristocracy. Multiple assassination attempts were hatched, though they all failed. One of the major attempts happened in 182. Instigated by his own sister, Lucilla, who was furious with the emperor's excesses, the plot involved several senators. The plan was to perhaps recreate the assassination of Julius Caesar, as the conspirators were to stab the emperor with a dagger. Unfortunately, one of the conspirators had cold feet at the last minute. Commodus survived, and Lucilla was exiled and executed later on.

The second attempt took place in 187, but it resulted in a harsh purge. Instead of ridding Rome of the cruel emperor, the foiled assassination conspiracy led to the murder of dozens of senators. Another attempt was made in 192, and this one was almost a success. By this point in time, Commodus had distanced himself from almost everyone in power. The coup was spearheaded by two of his most trusted high-ranking officials, Laetus and Eclectus. After securing an allegiance with the emperor's mistress, Marcia, the conspirators made haste to save the empire before Commodus could do more harm.

Poison was their first weapon of choice. They slipped a lethal dose into his wine or beef. Yet, the emperor managed to vomit out the meal, so the poison failed to kill him. Not planning on letting the plan fail, the conspirators turned to Narcissus, a professional wrestler, to finish the job. Commodus, now weakened by the poison, was resting in his chamber when Narcissus entered. The wrestler strangled the emperor to death.

And so, Rome was finally free from its luxury-loving emperor, the one who thought of himself as Hercules reborn. He died at the age of thirty-one, and his departure marked the end of the Antonine dynasty.

Chapter 9 – Smugglers, Pirates, and Underground Markets

A merchant ship could be seen calmly entering the bustling port of Ostia. There was nothing special about its cargo–just another set of crates filled with pottery. The crew moved quickly, unloading the goods under the watchful eyes of the Roman customs officials. It all looked normal, but the crew could feel their hearts beating faster than usual. Apart from the pottery, which looked like they were destined for the market, the merchant ship also secretly carried sacks of Egyptian grain, olive oil, and even spices that they had not declared. They knew the risks of smuggling, but they were more attracted to the rewards.

The ruins of a marketplace in Ostia, where merchants from across continents flocked to. [134]

The Eternal City was popularly known for its tariffs and taxes. Goods flowed in from distant provinces like Egypt, Hispania, and Syria, but these goods were heavily taxed, making certain imports almost prohibitively expensive. Grain from Egypt, for instance, was taxed heavily after the region was annexed by the empire. Other valuable goods coming from the East, including olive oil and exotic spices, were also targets for high taxation. The Roman government relied on its ports and taxes to fill its treasury. Yet, for the merchants, the heavy taxes were burdensome. They found the allure of avoiding taxes too great to resist.

This was where smugglers came into the picture. Those who chose this as a career were not typical criminals who lurked in dark alleys. Instead, they were often seasoned traders who understood the Roman trading system. To become a smuggler, one needed to master two main skills: forging shipping documents and disguising valuable goods as everyday items. Another skill was to have a keen eye; smugglers had to look for port officials who might abandon the law for the sake of money.

Smugglers had to keep a careful eye on their rivals. Perhaps hoping to gain favor with the authorities, they might tip off Roman officials and ruin the plan entirely. Once smuggling activity was discovered, punishment was swift. Although the punishment varied depending on the nature of the crime, the status of the person involved, and the goods being smuggled, the most common punishments were fines, the confiscation of goods, and imprisonment, especially for repeat offenders. Execution was reserved for more severe cases, especially for those who smuggled items seen as an affront to state security. This included military goods, weapons, and other contraband that could be used to undermine Rome's stability.

Despite the serious punishments, the underground trade network continued to flourish. The elites depended on a steady supply of luxury goods, and the official markets could not always meet the demand. The grain shortage in 22 CE, for instance, brought fortune to smugglers. The wealthy Romans were able to continue hosting banquets and feed their households because of smugglers. The commoners might have cursed the shortages and the spike in prices due to scarcity, but the elites were never hungry, thanks to the underground economy.

The most famous episode of smuggling came in the 6th century CE when the empire was already split into two halves: the Western Roman Empire and the Eastern Roman Empire (better known as the Byzantine Empire). During this period of time, silk was considered one of the most valuable materials in the world, but the secret of producing it was guarded by China. The only way to import it was through the Silk Road, making silk extremely expensive and difficult to obtain.

When two Christian monks who had traveled to China finally learned of the process of making silk, Emperor Justinian I ordered them to smuggle silkworm eggs back to the Byzantine Empire. The silkworm eggs were hidden inside hollow bamboo canes and safely brought to Constantinople, allowing the Byzantines to produce their own silk. This broke China's monopoly and benefitted the Roman Empire tremendously.

Other than food supplies and luxury items, the smuggling networks in Rome also extended to one of the empire's most lucrative yet controversial commodities: slaves. Activities of smuggling slaves thrived, especially during times of war or in regions where slavery was more tightly controlled. Using hidden routes, smugglers who carried slaves aboard their ships were able to avoid Roman checkpoints. Once docked, they sold these unfortunate slaves in secret auctions.

Piracy in Ancient Rome

While smugglers were the champions of Roman black markets, pirates ruled the open seas. Piracy's roots stretched back before the rise of the Roman Empire. Since the earliest days of maritime trade, when merchant vessels began crossing the Mediterranean, piracy flourished as a dark counterpart to legitimate commerce. Some might agree that piracy is almost as old as seafaring itself. Records from ancient Egypt, Greece, and even Phoenicia talk about raids on ships and coastal settlements. Many may imagine pirates as lawless marauders—thanks to the cinema— however, they were far more than that. They were, in fact, skilled seamen and opportunists who were well versed in the complexities of maritime trade.

Of course, piracy was a persistent threat to Roman commerce, especially once Rome established its dominance over the Mediterranean, which the Romans referred to as Mare Nostrum. The waters surrounding Cilicia, Crete, and Sicily were notorious nests for pirates. Since these locations had rocky coastlines and many hidden coves, it was easy for pirates to launch surprise attacks on unsuspecting merchant ships.

Ever strategic opportunists, these pirates would only target vessels that carried the most valuable and heavily taxed goods. So, ships carrying Egyptian grain shipments, which were a need for ancient Romans, spices from the East, and silks from Asia became their main targets. However, goods were not the only things they would get their hands on. Pirates in the Roman era would also capture those aboard. They would either demand ransom or sell their captives into slavery in black markets across the empire.

What made the pirates so successful was the geography of the Mediterranean, corrupt local officials, and defiant yet ambitious merchants. Most of the time, these pirates operated in coordination with Roman elites who chose to turn a blind eye to their activities. In return for their ignorance, the pirates gave them a cut of their profits. The Roman state publicly condemned piracy, as it was seen as a major threat to the empire's economic stability. However, it was different in private; many within the government did not hesitate to earn benefits from the illegal spoils. Because of these greedy officials, pirates were able to receive insider information; they would know which ship to attack and which ones were laden with the most expensive cargo.

As piracy became rampant in Rome, harming both the republic itself and its allies, Marcus Antonius Orator (the grandfather of Mark Antony) was sent to deal with the pirates in 102 BCE. Antonius was able to suppress pirate activity in Cilicia, making the region safer again for Roman trade and shipping. His success was appreciated to the point where the Senate agreed to hold a naval triumph in his honor.

However, this was not the end of the piracy infestation in Rome. When the pirates loomed large again a few decades later, another figure was sent to the Mediterranean to undergo a pirate-hunting campaign. This time around, the responsibility was given to Marcus Antonius Creticus (the son of Marcus Antonius Orator and the father of Mark Antony) in 74 BCE. However, he failed to mirror his father's success.

After being bestowed with the title of proconsul, Antonius Creticus was tasked with eradicating pirates operating around Crete. Unfortunately, the campaign turned into a disaster. Seeing an opportunity for personal enrichment, he abused his power and plundered the provinces he was supposed to protect from the pirates. The Cretans, however, had secured allegiance with the pirates; after all, the island was the pirates' stronghold. They were able to defeat Antonius Creticus and his forces.

News of his failure was made known to everyone back in the Eternal City. He became a subject of ridicule among the Roman officials. They even sarcastically gave him the cognomen (third name of a Roman citizen) "Creticus," which means the conqueror of Crete.

The pirate threat grew only more dangerous and pervasive. Aside from the usual raids and plundering, piracy had become deeply entwined with the corruption that plagued the Roman elite. Even senators were not free from this tempting path to achieve immense wealth. Eager to expand their power and influence without having to go through the long journey, they hired pirates to carry out their dirty work.

It was only when Pompey the Great rose to prominence that the pirates finally met a formidable opponent. Already a military commander of immense skill with a growing reputation, the Romans had high hopes for Pompey to finally eradicate piracy once and for all. He wasted no time in launching a campaign in 67 BCE.

Perhaps what set Pompey apart from his predecessors was his strategic brilliance. By organizing the Mediterranean into various sectors and assigning different commanders to each region, he was able to create a powerful naval force to hunt down pirates. His ability to unite Rome's military might was indeed impressive. He was able to not only pursue the pirates on open seas but also strike them down at their own bases of operations.

Pompey never hesitated. He swiftly cut off pirate access to key trade routes and blockaded pirate ports. When the opportunity arose, he attacked the pirate fleets with overwhelming force. It took him only forty days to clear the western Mediterranean of pirate activity. He then turned his gaze to the eastern Mediterranean, where piracy was more deeply rooted.

Cilician pirates were undeniably more organized and powerful. Their strongholds and hideouts, which were located in rugged areas, made them hard to penetrate. However, Pompey was not one to easily back down. His decisive victory eventually came when he successfully defeated the pirates at their main base in Cilicia. He struck down dozens of pirates, and those who survived were taken prisoner. Now that the pirates' territory was seized, Pompey established a city he named Pompeiopolis to further secure the region.

The entire campaign of subduing pirates in the Mediterranean lasted for only three months. Knowing that there was a possibility for the pirates to rise again and threaten the republic once more, Pompey resorted to a more lenient and pragmatic approach after he was done with the campaign. Instead of executing or locking up each surviving pirate, he offered them a chance to start again. Those who agreed to surrender were allowed to resettle in Roman colonies with their families. This helped the Roman Republic in securing long-term stability.

Rome's trade routes were made safe again, and the grain supply was greatly restored. As for Pompey, his success in eliminating the pirate threat awarded him immense wealth and unimaginable fame. Today, he is known as one of Rome's greatest military commanders. Ironically, his own son, Sextus Pompey, would later be described by ancient historians as one of the most notorious pirates in Roman history, although Sextus might not have viewed himself as one.

Known in full as Sextus Pompeius Magnus Pius, he was the younger son of Pompey the Great. His story could also be a study of how a man born into prominence could be both praised and condemned by ancient Rome.

It all began with his father's defeat at the hands of Julius Caesar at the Battle of Pharsalus in 48 BCE. Pompey was once a champion of the Roman Republic and the mighty conqueror of the Mediterranean pirates, but he was left with no choice but to seek refuge under a foreign power. Perhaps desperate, the military commander put his trust in the young Egyptian pharaoh to protect him from Caesar's hunt. However, this trust was misplaced, and it cost him his life.

Pompey's death. [125]

With his father's unfair death, Sextus was forced into hiding. However, he was not planning on letting his father's legacy be stained. In Hispania, he fought Caesar's generals and built a reputation based on his success in guerilla warfare. Unfortunately for Sextus, Caesar's forces were strong, and he was eventually defeated. Despite being forced to flee again, he was determined to undo Caesar's carefully crafted story that depicted Pompey the Great as a defeated and irrelevant figure of the old republic. After Caesar's assassination, he gathered what remained of his father's supporters and began working on consolidating his power in the provinces where Pompey was held in high regard, particularly in Sicily and the surrounding areas.

The republic had always valued Sicily; it was considered Rome's breadbasket. In Sextus's mind, taking control of Sicily would grant him a firm foothold in the Mediterranean. He who controlled Rome's grain supply could either make or break the republic's stability. In other words, when Sextus seized Sicily, he effectively held Rome hostage.

His extraordinary fleet soon became a formidable force in the Mediterranean. He was supported by Pompey's loyalists and defectors from various factions who were against the Second Triumvirate (Mark Antony, Octavian, and Lepidus).

From his base in Sicily, Sextus launched naval raids against military convoys and Rome's commercial ships. Some may agree that his tactics mirrored those of the pirates his father had once fought against. However, Sextus did not view himself as one; he thought of himself as the rightful heir to Pompey the Great's cause. His father was the last defender of the Roman Republic, and he was proud to stand against the forces of tyranny led by the Second Triumvirate.

Sextus and his forces became so powerful that Octavian and Antony were forced to head to the negotiating table. The Treaty of Misenum was signed in 39 BCE, which allowed Sextus to control Sicily, Sardinia, and Corsica. This gave him legitimate power and de facto control over the western Mediterranean. In return for these terms, Sextus agreed to end his raids and unblock the grain supply to the Eternal City.

However, the treaty did not give Rome permanent peace. Octavian and Mark Antony never viewed Sextus as a legitimate ruler. Both saw him as a thorn in their sides. Octavian married Scribonia in 37 BCE. Since she was related to Sextus, the union was intended to reinforce the fragile peace. Yet, it did little. Octavian and Mark Antony signed the Treaty of Tarentum, which provided them with renewed military power. Antony himself provided ships to Octavian. Along with the leadership of Marcus Vipsanius Agrippa in his fleet, Octavian finally had the resources to challenge Sextus on the high seas. To Sextus, this was an invitation for a confrontation. He knew a war was on the horizon, so he resumed his naval blockade. Rome was cut off from its grain supply once more.

The Eternal City began to witness a scene of unrest when grain shortages became an issue. This forced Octavian to act. The future emperor launched an attack on Messina in 36 BCE, which was a key Sicilian stronghold controlled by Sextus. A full-scale naval war was set in motion. In the beginning, Sextus seemed to have gained the upper hand; using his superior fleet, he launched a series of counterattacks and struck at Octavian's supply lines. This was the very moment where many would suggest that Octavian was no match for Sextus on the open sea.

Fortunately for Octavian, he had Marcus Vipsanius Agrippa by his side. Regarded as one of Rome's most skilled military commanders and the future emperor's most trusted ally, the tides of war slowly changed. Agrippa made use of vessels equipped with *corvi* (grappling hooks) and *harpax* (a type of catapult-launched harpoon) to latch onto Sextus's ships. This reduced the mobility advantage of Sextus's fleet. Agrippa's men were also highly efficient in close combat, so they were well prepared for critical naval engagements.

Sextus was eventually defeated in the Battle of Naulochus in 36 BCE. Again, he fled to the Aegean Sea before making his way eastward, particularly to areas controlled by Mark Antony. Sextus knew that tensions were brewing between Mark Antony and Octavian. Thus, he hoped to get on Antony's good side and benefit from the political rivalry between the two. But, in the end, Sextus was captured by Mark Antony's own general, Marcus Titius. Titius was believed to have had a personal grudge against Sextus—he had killed Titius's father in an earlier conflict.

This was the end of the road for Sextus Pompey. He was executed in 35 BCE. Just as he had feared, his memory was deliberately tarnished by Octavian and the Augustan writers. Sextus held great importance in the politics and military of the republic, but he was reduced to a mere pirate. Instead of being a legitimate contender in the civil war, he was described by ancient historians and poets (especially those who supported Augustus) as nothing more than a nuisance who disrupted Rome's stability. Writers like Velleius Paterculus and Appian, for example, wrote him as little more than a brigand, dismissing his military prowess and downplaying the threat he posed. As for Augustus, this portrayal of Sextus served him well.

Chapter 10 – The Ghosts of Pompeii

The sun had just risen, shining its first ray of light over the cobbled streets of Pompeii. A man named Lucius was all ready for the day. Lucius, a modest yet well-respected merchant in the city, adjusted his tunic before stepping out of his villa. His home was typical of the Pompeian elite. It was a small domus yet comfortable enough for his family of four. It featured a courtyard adorned with delicate frescoes that narrated the stories of Roman gods and heroes. Lucius could smell the freshly baked bread made by the local baker right across from his villa. He took a whiff and continued his walk. He was accompanied by the salty breeze from the nearby Bay of Naples.

Life was relaxing in Pompeii. It was, after all, a popular coastal city for wealthy Romans seeking leisure and relaxation. However, Lucius's day was different from that of the aristocrats on vacation. His day was a healthy balance between work, social obligations, and personal indulgence.

As he got closer to the center of Pompeii, Lucius was greeted by the sounds of laborers pushing their carts filled with fruits, vegetables, and spices. Along the streets, one could find a line of shops complete with vendors hawking their goods. He made his way through the forum, the city's nucleus. It was a public square where events took place, ranging from political meetings to religious festivals to lively markets. Its amphitheater and theater were also among the largest in the Roman world, showcasing the city's love for entertainment and culture.

The forum was always alive, with people walking around and conducting business. The look of this location was a sight to behold; each corner featured statues of the city's benefactors all dressed in togas. It is safe to say that Pompeii was, in many ways, a reflection of the Eternal City itself, though it was smaller in scale.

The city of Pompeii was an important city in the empire. It was originally founded by the Oscans and later influenced by the Greeks and Etruscans. The city's greatest quality was its strategic location on the coast. Its close proximity to Naples made it an attractive destination for rich Romans. They often traveled to Pompeii for vacation and built luxurious villas overlooking the bay. However, Pompeii was not a provincial town reserved only for the wealthy. Since it flourished as a trade hub, receiving ships from all corners of the known world, the city was also a land of opportunity for the plebeians and freedmen. They could work and earn enough to live a decent life. Some might even get lucky enough to be able to climb up the Roman hierarchy. Lucius himself had risen from a modest background to become a respected merchant through his dealings in olive oil and textiles.

A short distance away from the forum, one could set eyes on one of Pompeii's most revered landmarks. Known as the Temple of Jupiter, it perched on a hill overlooking the bustling marketplace. The temple was dedicated to Jupiter (equivalent to Greek Zeus).

The ruins of the once glorious Temple of Jupiter. [196]

In the eyes of the Romans, Jupiter was not merely a divine being; he was the protector of the state, and his name was often called upon during political and military decisions. It should not come as a surprise that the Romans paid extra care in constructing the temple. Although its design was typical of Roman architecture (it bore a striking resemblance to the great Capitoline Temple in Rome), its grand flight of steps that led up to the main platform impressed anyone who laid eyes on it. The temple was also flanked by towering Corinthian columns, which featured exquisitely carved reliefs of mythological scenes, the most important one being an image of Jupiter's victories over the Titans.

Inside the temple was a grand statue of the god looming over the altar. His figure was imposing and majestic—fitting for his status as the king of the gods. The statues must have required a substantial amount of money and resources to be built. It was sculpted from marble and adorned with leaves made out of pure gold. Jupiter was depicted seated on his throne with a thunderbolt firmly held in one of his hands while the other held a scepter. The builders of the statue also carved Jupiter's eyes with such detail that the god appeared as if he was watching over the city.

A wall painting of Jupiter recovered from Pompeii. [197]

Jupiter was accompanied by statues of his consort, Juno (the Greek Hera), and his daughter, Minerva (the Greek Athena)—these three deities made up the Capitoline Triad. Since Pompeii had been a Roman colony since 80 BCE, the city had adopted the worship of the Capitoline Triad as a central part of its identity. Because of this, temples in Pompeii were more than a place where religious ceremonies were held. The Temple of Jupiter was deeply tied to the city's civic life. Public speeches, political meetings, and even official proclamations often took place in front of the temple.

The temple was also a gathering place whenever the city was thrown into a crisis. Whenever there were natural disasters or military threats, the Pompeiians would flock to this temple, where they would offer sacrifices. This was done in hopes of appeasing Jupiter and securing his favor. Animal sacrifices were common. Bulls were often used, as they were believed to be the best choice to offer to the god of lightning.

When Lucius finally arrived at his store, he wasted no time in beginning his daily routine. He supervised his slaves and workers as they arranged the fine goods imported from vast provinces across the empire. Lucius had almost everything in his store; there were exquisite wines from Gaul, olive oil from Hispania, and unique glassware from Egypt. Once he was done checking his inventory, Lucius got himself ready for another walk.

This time, he made his way to the city's public baths. Spending some time in the public baths was an important relaxation ritual back then. The baths were where Romans would socialize. Senators, merchants, and craftsmen would gather around to discuss all sorts of matters, be it about the state of Roman politics and the emperor or even gossip about the elites. As for Lucius, he always had his ears open. The empire was full of intrigues, so it was always good to stay up to date on the whispers going around.

The Roman Baths at Bath, England. [128]

In the evening, Lucius attended a banquet hosted by his dear friend. He mingled with guests and feasted on roasted meats, fresh fish, and fruits. Soothing tunes filled the air, as talented musicians were hired to play their lyres and flutes. Amidst the crowd was an extremely wealthy patron who had spoken at length about his wish to sponsor a new gladiatorial game in the city. Lucius listened attentively. To the merchant, these games were not merely entertainment. Since the games would be hosted for weeks, crowds from across the region would come to Pompeii. Lucius's business would boom as a result.

However, little did they know that the gods had another plan for them, and subtle signs had already started to show. Occasionally, the ground would tremble. Lucius, like many others, had grown accustomed to these tremors; the Pompeiians often shrugged it off as nothing more than just a minor natural occurrence. The inhabitants went about their lives as usual—merchants would tend to their businesses while others would attend theatrical performances or socialize at the baths. They truly had no idea what Mother Nature would soon unleash upon them.

Pompeii with Mount Vesuvius in the background. [199]

At noon on August 24th, 79 CE, the first sign of catastrophe began to worry the Pompeiians. Mount Vesuvius had erupted with such force that a plume of ash, rock, and scorching-hot volcanic gasses rose high up in the sky. This could be seen by those living hundreds of miles away. The blast was sudden, and the towering column of ash and rock loomed over the region for hours, leading the Pompeiians to wonder whether this was an ominous sign sent by the gods.

As the column cooled, the dark soot began to drift back to earth. At first glance, it appeared to be fine-grained ash raining gently on the streets and covering the marble buildings of Pompeii like dust. The situation in the city was still calm. The citizens were confused, but they were also in awe since they had never witnessed this occurrence before. Unbeknownst to them, this was only the beginning. As the ash thickened, Pompeii witnessed chunks of pumice and other lightweight rocks falling from the sky. Before they knew it, roofs began to collapse, and statues lost their limbs.

A surge of panic hit the inhabitants of Pompeii. They had some time to flee, and many did. Many took their belongings before fleeing on foot. Some chose to take a boat and seek refuge in neighboring towns. As for Lucius, he quickly made his way back to his family, where they were already in the midst of packing their valuables. They could only hope that they were just in time to leave the city and save themselves. No one could predict that this was the prelude to one of the world's most terrifying natural disasters.

The Last Day of Pompeii by the Russian painter Karl Bryullov. [180]

The eruption was witnessed firsthand by Pliny the Elder, the famed Roman author of the first natural encyclopedia. He was stationed at Misenum across the Bay of Naples. As the commander of a Roman fleet, Pliny was there to oversee naval operations. Since he was a scholar and a naturalist, Pliny's curiosity quickly took over the moment he saw the massive cloud rise from Vesuvius. Perhaps driven by his scientific instincts, he ordered his ships to sail toward the eruption. He intended to observe and study the phenomenon, but when he saw the danger people were in, he made it his mission to rescue the Romans trapped by the falling debris.

Unfortunately, the rescue operation went south. Pliny found it extremely difficult to navigate the waters as they approached the coast. This was largely due to the falling ash and pumice. While the sea churned with volcanic debris, the air was filled with toxic gasses. The sky turned dark, making it difficult for the crew to adjust their sight. Nevertheless, Pliny did not give up; he ordered his crew to press on. He was intent on saving those trapped in the towns around Pompeii.

But Mother Nature was not yet done. The closer they got to land, the worse their condition became. The air was suffocating, as sulfurous gasses burned their lungs. Pliny was overcome by the toxic fumes when he attempted to disembark and rescue survivors. The great scholar and commander died, succumbing to the very disaster he initially wished to investigate.

As for those trapped in Pompeii, their situation did not get any better. The rain of ash and pumice soon gave way to something far more deadly. The Pompeiians saw fast-moving surges of superheated gas and ash racing down the slopes of Vesuvius. Known as pyroclastic flows, they obliterated everything that stood in their path. The heat was so intense that flesh vaporized instantly when it came in contact with the volcanic matter. Those who perished left only their hardened forms.

Lucius and his family were among the many who managed to make their way into the streets. However, there was no way out. The air was thick with ash, and they could only see darkness. The ground continued to tremble as the pyroclastic flows neared. Lucius and the rest tried to find shelter, but everything had collapsed. Seeing that the end was near, Lucius held his family tightly as the torrent of ash and debris buried them. Their bodies were frozen in time, much like the rest of the city's inhabitants. In just a matter of hours, the once flourishing city was transformed into a graveyard, with victims entombed under layers of volcanic material.

Of course, Pompeii was not the only city that fell to the wrath of the volcanic eruption. Nearby towns like Herculaneum suffered a similar fate. While Pompeii was covered in ash and pumice, Herculaneum was buried under a thick layer of volcanic mud, which preserved buildings, organic materials, and even human remains.

John Martin's Destruction of Pompeii and Herculaneum. [181]

Interestingly, the horror that struck these cities was witnessed by another figure: Pliny the Younger. The nephew of Pliny the Elder, he was also stationed at Misenum when the disaster erupted. He was safe across the bay—a fate that was not shared with his uncle—yet the sight of the volcanic eruption was enough to terrify the Roman author. Pliny the Younger described the disaster in great detail when he wrote to the historian Tacitus. He told the historian of his feeling when he first saw the immense cloud of ash and gas rise higher as the seconds passed by. Pliny said he thought the world was coming to an end.

Because of Pliny's letters—though they were written years after the event—we get a detailed firsthand account of the eruption of Mount Vesuvius. He described the disaster as beginning with the appearance of a towering cloud in a shape that resembled the massive trunk of a pine tree (this is similar to what we call a mushroom cloud). Pliny also mentioned the bravery of his uncle and his tragic death in his letters.

Back in the Eternal City, the reaction was swift. The moment news of the eruption reached Emperor Titus, who had just ascended to the throne in the same year, he was quick to dispatch relief efforts to the region. The scale of the destruction undoubtedly shocked the empire. In the aftermath of the eruption, scholars agree that Rome lost at least sixteen thousand people. Pompeii was home to approximately eleven thousand to fifteen thousand inhabitants, and Herculaneum had a population of at least four thousand people. This eruption was one of the deadliest natural disasters to ever occur in the ancient world.

Titus was said to have personally overseen the distribution of aid. He even ordered a special investigation into the disaster. Nonetheless, despite his efforts, Pompeii and a few other towns never saw light again. They were never rebuilt and left forgotten. Pompeii was buried underneath layers of volcanic ash and pumice for nearly 1,700 years.

The rediscovery of Pompeii took place in 1748 when workers were digging for a foundation near the town of Resina (modern-day Ercolano). The discovery was more or less accidental, but it quickly garnered the attention of a Spanish military engineer named Roque Joaquín de Alcubierre. Working under the Bourbon King Charles III of Spain, Alcubierre was already familiar with stories of cities buried by the eruption. By the time of the discovery, the Spanish engineer was supervising the excavation of Herculaneum. Alcubierre quickly shifted his attention to the newly discovered site, marking the beginning of one of the most significant archaeological excavations in history.

Excavations were not an easy walk in the park. Workers had to clear away multiple layers of ash and rock that had been there untouched for centuries. However, once they were done, the city emerged almost perfectly preserved. It was as if time had been frozen. Buildings that did not collapse stood intact, complete with their elaborate frescoes and mosaics that adorned the walls. Archaeologists also discovered everyday objects, including tools, pottery, and various household items.

The most haunting discoveries were the bodies of the victims. When archaeologists poured plaster into the cavities left behind by the decayed bodies, they created eerily lifelike casts of people in their final moments. Some were crouching or lying down, while others died holding their family in a tight hug as the pyroclastic flows surged toward them. Many were clutching their most prized possessions, perhaps hoping to escape by sea and eventually start a new life in another town.

It is undeniable that the most remarkable aspect of the rediscovery was the city's state. Despite the eruption that had claimed the lives of many, Pompeii appeared almost exactly as it had almost two thousand years ago. It differs greatly from other archaeological sites around the globe, where structures and buildings were often corroded by the passage of time. Ironically, Pompeii was preserved by the very force that annihilated it. The ash and pumice that buried the city had sealed it off from the elements, protecting its structures, art, and artifacts from decay. Today, Pompeii is open to the public. Curious visitors can walk through the streets and enter the homes once resided by the ancient Romans. The city has essentially become a living museum, offering a window into the lives of those who lived during the flourishing empire.

The casts of victims in Pompeii. [188]

To this day, archaeologists and historians are still uncovering more about the daily lives of the Pompeiians before the disaster struck. Perhaps one of the most recent debates was about the actual date of the eruption of Mount Vesuvius. For centuries, scholars accepted the date of the eruption as sometime in August 79 CE. This was largely based on a letter written by Pliny the Younger. However, new evidence emerged that indicated that the eruption might have happened in a different month.

The discovery of preserved remains of fruits, including pomegranates and walnuts, indicates that the eruption likely occurred sometime between October and November, as it was impossible for these fruits to have ripened by August. The victims also wore clothing that was better suited for a cooler autumn day rather than a hot summer day. Other clues, such as a coin found in the ruins with markings dating to mid-September, have also led scholars to question the traditional date.

Regardless of the exact timing of the eruption, it is hard to dismiss that Pompeii's rediscovery provided us with a substantial understanding of the ancient world. The preserved remains of the victims and structures in the city give us clearer insights into their art, architecture, daily life, social structure, and the very nature of Roman urban existence.

Conclusion

Now that we have reached the end of the book, it is sufficient to say that Rome was far more than just its famed achievements. It is true that Rome is often celebrated and remembered for its glory, but its lesser-known episodes are just as captivating.

Through these forgotten stories, we are able to take a better glimpse of the empire. The Eternal City gave birth to a long list of powerful figures that history could never forget, yet the individuals explored in this book held equal importance to the shaping of the empire. They each had their own ways of navigating the treacherous path to power and, for some, to freedom. Descriptions of the daily lives of ordinary citizens tend to be removed from the majority of narratives of grand historical events. The citizens, from merchants to farmers and from craftsmen to entertainers, had a hand in shaping the social and economic structure of Rome.

People often speak of Rome's might, but beneath those triumphs lay many episodes of vulnerability. The Eternal City was constantly fraught with internal challenges. Economic strain, social unrest, and leadership crises were common sights that exposed the city's fragility. The natural world was also not merciful; fires, plagues, and earthquakes often shook the empire to its foundations. Even the Roman legions, often described to be invincible, were not free from defeat and disasters. Take the mysterious disappearance of the Ninth Legion as an example. Despite being feared for centuries, its theories of how it disappeared serve as striking evidence that Rome was not untouchable.

The history of Rome is extensive and complex. It spanned over a millennium, beginning from its legendary founding in 753 BCE to the fall of the Western Roman Empire in 476 CE. Its history covers centuries of wars, political affairs, conspiracies, and cultural transformations. To tell its story properly would require hundreds of pages, and even that would only scratch the surface of Rome's magnificence. Even so, these lesser-known stories offer a meaningful glimpse into the unique history of the empire. Although they might not include the most popular individuals and incidents, these stories provide readers with a small window into how the Romans once lived.

Here's another book by Matt Clayton that you might like

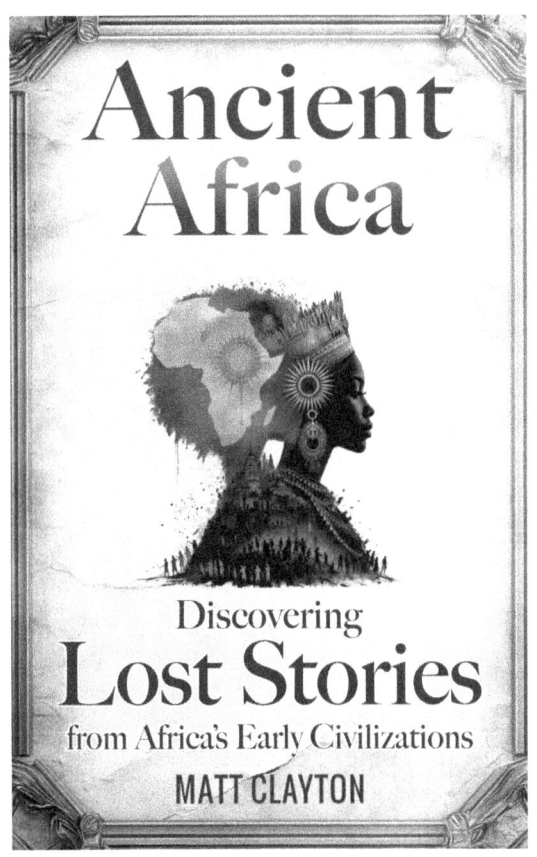

Ancient
Africa

Discovering
Lost Stories
from Africa's Early Civilizations
MATT CLAYTON

Free Bonus from Captivating History (Available for a Limited time)

Hi History Lovers!

Now you have a chance to join our exclusive history list so you can get your first history ebook for free as well as discounts and a potential to get more history books for free!

Simply visit the link below to join.

Or, Scan the QR code!

<u>captivatinghistory.com/ebook</u>

Also, make sure to follow us on Facebook, X, and YouTube by searching for Captivating History.

Bibliography

Part 1: Ancient Egypt

Bárta, Miroslav. "The Search for Imhotep: Tomb of Architect-Turned-God Remains a Mystery." *ARCE*, Accessed January 1. arce.org/resource/search-imhotep-tomb-architect-turned-god-remains-mystery.

Barton, Marc. "Imhotep – the First Physician - Past Medical History." *Past Medical History*, April 28, 2018. www.pastmedicalhistory.co.uk/imhotep-the-first-physician.

Cummins, Elizabeth. "Tutankhamun's Tomb (Innermost Coffin and Death Mask)." *Smart History*. Accessed January 28, 2025. smarthistory.org/tutankhamuns-tomb-innermost-coffin-and-death-mask.

De Lazaro, Enrico. "Mystery Surrounding Lost Army of Persian King Cambyses II May Have Been Solved." *Sci.News*, June 19, 2014. www.sci.news/archaeology/science-lost-army-persian-king-cambyses-ii-02002.html.

Escolano-Poveda, Marina. "Imhotep: A Sage Between Fiction and Reality." *ARCE*, Accessed January 10, 2025. arce.org/resource/imhotep-sage-between-fiction-and-reality.

Gillan, Joanna. "The Lost Labyrinth of Ancient Egypt – Part 1." *Ancient Origins*. January 13, 2020. https://www.ancient-origins.net/ancient-places-africa/lost-labyrinth-ancient-egypt-part-1-002033.

HistoricalEve. "Ramses III Against the Sea Peoples." *The Archaeologist*, October 27, 2022. www.thearchaeologist.org/blog/ramses-iii-against-the-sea-peoples?utm_source=chatgpt.com#google_vignette.

Holloway, April. "The Lost Labyrinth of Ancient Egypt – Part 2." *Ancient Origins.* September 3, 2014. https://www.ancient-origins.net/ancient-places-africa/lost-labyrinth-ancient-egypt-part-2-002034

Holloway, April. "The Lost Labyrinth of Ancient Egypt – Part 3: Uncovering Its Location." *Ancient Origins.* September 4, 2014. https://www.ancient-origins.net/ancient-places-africa/lost-labyrinth-ancient-egypt-part-3-uncovering-its-location-002039

Litecky, Tessa. "The Opet Festival: Rejuvenation of the Gods." *Mused.* Accessed February 3, 2025. mused.com/stories/127/the-opet-festival-rejuvenation-of-the-gods.

Lorenzi, Rossella. "Vanished Persian Army Said Found in Desert." *NBC News,* Nov 10, 2009. www.nbcnews.com/id/wbna33791672.

Mana, Davide. "The Lost Army of Cambyses." *Karavansara,* Sept 30, 2021. karavansara.live/2021/09/30/the-lost-army-of-cambyses.

Margaret. "'Seeking Senenmut: Statues, Status and Scandal' Campbell Price (EEG Meeting Talk)." *Other People's Tales,* June 15, 2016. writeups.talesfromthetwolands.org/2016/06/15/seeking-senenmut-statues-status-and-scandal-campbell-price-eeg-meeting-talk.

Mark, Joshua J., and RÃ©Mih. "Deir el-Medina." *World History Encyclopedia,* Feb. 2025, www.worldhistory.org/Deir_el-Medina.

Mark, Joshua J. "Imhotep." *World History Encyclopedia,* Feb 16, 2016. www.worldhistory.org/imhotep.

Mark, Joshua J. "Sea Peoples." *World History Encyclopedia,* September 2, 2009. https://www.worldhistory.org/Sea_Peoples/.

Mark, Joshua J. "The Battle of Pelusium: A Victory Decided by Cats." *World History Encyclopedia,* July 10,. 2017. www.worldhistory.org/article/43/the-battle-of-pelusium-a-victory-decided-by-cats.

Mark, Joshua J. "Third Intermediate Period of Egypt." *World History Encyclopedia,* October 11, 2016. www.worldhistory.org/Third_Intermediate_Period_of_Egypt.

Maydana, Sebastián. "Devouring Gods! What Was the Ancient Egyptian Cannibal Hymn?" *TheCollector,* September 20, 2022. www.thecollector.com/ancient-egyptian-cannibal-hymn.

Penner, Jay. *"The Story of the Lost Army of Cambyses." Jay Penner.* Accessed February 2, 2025. jaypenner.com/blog/the-story-of-the-lost-army-of-cambyses.

Ryan, Donald P. "24 Hours in Ancient Egypt: A Day in the Life of the People Who Lived There." Michael O'Mara Books.

Samir, Samar. "Famine Stela: A Piece of Pharaonic Diary." *EgyptToday,* July 15, 2018. www.egypttoday.com/Article/4/54056/Famine-Stela-A-piece-of-Pharaonic-diary.

"Imhotep Vizier of Works." *The Curious Egyptologist*, July 4, 2022. thecuriousegyptologist.com/2022/07/04/imhotep-vizier-of-works.

"Pyramid of Unas." *Lonely Planet.* Accessed January 25, 2025. www.lonelyplanet.com/egypt/saqqara-memphis-dahshur/attractions/pyramid-of-unas/a/poi-sig/1501661/1330429.

"Tantamani: The Last Pharaoh of the 25th Dynasty of Egypt." *World History Edu*, November 5, 2024. worldhistoryedu.com/tantamani-the-last-pharaoh-of-the-25th-dynasty-of-egypt.

"The Cannibalism Hymn of Pharaoh Unas: Ancient Egypt's Most Disturbing Inscription." *History Skills*, Accessed January 14, 2025. www.historyskills.com/classroom/ancient-history/cannibalism-hymn-of-unas/?srsltid=AfmBOopDtQadOkSUkm0H_sTltw9Mw-YqD5kPeLd7d1M-vwQXHzcRUiuo.

"The Lost Labyrinth of Ancient Egypt." *Historical Eve.* June 22, 2021. https://historicaleve.com/lost-labyrinth-of-ancient-egypt/

"The Sacred Lake in Karnak Temple Luxor | History, Facts, Pharaonic Temples." *Goota Travel*, September 3, 2022. gootatravel.com/ancient-egypt-civilization/pharaonic-temples/the-sacred-lake-in-karnak-temple-luxor.

"The Sea Peoples: Who Were They, and How Much Chaos Did They Create in the Bronze Age?" *World History Edu*, October 10, 2024. worldhistoryedu.com/the-sea-peoples/

Part 2: Ancient Greece

Bogaard, Cecilia. "Empedocles of Acragas Commits Suicide by Jumping into a Volcano." *Ancient Origins,* August 28, 2022. https://www.ancient-origins.net/weird-facts/empedocles-acragas-0017197

Cartwright, Mark. "Battle of Marathon." *World History Encyclopedia*, May 19. 2013. www.worldhistory.org/marathon.

Cartwright, Mark. "Hetaira." *World History Encyclopedia*, January 22. 2021. www.worldhistory.org/Hetaira.

Chaliakopoulos, Antonis. "Heraclitus of Ephesus: The Philosopher of Change (Bio and Quotes)." *TheCollector*, March 5, 2023. www.thecollector.com/greek-philosopher-heraclitus-ephesus-quotes.

Copeland, Cody. "The Bizarre Death of Milo of Croton." *Grunge*, February 10, 2021. www.grunge.com/331467/the-bizarre-death-of-milo-of-croton.

Daley, Jason. "Was Alexander the Great Pronounced Dead Prematurely?" *Smithsonian Magazine*, February 5, 2019. www.smithsonianmag.com/smart-news/was-alexander-great-pronounced-dead-prematurely-180971419.

Davis, Lori. "4.2 Neaira: A Slave in Ancient Greece." *Her Half of History*, September 16, 2021. herhalfofhistory.com/2021/09/16/neaira-a-slave-in-ancient-greece.

Dilouambaka, Ethel. "This Greek Philosopher Died Laughing at His Own Joke." *Culture Trip*, October 29, 2024. theculturetrip.com/europe/greece/articles/this-greek-philosopher-died-laughing-at-his-own-joke.

Garlinghouse, Thomas S. "On The Ocean: The Famous Voyage of Pytheas." *World History Encyclopedia*, July 14, 2017. www.worldhistory.org/article/1078/on-the-ocean-the-famous-voyage-of-pytheas.

Hewitt, Nathan. "Alexander the Not-Feeling-Great: How Did Alexander the Great Die?" *TheCollector*, January 8, 2024, www.thecollector.com/how-did-alexander-the-great-die.

Marchant, Jo. "Decoding the Antikythera Mechanism, the First Computer." *Smithsonian Magazine*, February 2015. www.smithsonianmag.com/history/decoding-antikythera-mechanism-first-computer-180953979.

Mark, Joshua J. "Thucydides on the Plague of Athens: Text and Commentary." *World History Encyclopedia*, April 1, 2020. www.worldhistory.org/article/1535/thucydides-on-the-plague-of-athens-text--commentar.

Nel, Aiden. "Alcibiades: His Relationship With Socrates, Political Life, and Scandals." *TheCollector*, September 21, 2022. www.thecollector.com/alcibiades-general-and-lover.

Nel, Aiden. "Orpheus and the Mystery Cult of Orphism (Myths, Beliefs, Practices)." *TheCollector*, January 25, 2023, www.thecollector.com/orpheus-cult-orphism.

Nugent, Addison. "Why Heron's Aeolipile Is One of History's Greatest Forgotten Machines." *Popular Mechanics*, Nov 29, 2020. www.popularmechanics.com/science/energy/a34554479/heron-aeolipile.

Pruitt, Sarah. "Alexander the Great Died Mysteriously at 32. Now We May Know Why." *HISTORY*, February 5, 2024. www.history.com/news/alexander-the-great-death-cause-discovery.

Rees, Owen. "Did The Spartans Throw Babies Down Mountains?" *Bad Ancient*, Aug 31, 2020. www.badancient.com/claims/spartans-throw-babies-mountains.

Sahir. "Did Pythagoras' Bizarre Fear of Fava Beans Contribute to his Death?." *Ancient Origins*, July 24, 2022. https://www.ancient-origins.net/history-famous-people/pythagoras-beans-0017052

Scandelius, Carl. "The Sicilian Expedition." *The 1440 Review*, May 6, 2022. 1440review.com/2022/05/06/the-sicilian-expedition.

Silver, Carly. "The Ancient Spartans Had a Murderous Secret Police." *ThoughtCo*, Mar 7, 2017. www.thoughtco.com/ancient-spartans-murderous-secret-police-1031226.

Starkston, Judith. "Samothrace Mystery Cult." *Judith Starkston*, October 6, 2021. www.judithstarkston.com/2021/10/06/samothrace-mystery-cult.

"16 Dramatic and Bizarre Ways People Died in Ancient Greece and the Hellenistic World" *History Collection*, accessed December 10, 2024. historycollection.com/16-dramatic-and-bizarre-ways-people-died-in-ancient-greece-and-the-hellenistic-world.

"Battle of Marathon." *HISTORY*, July 13, 2023. www.history.com/topics/ancient-greece/battle-of-marathon.

"Battle of Tegyra (375 BC) – Breaking the Myth of Spartan Invincibility." *HistoryForce*, Nov 4, 2022. historyforce.com/battle-of-tegyra375-bc-breaking-the-myth-of-spartan-invincibility.

"Death of Alcibiades." *Heritage History,* Accessed December 12, 2024. www.heritage-history.com/index.php?c=read&author=guerber&book=greeks&story=alcibiades2.

"Odometer Was Invented in Ancient Greece." *Greek Boston,* accessed December 20, 2024. www.greekboston.com/culture/ancient-history/odometer.

"Secret Assassins of Ancient Sparta: The Krypteia and Their Murderous Missions." *History Skills*, Accessed December 8, 2024. www.historyskills.com/classroom/ancient-history/krypteia/?srsltid=AfmBOorPlAt3_m9Mk60TFMUvZRbwWL1-19POqA9NIqi5yIUo3Ot8Sj9g.

"The Battle of Marathon." *Heritage History,* Accessed December 9, 2024. www.heritage-history.com/index.php?c=read&author=macgregor&book=greece&story=marathon.

"The Diolkos, a Corinthian Curiosity. - AncientBlogger." *Ancient Blogger*, June 19, 2024. ancientblogger.com/the-diolkos-a-corinthian-curioisity.

"The Plague of Athens as Told by Thucydides: A Timeless Analysis of an Epidemic." *Greek News Agenda*, May 21, 2020. www.greeknewsagenda.gr/the-plague-of-athens-as-told-by-thucydides.

Part 3: Ancient Rome

Addis, Ferdinand. "Rome: Eternal City." *Bloomsbury Publishing*, 2018.

Adhamy, Amir. "Agrippina the Younger: the first true empress of Ancient Rome." *HistoryExtra*, November 15, 2023. https://www.historyextra.com/period/roman/agrippina-younger-empress-ancient-rome-empress-nero-caligula/.

Andrews, Evan. "8 Things You May Not Know About Emperor Claudius." *History,* September 11, 2023. https://www.history.com/news/8-things-you-may-not-know-about-emperor-claudius.

Bileta, Vedran. "Agrippina the Younger: Rome's first true Empress." *TheCollector,* October 18, 2021. https://www.thecollector.com/agrippina-the-younger/.

Bileta, Vedran. "Caligula: 18 Facts on the 'Mad' Roman Emperor." *TheCollector,* August 16, 2023. https://www.thecollector.com/caligula/.

Dash, Mike. "King, Magician, General ... Slave: Eunus and the First Servile War Against Rome." *A Blast From the Past,* July 16, 2016. https://mikedashhistory.com/2016/07/16/king-magician-general-slave-eunus-and-the-first-servile-war-against-rome/.

Daugherty, Greg. "Was Commodus the Worst Emperor in Ancient Roman History?" *History,* August 18, 2022. https://www.history.com/news/commodus-worst-roman-emperor-gladiator.

De Abreu, Kristine. "Exploration Mysteries: Disappearance of the Ninth Legion." *Explorersweb,* March 8, 2023. https://explorersweb.com/exploration-mysteries-disappearance-of-the-ninth-legion/.

Dunn, Daisy. "The truth behind Ancient Rome's most controversial woman," *BBC,* May 7, 2021. https://www.bbc.com/culture/article/20210506-the-truth-behind-ancient-romes-most-controversial-woman.

Kings and Generals. "Before Spartacus: Second Servile War Against the Roman Republic," YouTube video, October 24, 2019. https://www.youtube.com/watch?v=jhLXhrOiLmk.

Mark, Joshua J. "The Spartacus Revolt." *World History Encyclopedia,* March 4, 2016. https://www.worldhistory.org/article/871/the-spartacus-revolt/.

Meddings, Alexander. "Messalina – the Empress Who Remarried While the Emperor Was Out of Town." *Walks Inside Rome,* accessed September 19, 2024. https://www.walksinsiderome.com/blog/messalina-the-empress-who-remarried-while-the-emperor-was-out-of-town/?fbclid=IwZXh0bgNhZW0CMTEAAR2RcEUXpymZEx-Wgv9p6eJfIjRs1YWFXAmQeVdfAmW5sypsqsI3wKnL7to_aem_COQPseaOLhN_AwEFHhuoyQ.

Sullivan, Missy. "Pompeii" *History,* July 29, 2022. https://www.history.com/topics/ancient-rome/pompeii.

Wasson, Donald L. "Legio IX Hispana." *World History Encyclopedia,* July 16, 2021. https://www.worldhistory.org/Legio_IX_Hispana/.

Wasson, Donald L. "Livia Drusilla." *World History Encyclopedia,* May, 13, 2016. https://www.worldhistory.org/Livia_Drusilla/.

Wolfson, Aaron. "Julia Domna." *World History Encyclopedia,* September 18, 2020. https://www.worldhistory.org/Julia_Domna/

Wright, Jennifer. "Locusta of Gaul: Rome's Imperial Poisoner and Possibly the World's First Serial Killer," *CrimeReads.* November 2, 2021. https://crimereads.com/locusta-of-gaul-romes-imperial-poisoner-and-possibly-the-worlds-first-serial-killer/.

"Claudius." *PBS,* accessed September 9, 2024. https://www.pbs.org/empires/romans/empire/claudius.html#:~:text=Disfigured%2C%20awkward%20and%20clumsy%2C%20Claudius,women%20would%20prove%20his%20undoing.

"Spartacus." *National Geographic,* accessed September 10, 2024. https://education.nationalgeographic.org/resource/spartacus/.

"The mystery of Rome's lost Ninth Legion: what really happened to them?," *History Skills,* accessed September 4, 2024. https://www.historyskills.com/classroom/ancient-history/ninth-legion/?srsltid=AfmBOorsceGcsIGCwlZ7gE9V7T4-xZZV91bguUkZ897nTOJhl4qGsnrc.

Image Sources

1 The Wellcome Collection, CC BY 4.0
<https://creativecommons.org/licenses/by/4.0>, via Wikimedia Commons:
https://commons.wikimedia.org/wiki/File:An_invocation_to_I-em-
hetep,_the_Egyptian_deity_of_medicine._Wellcome_V0018149.jpg

2 Mastaba.jpg: Unknown. Originally uploaded by Oesermaatra0069 at 2006-03-
12.derivative work: Master Uegly, CC BY-SA 3.0
<http://creativecommons.org/licenses/by-sa/3.0/>, via Wikimedia Commons:
https://commons.wikimedia.org/wiki/File:Mastaba_schematics.svg

3 Francisco Anzola, CC BY 2.0 <https://creativecommons.org/licenses/by/2.0>, via
Wikimedia Commons: https://commons.wikimedia.org/wiki/File:Zoser_Pyramid_
(2347235367).jpg

4 Morburre, CC BY-SA 3.0 <https://creativecommons.org/licenses/by-sa/3.0>, via
Wikimedia Commons: https://commons.wikimedia.org/wiki/File:Sehel-
steleFamine.jpg

5 Metropolitan Museum of Art, CC0, via Wikimedia Commons:
https://commons.wikimedia.org/wiki/File:Imhotep,_donated_by_Padisu_MET_DP1
64134.jpg

6 https://commons.wikimedia.org/wiki/File:Edwin_Smith_Papyrus_v2.jpg

7 Aidan McRae Thomson, CC BY-SA 2.0 <https://creativecommons.org/licenses/by-
sa/2.0>, via Wikimedia Commons: https://commons.wikimedia.org/wiki/File:
Pyramid_Texts_in_Unas%E2%80%99_Pyramid_2017.jpg

8 Olaf Tausch, CC BY 3.0 <https://creativecommons.org/licenses/by/3.0>, via
Wikimedia Commons: https://commons.wikimedia.org/wiki/File:Unas-
Pyramide_(Sakkara)_13.jpg

9 https://commons.wikimedia.org/wiki/File:01_unas_causeway.jpg

10 Rama, CC BY-SA 3.0 FR <https://creativecommons.org/licenses/by-sa/3.0/fr/deed.en>, via Wikimedia Commons: https://commons.wikimedia.org/wiki/File:Bedouins_starving_in_the_desert-E_17381-IMG_9845-gradient.jpg

11 ArdadN, Jeff Dahl, CC BY-SA 3.0 <https://creativecommons.org/licenses/by-sa/3.0>, via Wikimedia Commons: https://commons.wikimedia.org/wiki/File:Egypt_NK_edit.svg

12 https://commons.wikimedia.org/wiki/File:Medinet_Habu_Ramses_III._Tempel_Nordostwand_Abzeichnung_01.jpg

13 Andrew®, CC BY 2.0 <https://creativecommons.org/licenses/by/2.0>, via Wikimedia Commons: https://commons.wikimedia.org/wiki/File:Deir_el-Medina_ruins_(2009a).jpg

14 Fotograf/Photographer: Peter J. Bubenik (1995), CC BY-SA 2.0 <https://creativecommons.org/licenses/by-sa/2.0>, via Wikimedia Commons: https://commons.wikimedia.org/wiki/File:Luxor,_Tal_der_K%C3%B6nige_(1995,_860x605).jpg

15 EditorfromMars, CC BY-SA 4.0 <https://creativecommons.org/licenses/by-sa/4.0>, via Wikimedia Commons: https://commons.wikimedia.org/wiki/File:Inside_Pharaoh_Tutankhamun%27s_tomb,_18th_dynasty.jpg

16 Ad Meskens, CC BY-SA 3.0 <https://creativecommons.org/licenses/by-sa/3.0>, via Wikimedia Commons: https://commons.wikimedia.org/wiki/File:Mortuary_Temple_of_Hatshepsut_01.jpg

17 Osama Shukir Muhammed Amin FRCP(Glasg), CC BY-SA 4.0 <https://creativecommons.org/licenses/by-sa/4.0>, via Wikimedia Commons: https://commons.wikimedia.org/wiki/File:Stone_inscribed_with_the_name_of_Senenmut,_from_Thebes,_Egypt._Neues_Museum,_Berlin.jpg

18 British Museum, CC BY-SA 3.0 <http://creativecommons.org/licenses/by-sa/3.0/>, via Wikimedia Commons: https://commons.wikimedia.org/wiki/File:BlockStatueOfSenenmutAndNeferura-LeftProfile-BritishMuseum-August19-08.jpg

19 Metropolitan Museum of Art, CC0, via Wikimedia Commons: https://commons.wikimedia.org/wiki/File:Seated_Statue_of_Hatshepsut_MET_Hatshepsut2012.jpg

20 Kimberlym21, CC BY-SA 4.0 <https://creativecommons.org/licenses/by-sa/4.0>, via Wikimedia Commons: https://commons.wikimedia.org/wiki/File:Mortuary_Temple_of_Hatshepsut,_Egypt.jpg

21 Edal Anton Lefterov, CC BY-SA 3.0 <https://creativecommons.org/licenses/by-sa/3.0>, via Wikimedia Commons: https://commons.wikimedia.org/wiki/File:Tomb-of-Senenmut.jpg

22 Keith Schengili-Roberts, CC BY-SA 3.0 <http://creativecommons.org/licenses/by-sa/3.0/>, via Wikimedia Commons:

https://commons.wikimedia.org/wiki/File:Senenmut-BrownQuartziteSarcophagus_MetropolitanMuseum.png

23 Toni Pecoraro, CC BY-SA 4.0 <https://creativecommons.org/licenses/by-sa/4.0>, via Wikimedia Commons: https://commons.wikimedia.org/wiki/File:Egyptian_labyrinth.jpg

24 https://commons.wikimedia.org/wiki/File:%D0%9B%D0%B0%D0%B1%D1%96%D1%80%D0%B8%D0%BD%D1%82_%D0%B2_%D0%A5%D0%B0%D0%B2%D0%B0%D1%80%D1%96,_%D0%BE%D0%BF%D0%B8%D1%81D0%B0%D0%BD%D0%B8%D0%B9_%D0%93%D0%B5%D1%80%D0%BE%D0%B4%D0%BE%D1%82%D0%BE%D0%BC.jpg

25 LassiHU, CC BY-SA 4.0 <https://creativecommons.org/licenses/by-sa/4.0>, via Wikimedia Commons: https://commons.wikimedia.org/wiki/File:Gebel_Barkal.jpg

26 Bertramz, CC BY 3.0 <https://creativecommons.org/licenses/by/3.0>, via Wikimedia Commons: https://commons.wikimedia.org/wiki/File:Al-Kurru,main_pyramid.jpg

27 Cornell University Library, CC BY 2.0 <https://creativecommons.org/licenses/by/2.0>, via Wikimedia Commons: https://commons.wikimedia.org/wiki/File:Temple_Complex_at_Karnak.jpg

28 René Hourdry, CC BY-SA 4.0 <https://creativecommons.org/licenses/by-sa/4.0>, via Wikimedia Commons: https://commons.wikimedia.org/wiki/File:Temple_de_Louxor_53.jpg

29 Sara Nabih, CC BY-SA 4.0 <https://creativecommons.org/licenses/by-sa/4.0>, via Wikimedia Commons: https://commons.wikimedia.org/wiki/File:Karnak_Temple,_Ram_Road.JPG

30 Dennis G. Jarvis, CC BY-SA 2.0 <https://creativecommons.org/licenses/by-sa/2.0>, via Wikimedia Commons: https://commons.wikimedia.org/wiki/File:Egypt-3B-009_-_Festival_Hall_of_Tuthmosis_III_(2216561709).jpg

31 Warren LeMay from Chicago, IL, United States, CC0, via Wikimedia Commons: https://commons.wikimedia.org/wiki/File:Sacred_Lake,_Karnak_Temple,_Luxor,_LG,_EGY_(48009488536).jpg

32 Warren LeMay from Chicago, IL, United States, CC0, via Wikimedia Commons: https://commons.wikimedia.org/wiki/File:Osrian_Temple_of_Taharqa,_Karnak_Temple,_Luxor,_LG,_EGY_(48009600862).jpg

33 https://commons.wikimedia.org/wiki/File:Luxor_temple_2.JPG

34 https://commons.wikimedia.org/wiki/File:Le_roi_Cambyse_au_si%C3%A8ge_de_P%C3%A9luse_par_Paul-Marie_Lenoir.jpg

35 Pergamon Museum, CC BY 2.0 <https://creativecommons.org/licenses/by/2.0>, via Wikimedia Commons: https://commons.wikimedia.org/wiki/File:Persian_warriors_from_Berlin_Museum.jpg

36 Map_athenian_empire_431_BC-fr.svg: Marsyasderivative work: Once in a Blue Moon, CC BY-SA 2.5 <https://creativecommons.org/licenses/by-sa/2.5>, via

Wikimedia Commons: https://commons.wikimedia.org/wiki/File:Map_athenian_empire_431_BC-en.svg

37 https://commons.wikimedia.org/wiki/File:Pelopennesian_War,_Walls_Protecting_the_City,_431_B.C..JPG

38 https://commons.wikimedia.org/wiki/File:Plague_in_an_Ancient_City_LACMA_AC1997.10.1_(1_of_2).jpg

39 George E. Koronaios, CC BY-SA 4.0 <https://creativecommons.org/licenses/by-sa/4.0>, via Wikimedia Commons: https://commons.wikimedia.org/wiki/File:Kerameikos_Cemetery_on_July_28,_2019.jpg

40 https://commons.wikimedia.org/wiki/File:Discurso_funebre_pericles.PNG

41 Generic Mapping Tools, CC BY-SA 3.0 <http://creativecommons.org/licenses/by-sa/3.0/>, via Wikimedia Commons: https://commons.wikimedia.org/wiki/File:MacedonEmpire.jpg

42 https://commons.wikimedia.org/wiki/File:Le_Brun,_Alexander_and_Porus.jpg

43 Peter Paul Rubens, CC0, via Wikimedia Commons: https://commons.wikimedia.org/wiki/File:Sir_Peter_Paul_Rubens,_Pan_Reclining,_possibly_c._1610,_NGA_56608.jpg

44 https://commons.wikimedia.org/wiki/File:Greek_Phalanx.jpg

45 https://commons.wikimedia.org/wiki/File:Les_H%C3%A9ros_de_Marathon_Georges_Rochegrosse_1859.jpg

46 https://commons.wikimedia.org/wiki/File:Phidippides.jpg

47 Sailko, CC BY-SA 4.0 <https://creativecommons.org/licenses/by-sa/4.0>, via Wikimedia Commons: https://commons.wikimedia.org/wiki/File:Volterra,_urna_cineraria_con_scena_di_combattimento_(guerriero_con_aratro)_01.jpg

48 https://commons.wikimedia.org/wiki/File:Antique_Map_of_Classical_City_of_Sparta.jpg

49 https://commons.wikimedia.org/wiki/File:Jean-Pierre_Saint-Ours_-_Gericht_%C3%BCber_die_Neugeborenen_Spartas_-_2358_-_Bavarian_State_Painting_Collections.jpg

50 AlMare, CC BY-SA 2.5 <https://creativecommons.org/licenses/by-sa/2.5>, via Wikimedia Commons: https://commons.wikimedia.org/wiki/File:Taygetos_From_Sparti.jpg

51 Metropolitan Museum of Art, CC BY 2.5 <https://creativecommons.org/licenses/by/2.5>, via Wikimedia Commons: https://commons.wikimedia.org/wiki/File:Banqueters_Met_1979.11.8.jpg

52 https://commons.wikimedia.org/wiki/File:Jean-L%C3%A9on_G%C3%A9r%C3%B4me,_Phryne_revealed_before_the_Areopagus_(1861)_-_01.jpg

53 https://commons.wikimedia.org/wiki/File:The_story_of_the_greatest_nations;_a_comprehensive_history,_extending_from_the_earliest_times_to_the_pres

ent,_founded_on_the_most_modern_authorities,_and_including_chronological_su
mmaries_and_(14783288925).jpg

54 https://commons.wikimedia.org/wiki/File:Do_Not_Eat_Beans.jpg

55 https://commons.wikimedia.org/wiki/File:Alcibades_being_taught_by_
Socrates,_Fran%C3%A7ois-Andr%C3%A9_Vincent.jpg

56 https://commons.wikimedia.org/wiki/File:La_mort_d%27Alcibiade_
Philippe_Ch%C3%A9ry_1791.jpg

57 https://commons.wikimedia.org/wiki/File:Greek_triremes_at_Salamis.jpg

58 https://commons.wikimedia.org/wiki/File:Illustrerad_Verldshistoria_band_
I_Ill_116.png

59 https://commons.wikimedia.org/wiki/File:Canova_-
_Urania,_the_Muse_of_Astronomy_Reveals_to_Thales_the_Secrets_of_the_Skies,_
1798-1799_(crop).jpg

60 Jean Housen, CC BY-SA 3.0 <https://creativecommons.org/licenses/by-sa/3.0>, via
Wikimedia Commons: https://commons.wikimedia.
org/wiki/File:20140415_ioannina524.JPG

61 https://commons.wikimedia.org/wiki/File:The-Siege-Of-Sparta-By-Pyrrhus-319-272-
Bc-1799-1800.jpg

62 https://commons.wikimedia.org/wiki/File:Franc_Kav%C4%8Di%C4%8D_-
_Dekle_re%C5%A1i_Aristomena_iz_ujetni%C5%A1tva.jpg

63 Steve Swayne, CC BY 2.0 <https://creativecommons.org/licenses/by/2.0>, via
Wikimedia Commons: https://commons.wikimedia.org/wiki/File:
The_Parthenon_in_Athens.jpg

64 https://commons.wikimedia.org/wiki/File:1868_Lawrence_Alma-Tadema_-
_Phidias_Showing_the_Frieze_of_the_Parthenon_to_his_Friends.jpg

65 InSapphoWeTrust from Los Angeles, California, USA, CC BY-SA 2.0
<https://creativecommons.org/licenses/by-sa/2.0>, via Wikimedia Commons:
https://commons.wikimedia.org/wiki/File:Scale_model_of_Parthenon_Athena,_Roya
l_Ontario_Museum_(6222386828).jpg

66 Marsyas, CC BY-SA 2.5 <https://creativecommons.org/licenses/by-sa/2.5>, via
Wikimedia Commons: https://commons.wikimedia.org/wiki/File:
AGMA_Clepsydre.jpg

67 No machine-readable author provided. Marsyas assumed (based on copyright
claims)., CC BY-SA 3.0 <http://creativecommons.org/licenses/by-sa/3.0/>, via
Wikimedia Commons: https://commons.wikimedia.org/wiki/File:
NAMA_Machine_d%27Anticyth%C3%A8re_1.jpg

68 https://commons.wikimedia.org/wiki/File:Aeolipile_(from_Pneumatica).jpg

69 Zdravko Pečar, CC BY-SA 4.0 <https://creativecommons.org/licenses/by-sa/4.0>, via
Wikimedia Commons: https://commons.wikimedia.org/wiki/File:
Irrigation_Pump_in_Egypt_-_1950s.tiff

---

70 Dan Diffendale, CC BY-SA 2.0 <https://creativecommons.org/licenses/by-sa/2.0>, via Wikimedia Commons: https://commons.wikimedia.org/wiki/File:Diolkos,_Western_End._Pic_04.jpg

71 Gts-tg, CC BY-SA 4.0 <https://creativecommons.org/licenses/by-sa/4.0>, via Wikimedia Commons: https://commons.wikimedia.org/wiki/File:Vitruve%27s_odometer,_1st_century_BC,_Roma_(reconstruction).jpg

72 https://commons.wikimedia.org/wiki/File:Plaque_Campana_-_Initiation_aux_myst%C3%A8res_d%27Eleusis_(Louvre,_Cp_4154).jpg

73 https://commons.wikimedia.org/wiki/File:%27Thesmophoria%27_by_Francis_Davis_Millet,_1894-1897.jpg

74 https://commons.wikimedia.org/wiki/File:Regius_-_Orpheus_Beasts.jpg

75 https://commons.wikimedia.org/wiki/File:DSC00355_-_Orfeo_(epoca_romana)_-_Foto_G._Dall%27Orto.jpg

76 No machine-readable author provided. Marsyas assumed (based on copyright claims)., CC BY-SA 3.0 <http://creativecommons.org/licenses/by-sa/3.0/>, via Wikimedia Commons: https://commons.wikimedia.org/wiki/File:Samothraki_Arsinoe_rotunda.jpg

77 https://commons.wikimedia.org/wiki/File:The_Death_of_Empedocles_by_Salvator_Rosa.jpg

78 https://en.wikipedia.org/wiki/File:Death_of_Aeschylus_in_Florentine_Picture_Chronicle.jpg#Licensing

79 https://commons.wikimedia.org/wiki/File:Draco.webp

80 https://commons.wikimedia.org/wiki/File:Chrysippos_BM_1846.jpg

81 https://commons.wikimedia.org/wiki/File:Utrecht_Moreelse_Heraclite.JPG

82 Ishkabibble at the English Wikipedia, CC BY-SA 3.0 <http://creativecommons.org/licenses/by-sa/3.0/>, via Wikimedia Commons: https://commons.wikimedia.org/wiki/File:Antikythera_philosopher.JPG

83 https://commons.wikimedia.org/wiki/File:Suv%C3%A9e,_Joseph-Benoit_-_Milo_of_Croton.jpg

84 Staatliche Antikensammlungen, CC BY-SA 3.0 <http://creativecommons.org/licenses/by-sa/3.0/>, via Wikimedia Commons: https://commons.wikimedia.org/wiki/File:Pankratiasten_in_fight_copy_of_greek_statue_3_century_bC.jpg

85 Rvalette, CC BY-SA 3.0 <https://creativecommons.org/licenses/by-sa/3.0>, via Wikimedia Commons: https://commons.wikimedia.org/wiki/File:Pyth%C3%A9as.jpg

86 Photo taken by Alexandre Mirgorodski for http://www.taganrogcity.com Courtesy of Taganrog Local Government. © TaganrogCity.Com, https://commons.wikimedia.org/wiki/File:Sundial_Taganrog.jpg

87 Hans Kylberg from Stockholm Bagarmossen, Sweden, CC BY 2.0 <https://creativecommons.org/licenses/by/2.0>, via Wikimedia Commons: https://commons.wikimedia.org/wiki/File:Islossning_(119329313).jpg

88 https://commons.wikimedia.org/wiki/File:M443922_Julius-Caesar-taken-prisoner-by-Cilician-pirates-while-crossing-the-Aegean-Sea-c75-BC.jpg

89 https://commons.wikimedia.org/wiki/File:RomanRepublic40BC.jpg

90 https://commons.wikimedia.org/wiki/File:Cicero_Denounces_Catiline_in_the_Roman_Senate_by_Cesare_Maccari.png

91 https://commons.wikimedia.org/wiki/File:CaesarRefusesTheDiadem Ridpathdrawing.jpg

92 https://commons.wikimedia.org/wiki/File:Cleopatra_and_Caesar_by_Jean-Leon-Gerome.jpg

93 Miguel Hermoso Cuesta, CC BY-SA 4.0 <https://creativecommons.org/licenses/by-sa/4.0>, via Wikimedia Commons: https://commons.wikimedia.org/wiki/File:Livia_y_Tiberio_M.A.N._01.JPG

94 Classical Numismatic Group, Inc. http://www.cngcoins.com, CC BY-SA 2.5 <https://creativecommons.org/licenses/by-sa/2.5>, via Wikimedia Commons: https://commons.wikimedia.org/wiki/File:Caligula_sestertius_RIC_33_680999.jpg

95 https://commons.wikimedia.org/wiki/File:Georges_Antoine_Rochegrosse_The_Death_of_Messalina_1916.jpg

96 Carlos Delgado, CC BY-SA 3.0 <https://creativecommons.org/licenses/by-sa/3.0>, via Wikimedia Commons: https://commons.wikimedia.org/wiki/File:Ner%C3%B3n_y_Agripina.jpg

97 José Luiz Bernardes Ribeiro: https://commons.wikimedia.org/wiki/File:Portrait_of_family_of_Septimius_Severus_-_Altes_Museum_-_Berlin_-_Germany_2017.jpg

98 T8612, CC BY-SA 4.0 <https://creativecommons.org/licenses/by-sa/4.0>, via Wikimedia Commons: https://commons.wikimedia.org/wiki/File:First_Servile_War_(135-132_BC).png

99 https://commons.wikimedia.org/wiki/File:Mario_vincitore_dei_Cimbri.jpg

100 https://commons.wikimedia.org/wiki/File:Tod_des_Spartacus_by_Hermann_Vogel.jpg

101 Fabien1309, CC BY-SA 2.0 FR <https://creativecommons.org/licenses/by-sa/2.0/fr/deed.en>, via Wikimedia Commons: https://commons.wikimedia.org/wiki/File:Statue-vercingetorix-jaude-clermont.jpg

102 Modern portrayal of Roman soldiers (legionaries), CC0, via Wikimedia Commons: https://commons.wikimedia.org/wiki/File:Roman_holiday_birthplace_of_rome_roman_soldiers-883133.jpg!d.jpg

103 Carole Raddato from FRANKFURT, Germany, CC BY-SA 2.0 <https://creativecommons.org/licenses/by-sa/2.0>, via Wikimedia Commons: https://commons.wikimedia.org/wiki/File:Statue_of_a_Gaulish_soldier_wearing_a_C

eltic_torc_necklace,_Roman_clothes_and_holding_a_Gallic_shield,_most_likely_a_ Gallic_aristocrat_recruited_into_the_Roman_auxiliaries,_Augustan_period_(501257 23031).jpg

104 Paul Walter, CC BY 2.0 <https://creativecommons.org/licenses/by/2.0>, via Wikimedia Commons: https://commons.wikimedia.org/wiki/File: Boudica_statue,_Westminster_(8433726848).jpg

105 Yorkshire Museum, CC BY-SA 4.0 <https://creativecommons.org/licenses/by-sa/4.0>, via Wikimedia Commons: https://commons.wikimedia.org/wiki/File: Fragment_of_Legio_IX_Hispana_Tablet_YORYM_1998_21.jpg

106 https://commons.wikimedia.org/wiki/File:Vincenzo_Camuccini_-_La_morte_di_Cesare.jpg

107 Homoatrox, CC BY-SA 4.0 <https://creativecommons.org/licenses/by-sa/4.0>, via Wikimedia Commons: https://commons.wikimedia.org/wiki/File:Calig2en.png

108 https://commons.wikimedia.org/wiki/File:The_Assassination_of_the_ Emperor_Caligula.jpg

109 https://commons.wikimedia.org/wiki/File:Robert,_Hubert_-_Incendie_%C3%A0_Rome_-.jpg

110 https://commons.wikimedia.org/wiki/File:Marcus_Tullius_Cicero_dragged_ from_his_litter_and_assassinated_by_soldiers_under_the_command_of_Marc_Anto ny_43_BCE.jpg

111 https://commons.wikimedia.org/wiki/File:Fulvia_y_Marco_Antonio,_o_La_ venganza_de_Fulvia_(Museo_del_Prado).jpg

112 https://commons.wikimedia.org/wiki/File:Ostia_Antica_Mithraeum.jpg

113 https://commons.wikimedia.org/wiki/File:Neuenheimer_Mithraeum.jpg

114 https://commons.wikimedia.org/wiki/File:Mosaic_museum_Istanbul_2007_011.jpg

115 https://commons.wikimedia.org/wiki/File:Gladiators_from_the_Zliten_ mosaic_3.JPG

116 https://commons.wikimedia.org/wiki/File:Jean-Leon_Gerome_Pollice_Verso.jpg

117 Pascal Radigue, CC BY-SA 3.0 <https://creativecommons.org/licenses/by-sa/3.0>, via Wikimedia Commons: https://commons.wikimedia.org/wiki/File:Plan_Rome_ Caen_Circus_Maximus_Colis%C3%A9e.jpg

118 https://commons.wikimedia.org/wiki/File:Jean_L%C3%A9on_G%C3% A9r%C3%B4me_-_Chariot_Race_-_1983.380_-_Art_Institute_of_Chicago.jpg

119 https://commons.wikimedia.org/wiki/File:Proclaiming_claudius_emperor.png

120 Chris 73, CC BY-SA 3.0 <https://creativecommons.org/licenses/by-sa/3.0>, via Wikimedia Commons: https://commons.wikimedia.org/wiki/File:Aqua_Claudia_05.jpg

121 my work, CC BY-SA 3.0 <https://creativecommons.org/licenses/by-sa/3.0>, via Wikimedia Commons: https://commons.wikimedia.org/wiki/File: Roman.Britain.campaigns.43.to.60.jpg

122 https://commons.wikimedia.org/wiki/File:The_Emperor_Commodus_
Leaving_the_Arena_at_the_Head_of_the_Gladiators_by_American_muralist_Edwi_
Howland_Blashfield_(1848-1936)_01_(cropped).jpg

123 Jofrey Rudel Marie-Lan Nguyen (Jastrow), CC0, via Wikimedia Commons:
https://commons.wikimedia.org/wiki/File:COMMODE_HERCULE.jpg

124 Jean-Pierre Dalbéra from Paris, France, CC BY 2.0
<https://creativecommons.org/licenses/by/2.0>, via Wikimedia Commons:
https://commons.wikimedia.org/wiki/File:La_place_des_corporations_(Ostia_Antica)
_(5900530118).jpg

125 https://commons.wikimedia.org/wiki/File:Death_of_Pompey_Magnus.jpg

126 Carla Brain, CC BY-SA 2.0 <https://creativecommons.org/licenses/by-sa/2.0>, via
Wikimedia Commons:
https://commons.wikimedia.org/wiki/File:Temple_of_Jupiter_(2).jpg

127 https://commons.wikimedia.org/wiki/File:Zeus_pompei.JPG

128 Diliff, CC BY-SA 3.0 <http://creativecommons.org/licenses/by-sa/3.0/>, via
Wikimedia Commons: https://commons.wikimedia.org/wiki/File:
Roman_Baths_in_Bath_Spa,_England_-_July_2006.jpg

129 Qfl247, CC BY-SA 3.0 <https://creativecommons.org/licenses/by-sa/3.0>, via
Wikimedia Commons:
https://commons.wikimedia.org/wiki/File:Pompeii%26Vesuvius.JPG

130 https://commons.wikimedia.org/wiki/File:Karl_Brullov_-
_The_Last_Day_of_Pompeii_-_Google_Art_Project.jpg

131 https://commons.wikimedia.org/wiki/File:Destruction_of_Pompeii_
and_Herculaneum.jpg

132 Lancevortex, CC BY-SA 3.0 <http://creativecommons.org/licenses/by-sa/3.0/>, via
Wikimedia Commons: https://commons.wikimedia.org/wiki/File:
Pompeii_Garden_of_the_Fugitives_02.jpg

www.ingramcontent.com/pod-product-compliance
Lightning Source LLC
Chambersburg PA
CBHW061553120626

46550CB00004B/1467

9 7 8 1 9 5 3 9 3 4 6 8 0